Women Working

An Anthology of Stories and Poems

Project Staff

SUE DAVIDSON, *Editor*

SHIRLEY FRANK, *Associate Editor*

MERLE FROSCHL, *Field-Testing Coordinator*

FLORENCE HOWE, *Director*

MARY MULROONEY, *Production Associate*

ELIZABETH PHILLIPS, *Editor*

SUSAN TROWBRIDGE, *Design and Production Director*

SANDY WEINBAUM, *Teaching Guide Editor*

Women Working

An Anthology of Stories and Poems

Nancy Hoffman

UNIVERSITY OF MASSACHUSETTS / BOSTON

Florence Howe

STATE UNIVERSITY OF NEW YORK / COLLEGE AT OLD WESTBURY

Illustrations by Ann Toulmin-Rothe

Collected by Elaine Hedges, Nancy Hoffman, Florence Howe, Joan Jensen, Paul Lauter, Tillie Olsen, Michele Russell, Deborah Rosenfelt, Kathleen Sands, and Barbara Smith

The Feminist Press

OLD WESTBURY, NEW YORK

The McGraw-Hill Book Company

NEW YORK, ST. LOUIS, SAN FRANCISCO

**Library of Congress
Cataloging in Publication Data**

Main entry under title:
Women working.

    (Women's lives / women's work)
    Includes index.
    1. American literature—Women authors.
2. Women—Literary collections. 3. Work—
Literary collections. I. Hoffman, Nancy.
II. Howe, Florence. III. Hedges, Elaine. IV.
Series.
PS508.w7w64   1978   810'.9'352   78-4636
ISBN 0-07-020431-4

Grateful acknowledgment is made for permission to reprint the following copyrighted material:

    Asch, Sholem, "The Triangle Fire." From
East River by Sholem Asch, copyright © 1946
by Sholem Asch. All rights reserved. Used by
permission.

    Ballantyne, Sheila, "They Call Me Mum-
my." Copyright © 1972 by Sheila Ballantyne. Originally published in *Aphra* in 1972.
Reprinted by permission of the author.

    Bambara, Toni Cade, "Raymond's Run."
Copyright © 1971 by Toni Cade Bambara. Re-
printed from *Gorilla, My Love* by Toni Cade
Bambara, by permission of Random House, Inc.

    Brown, Rosellen, "The Famous Writers
School Opens Its Arms in the Next Best Thing
to Welcome." Reprinted by permission from
Some Deaths in the Delta by Rosellen Brown.
Copyright © 1970 by The University of Massa-
chusetts Press.

    Crosby, Ranice Henderson, "Waitresses."
Copyright © 1975 by Ranice Henderson
Crosby. Reprinted by permission of the author.

    Cumming, Patricia, "Midsummer." From
Letter From an Outlying Province, Alice James
Books, © 1976 by Patricia Cumming.

    Davidson, Sue, "The Peace Walk." Origi-
nally published in *Northwest Review,* copyright © 1959 by Sue Davidson. Reprinted by
permission of the author.

(*Acknowledgments continued on page 270*)

Table of Contents

Publisher's Acknowledgments

EARLY IN 1973, Mariam Chamberlain and Terry Saario of the Ford Foundation spent one day visiting The Feminist Press on the campus of the State University of New York / College at Old Westbury. They heard staff members describe the early history of The Feminist Press and its goal—to change the sexist education of girls and boys, women and men, through publishing and other projects. They also heard about those books and projects then in progress; they felt our sense of frustration about how little we were able to do directly for the classroom teacher. Advising us about funding, Terry Saario was provocative. "You need to think of yourselves," she said, "in the manner of language labs, testing and developing new texts for students and new instructional materials for teachers." Our "language" was feminism, our intent to provide alternatives to the sexist texts used in schools. The conception was, in fact, precisely the one on which the Press had been founded.

Out of that 1973 meeting came the idea for the *Women's Lives / Women's Work* project. This project, which would not officially begin for more than two years, has allowed us to extend the original concept of The Feminist Press to a broader audience.

We spent the years from 1973 to 1975 assessing the needs for a publication project, writing a major funding proposal, steering it through two foundations, negotiating with the Webster Division of McGraw-Hill, our co-publisher. We could not have begun this process without the advice and encouragement of Marilyn Levy of the Rockefeller Family Fund from which we received a planning grant in 1973. (The Feminist Press received a second grant from the Rockefeller Family Fund in 1978, in order to help complete the project.) For one year, Phyllis Arlow, Marj Britt, Merle Froschl, and Florence Howe surveyed the needs of teachers for books about women, reviewed the sexist bias of widely used history and literature texts, and interviewed editorial staffs of major educational publishers about their intentions to publish material on women. The research accumulated provided a strong case for the grant proposal first submitted to the Ford Foundation in the summer of 1974.

During the winter of 1974–75, Merle Froschl, Florence Howe, Corrine Lucido, and attorney Janice Goodman (for The Feminist Press) negotiated a co-publishing contract with McGraw-Hill. We could not have proceeded without the strong interest of John Rothermich of McGraw-Hill's Webster Division. Our co-publishing agreement gives control over editorial content and design to The Feminist Press; McGraw-Hill is responsible for the wide distribution of the series.

In the summer of 1975, the final proposal—to produce for co-publication a series of twelve supplementary books and their accompanying teaching guides—was funded by the Ford Foundation and the Carnegie Corporation. Project officers Terry Saario and Vivien Stewart were supportive and helpful throughout the life of the project.

Once funding was obtained, The Feminist Press began its search for additional staff to work on the project. The small nucleus of existing staff working on the project was expanded as The Feminist Press hired new employees. The *Women's Lives / Women's Work* project staff ultimately included eight people who remained for the duration of the project: Sue Davidson, Shirley Frank, Merle Froschl, Florence Howe, Mary Mulrooney, Elizabeth Phillips, Susan Trowbridge, and Sandy Weinbaum. Two other people, Dora Janeway Odarenko and Michele Russell, were on the staff through 1977, and we wish to acknowledge their contributions. Helen Schrader, a Feminist Press staff member, participated on the project during its first year and kept financial records and wrote financial reports throughout the duration of the project.

The *Women's Lives / Women's Work* project staff adopted the methods of work and the decision-making structure developed by The Feminist Press staff as a whole. As a Press "work committee," the project met weekly to make decisions, review progress, discuss problems. The project staff refined the editorial direction of the project, conceptualized and devised guidelines for the books, and identified prospective authors. When proposals came in, the project staff read and evaluated the submissions, and made decisions regarding them. Similarly, when manuscripts arrived, the project staff read and commented on them. Project staff members took turns drafting memoranda, reports, and other documents. And the design of the series grew out of the discussions and the ideas generated at the project meetings. The books, teaching guides, and other informational materials had the advantage, at significant stages of development, of the committee's collective direction.

Throughout the life of the project, The Feminist Press itself continued to function and grow. Individuals on staff who were not part of the *Women's Lives / Women's Work* project provided support and advice to the project. All major project policy decisions about such matters as finance and personnel were made by The Feminist Press

Board at its monthly meetings. The Board includes all Feminist Press staff, and other individuals who have an ongoing relationship to the Press: Phyllis Arlow, Jeanne Bracken, Brenda Carter, Toni Cerutti, Ranice Crosby, Sue Davidson, Michelina Fitzmaurice, Shirley Frank, Merle Froschl, Barbara Gore, Brett Harvey, Ilene Hertz, Florence Howe, Paul Lauter, Carol Levin, Corrine Lucido, Mary Mulrooney, Dora Janeway Odarenko, Ethel Johnston Phelps, Elizabeth Phillips, Helen Schrader, Sylvia Stewart, Barbara Sussman, Susan Trowbridge, Sandy Weinbaum, Sharon Wigutoff, Jane Williamson, Sophie Zimmerman.

The process of evaluation by teachers and students before final publication was as important as the process for developing ideas into books. To this end, we produced testing editions of the books. Field-testing networks were set up throughout the United States in a variety of schools—public, private, inner-city, small town, suburban, and rural—to reach as diverse a student population as possible. We field tested in the following cities, regions, and states: Boston, Massachusetts; Tucson, Arizona; Seattle, Washington; Los Angeles, California; Tampa, Florida; Greensboro, North Carolina; Eugene, Oregon; Martha's Vineyard, Massachusetts; New York City; Long Island; New Jersey; Rhode Island. We also had an extensive network of educators—350 teachers across the country—who reviewed the books in the series, often using sections of books in classrooms. From teachers' comments, from students' questionnaires, and from tapes of teachers' discussions, we gained valuable information both for revising the books and for developing the teaching guides.

Although there is no easy way to acknowledge the devotion and enthusiasm of hundreds of teachers who willingly volunteered their time and energies, we would like to thank the following teachers—and their students—with whom we worked directly in the testing of *Women Working: An Anthology of Stories and Poems*. On Long Island: Eleanor Carlson, Olga Dufour, Renee Kasper, Merle Levine, and Eleanor Newirth. In Massachusetts, co-author Nancy Hoffman helped to contact the following teachers in the Boston area: Anne Froines, Marcia A. Luongo, Nadine Pluchinsky, and Gail Sarofen. In New Jersey, Nida E. Thomas, director of the Office of Equal Educational Opportunity, and Janet Emig, professor of education at Rutgers University—with the assistance of Judith Zamost and Deena Linett—helped to contact teachers throughout the state: Doris G. Egger, Patricia L. Gardner, Madeline Graber, Helaine L. Greenberg, Beverly J. Harris, Marcia Holtzman, Patricia Marino, Sylvia Oettle, Gaylene

Pepe, Sharon L. Rogan, Emilie B. Romney, Edwin Romond, Therese M. Snyder, Carole D. Yorke. In Rhode Island, Susan J. Sims and Frank Walker of the Office of Equal Educational Opportunity, and Sylvia D. Feldman, affirmative action officer at the University of Rhode Island, helped to contact teachers in and near Providence: Paul N. Dargie, Maryanne E. Flanagan, Ethel Friedman, Michael C. Gillespie, Deborah L. Jacobson, Nancy Mullen, Judith Preble, Jean Rayack, Katharine K. Russum, Maria D. Wilk.

Three times during the life of the *Women's Lives / Women's Work* project, an Advisory Board composed of feminist educators and scholars met for a full day to discuss the books and teaching guides. The valuable criticisms and suggestions of the following people who participated in these meetings were essential to the project: Millie Alpern, Rosalyn Baxandall, Peggy Brick, Ellen Cantarow, Elizabeth Ewen, Barbara Gates, Clarisse Gillcrist, Elaine Hedges, ,Nancy Hoffman, Susan Klaw, Alice Kessler-Harris, Roberta Kronberger, Merle Levine, Eleanor Newirth, Judith Oksner, Naomi Rosenthal, Judith Schwartz, Judy Scott, Carroll Smith-Rosenberg, Adria Steinberg, Barbara Sussman, Amy Swerdlow. We also want to express our gratitude to Shirley McCune and Nida Thomas, who acted in a general advisory capacity and made many useful suggestions; and to Kathryn Girard and Kathy Salisbury who helped to develop the teacher and student field-testing questionnaires.

Other people whom we want to thank for their work on *Women Working: An Anthology of Stories and Poems* are Flavia Rando for her photo research; the many photographers, listed individually in the photo acknowledgments on page 271, who permitted us to use their work without charge; Ruth Adam for restoring the historical photographs; Barbara Beckelman of Publishers Graphics for her suggestions on illustration. We thank also Linda Petillo and Emerson W. Madairy of Monotype Composition Company and Karen Romano of the production department of McGraw-Hill for their technical assistance; Walter Heitner of Faculty Press, the printer of the testing edition of the book; and Betty Barth, who typed the testing edition.

The assistance of the many people mentioned in these acknowledgments has been invaluable to us. We would also like to thank all of you who will read this book—because you helped to create the demand that made the *Women's Lives / Women's Work* project possible.

THE FEMINIST PRESS

Authors' Acknowledgments

THIS ANTHOLOGY was compiled with the assistance of an unusual group of people around the country who searched for appropriate selections. These "searchers" had one characteristic in common: an interest in and a knowledge of the literature of lost women writers. Several suggested identical works. Deborah Rosenfelt, who should be singled out for special acknowledgment, read twenty volumes of *The Best Short Stories of . . .* to discover, for example, "The Butcher." And Grace Paley located Wilma Shore, the author of "The Butcher," for us.

We wish to thank Elizabeth Phillips for her sensitive and careful editing and for her critical contributions to the ideas of the book. We are grateful also for Frances Kelley's valuable research assistance and for her preparation of the manuscript; she was the person without whom the deadlines could not have been met. We also thank Deborah Takis, who helped do research for the book.

Finally, for their interest and encouragement, we want to thank the two thousand teachers and students who field and network tested the book. We took their advice especially about what to cut from the testing edition. But of course the final responsibility for the volume, including its possible failures, is ours.

FLORENCE HOWE
NANCY HOFFMAN

Introduction

THE EDITORS OF THIS COLLECTION spent more than a year—with the assistance of many friends—searching for literature about women working. We insisted on imaginative literature, rather than history or documentary, for several reasons. Most important was the power of a story or a poem to catch the intensity of experience. Many of us remember significant romantic scenes in fiction; some of us remember sharply a solitary moment of pain expressed in a poem, or an individual moment of awakening in an autobiography. Could we find comparably powerful scenes and feelings in portraits of women at work?

We guessed that we would find most of this imaginative literature either buried in the lost or forgotten works of older or dead women writers, or emerging in the contemporary work of young women writing today. We supposed that most male writers did not focus on women working. Our search confirmed this and provided a second reason for insisting on literary works: helping to restore women writers to American literature. With a few notable exceptions, then, it is women writers who fill the pages of this volume. Some of them, like Sarah Orne Jewett, Zora Neale Hurston, and Anzia Yezierska, achieved recognition in their own day, then were lost from view until the current revival of interest in women writers. Others, like Ranice Crosby and Rikki Lights, are young writers publishing their early work.

The third reason for searching for literature about working women is that literature is a useful, though not always obvious, source of social history. Stories and poems written during or after a strike may be one significant source of information about that event. A whole group of stories and poems, written by different writers in different periods, may also be informative. As we shall see, certain themes—the fragmentation of women's work lives, for example—occur repeatedly. We recover another layer of social history from those repetitions.

Our final reason returns us to the first: we believe that women and men need to add to their imaginative vision images of women working—at jobs that are boring, exciting, heroic, oppressive, difficult, tedious, satisfying. In this society, a man's identity is commonly defined by the work he does while a woman's identity has often been based on her relationships to others—daughter, wife, mother. But such starkly stereotypical definitions are inadequate: for both women and men, work and relationships are essential aspects of human identity. In the future we will all continue to work—female and male alike. But jobs may be more equitably distributed both inside and outside the home. And our consciousness about our jobs and ourselves may be different. It is difficult to imagine such a future without examples from the past, examples long denied us. This volume, then, is one starting place.

What Is Women's Work?

Before we could begin to collect the pieces for this volume, we had to define the limits of our task. What *is* work? If it is labor that earns a paycheck, then what is the status of the housewife and mother? Is she a worker? What about people *training* for work, as in a medical school, or as in the daily routines of a runner? What of the unpaid work of a social activist? Should the work of all artists be included—quiltmakers and potters, for example, as well as writers or painters? And what of the work of children in families?

As the contents of this volume indicate, we decided on a broad definition of work, one that might raise questions beyond the usual ones of salaries and prestige. Women have always worked—poor women at paid jobs, though not at decent wages; middle-class Western women, for the past hundred and fifty years, at professional jobs, again usually at inequitable wages. But almost all women the world over have worked at unpaid jobs: as wives, mothers, housekeepers; farming land alongside those males known as "farmers"; as artists; and, for more than one hundred and fifty years, as workers in such causes as abolition, women's rights, labor-organizing, civil rights, and peace.

We decided also that we wanted literature that would raise questions about the quality of various kinds of work, about what it felt like to do certain jobs. In the United States, among young and old alike, it is commonly assumed that work is a burden that most people have to endure from nine until five, Monday through Friday, so that afterwards they may do what they *really* enjoy. Hence, it may be surprising to find among the selections an autobiographical account of a young woman who seems mainly to be having fun at a party. In fact, Zora Neale Hurston is collecting material for a volume of folklore that will be one day highly valued as anthropology and literature. But *is* that work? Similarly, readers may question the inclusion of a story by Toni Cade Bambara called "Raymond's Run." The heroine of this story might not be considered a worker on two counts: she is a child assigned by her family to look after her retarded brother; and she has organized a way of doing that and "working" at running exercises at the same time. Like Hurston, Squeaky enjoys what she is doing: it is the center of her life, occupying all her waking moments, as well as her dreams of the future. Can this be *work*?

While questions about anthropologists on field trips or unpaid writers, about siblings doing child-care chores or runners training may be asked both of female and male workers, unpaid domestic work has been traditionally women's province. As such, it has been ignored in most economic theories and also in most discussions of the value of work. We are all familiar with the housewife who denies her existence as a working person when she responds to the question "What do you do?" with the answer "I don't work; I'm only a housewife." Of course, she may be the mother of five children. Is being a mother *work*?

More than half the selections in this volume describe unpaid working women—mothers and wives, students, artists, social activists, athletes. All carry out purposeful, productive activity through either physical or mental effort. Most of these women do not identify themselves as workers. Nor do husbands, children, friends, neighbors, or community members dignify these women's activities with the name of "work." Superficially at least, the familiar characteristics of a job are lacking: these women workers appear to have no bosses, no set schedules; they punch no time cards; they fill no job descriptions that are annually evaluated. They usually work in isolation, even when they work in families. Without recognition as "workers," moreover, these women cannot negotiate changes in their working conditions, nor can they easily quit to choose a new job. Unpaid work, the selections reveal, has its own rules—and they are very different from those of paid work.

If we need a broad definition of work in order to reevaluate women's unpaid labor, the literature about paid labor suggests different problems. While women have worked at a wide variety of jobs, most paid women workers can be found in clothing factories, offices, hospitals, schools, restaurants, and in private households. And in most of these places (the exception being private households), men are in charge; women are considered temporary workers before marriage and workers who supplement their husbands' incomes after marriage. A few women in the labor force work at "exceptional" jobs—as manufacturers, for example, like Mary in Sarah Orne Jewett's story, "Tom's Husband," or as entertainers like Aretha, in Nikki Giovanni's poem. But, as the volume accurately suggests, most of our mothers and grandmothers, and most women today—who now make up nearly half of the paid labor force—work at low-paid menial jobs.

The Organization of This Book

Discussions about work, and the special nature and history of women's work, led us to the organization of this volume. The four divisions may not seem, and, in fact, are not, exactly parallel to one another. Indeed, all of the selections might have been organized into the first two divisions—"Oppressive Work" and "Satisfying Work," though, in some cases, it would have been difficult to decide where to place a particular story or poem in which, for example, a person does two kinds of work. We used the feelings and expressions of the central character as a yardstick for measuring the frustration or suffering caused by "Oppressive Work" and the joy or sense of well-being that comes from "Satisfying Work." Where those feelings are mixed, or shift in the course of the story or poem, we relied on our judgment. Even so, readers may find themselves challenging our placement of a particular story or poem. Placing Rikki Lights's "Medicine Man" in "Satisfying Work," for example, may obscure the fact that the heroine finds medical school exhausting, grueling, at times dehumanizing.

The last two divisions are quite different from the first two —and from each other—and again, selections placed in one category might also suit another. "Family Work" recognizes the significance of housework and child care in the lives of most women and allows for questions to be raised especially about the relationships of wives and husbands, mothers and children. It is interesting to note that twelve of the eighteen prose selections and nine of the sixteen poems in the entire volume are, in some measure, about family work.

"Transforming Work," the final division, is the most complex. We are thinking here of work that transforms lives by dignifying them with meaning and significance. We are thinking also of the challenge endemic to all workers—to transform the conditions under which they work, whether in a factory or in their own or another's home. Thus, some of the selections seem to be about work that is as oppressive as, and sometimes more dangerous than, work described in the first section. Two of these selections are about the kind of work that transforms individuals into parts of a working team. "I Was Marching" by Meridel Le Sueur is the autobiographical account of a middle-class woman who feels, for the first time, the power of a social movement—among workers of another class. The experience of working "anonymously" fills her "with fear and awe and at the same time hope." Similarly, though with a tragic end, Adrienne Rich's poem celebrates the accomplishments of a Soviet women's climbing team. In "Phantasia for Elvira Shatayev," the team's leader speaks through quoted sections of her diary:

In the diary as the wind   began to tear
at the tents over us   I wrote:
We know now we have always been in danger
down in our separateness
and now up here together   but till now
we had not touched our strength

That the team die in a storm is an accident for which we and the poet, as well as the surviving families, grieve; the poem celebrates the work of climbing that transforms individuals into parts of a working team.

A Brief History
of Women's Work

Although we did not select the literature in this anthology to
present an historical account of women's work, the selections
do provide glimpses of that work during the course of two centuries. The selections do not, of course, contain explicit analy-
ses of the relationship between shifts in the American economy and changes in women's lives. Literature, however, as
distinct from history, sociology, or economics, permits us to
enter into the lives of individuals, to observe both the representative and the singular experience.

In the preindustrial United States (before the 1840s), women
and men often worked in family groups, and, in certain ways,
unpaid family labor offered more satisfactions than family
work today. For one thing, the range of tasks women performed
—gardening, caring for animals, weaving, sewing, preserving,
nursing—varied more than the range of a contemporary housewife. Secondly, although women and men worked in separate
groups at different kinds of jobs, the work of both was visible
and valued. Women were responsible for making cloth as well
as clothing and bed linen; their work was essential to the family's ability to endure cold winters without the luxury of fac-
tory-prepared foods or easy shopping facilities. Women frequently left the privacy of home to market extra produce; they
handled money, and, on large farms, supervised the work of
others. Boys as well as girls learned adult work at home, boys
working alongside their fathers, girls with their mothers.

In two story-like excerpts from the biography of the famous
María, the potter of San Ildefonso, we catch a glimpse of the
harmonious family work life of Native American women at
the turn of the century. While her sister chooses to work the
land with her father, María helps her mother by going out alone
to sell cheese. Though the work is laborious and demands a
sense of responsibility, María finds the effort immensely satisfying; her contribution to family work is a source of five-year-
old dignity and pride.

On the other hand, we must not romanticize nineteenth-
century rural life. Many black women and men were slaves,
working unpaid on land they did not own. Women's farm work

was both unending and physically exhausting. Children's illnesses were prevalent and good nursing and prayer were the most common remedies. Hardly a family escaped the frequent presence of serious illness and death in their household.

If we were to recreate the work history of another farm woman, her story might be that of Aunt Mehetabel, a character in Dorothy Canfield Fisher's "The Bedquilt." A spinster who works, unpaid, as a servant in her brother's household, Aunt Mehetabel has never "for a moment known the pleasure of being important to anyone." Her life is a sequence of strenuous labors: Monday, washing the men's shirts; Tuesday, "all day ironing a monotonous succession of dish clothes and towels and sheets." Other days, she "stoned cherries incessantly, or hulled strawberries until her fingers were dyed red." A privilege it was "to be allowed to iron . . . the baby's white dresses or the fancy aprons of her young lady nieces." Indeed, the most common domestic work, until quite recently, was laundering, for oneself or for pay. The phrase "I'm all washed out" once referred literally to the exhaustion which came from building a fire, boiling water, scrubbing with home-made soap, wringing, hanging out, then bending over the ironing board.

Had Fisher's Aunt Mehetabel left her home and entered the world of middle-class culture in the mid-nineteenth century, she might have heard her life's work praised by Catharine Beecher. Although married women, not spinsters, were Beecher's "ideal," this immensely popular author of *Treatise on Domestic Economy* would have looked approvingly on Aunt Mehetabel's willingness to serve others and sacrifice herself. These characteristic female traits, Beecher assumed, provided a counterbalance to male egotism and selfishness in the competitive outside world. Miss Beecher, lecturer on female education, thought schooling should prepare a woman to be "chief minister of the family state" and custodian of moral virtue. True women, according to Beecher, had no political opinions, disparaged female antislavery societies, and argued against women's suffrage.

Small wonder, then, that when women began to enter the paid labor force in substantial numbers (and partly as a result of the nineteenth-century women's movement), they were relegated to jobs that were considered an extension of their domestic work. If women were defined as self-sacrificing, naturally patient, good at detailed, repetitive work with children and at home, then women could use those same virtues as maids, textile workers, stenographers, saleswomen, or teachers. Because a woman was supposed to work only until she married, employers excused her low wages and deplorable working conditions.

In the cities crowded with immigrants, it was mainly the boys who became entrepreneurs, got enough schooling for a profession, or worked out of doors. Sholem Asch's "The Triangle Fire" and Anzia Yezierska's "America and I" portray young immigrant women in need of food and shelter. Asch's Mary finds work in a cellar sweatshop. "There was no ventilation," no daylight: "Before twelve machines, each of them set below a naked electric bulb, hanging from the low ceiling, sat twelve girls—Irish, Jewish, Italian." The boss convinces them that "union shops wouldn't take them in." In this way, he exploits them. Finally, the girls graduate to a regular shirtwaist factory, the end of a female worker's journey. The only other kind of work available was marriage to a man with money—a diamond dealer, a shopkeeper, a salesman, even a peddler.

The entry of large numbers of poor immigrant women into the paid labor force renewed the seed of women's unionism planted by New England factory women a century earlier. Outside of their homes and beyond their ethnic neighborhoods, women factory workers recognized that the overwhelming similarities of their work conditions obliterated differences of culture, religion, and language. Women faced many difficulties in organizing that they still face today. Their double work load —taking care of house and children as well as working outside the home—allowed little time for union activity. And the male-controlled unions were not often receptive to women. But despite these and other problems, and against the often fierce resistance of unregulated big businesses, women joined unions, planned strikes, and took risky actions together. Their organizing required new skills—the courage to speak publicly, the wit to outsmart bosses and foremen, the intellect to reason out a politics of collective action.

While some women—about twenty-five percent—were working outside the home during the first few decades of the twentieth century, women's housework and child care were becoming increasingly isolating, not only in the growing suburbs, but also in the cities. In Wilma Shore's "The Butcher," Millie Patron no longer lives in a large, extended family. When she graduates from high school, Millie chooses between two "genteel" professions, stenography and teaching, with the conviction firm in her mind "that the only important thing was getting married, having her own house, and maybe a couple of kids, loving her husband, and getting to have the warmth and assurance she saw in her own mother." After marriage, Millie gives up her job as stenographer and devotes herself to house-furnishing, and then to cooking. She falls an early victim to the "disease" that Betty Friedan in *The Feminine Mystique* some decades later called "the problem that has no name." Millie feels inexplicably depressed and first puts on fifteen pounds, then takes them off. But she keeps reviewing the facts: she has "a good, kind husband," a new apartment fixed "just the way it had always looked in her mind," hours for baking, shining, straightening, reading magazines, and doing errands. She wonders how she can be unhappy and asks, "Is this all?" Millie does not recognize her own need for satisfying work.

It is not surprising that Millie thinks it is wrong for a married woman to work outside the home. The percentage of women doing paid work in 1940 was almost the same as the percentage doing that work in 1910. And of the twenty-five percent of women who worked for wages, the large majority were unmarried. These patterns changed dramatically during World War II, when new war industries demanded increased numbers of workers. Millions of men preparing for the soldiers' life were not available to fill the jobs; women, therefore, began working outside the home in record numbers, and many of them retained their positions in the paid labor force even after the war. By 1949, the percentage of women working for pay rose to thirty-two percent; in 1950, for the first time in American history, the majority of women workers were married.

Since World War II, the reality of women's lives has increasingly included paid work. We do not need "manpower" spe-

cialists to tell us that women's entry into the paid labor force
in the past few years is "the single most outstanding phenom-
enon of our century. Its long-term implications are . . . unchart-
able."[1] For almost half of adult American women, paid work is
now mainly a necessity, not a choice. And yet, of the handful of
stories in this collection written in the 1960s and 1970s, surprisingly only one contains a portrait of a paid worker. Like
4.2 million other American women, the hero of Judith Higgins's
"The Only People" is a typist whose attitude toward work is
shared by many. Lacking any special skill besides typing, Jane
has shifted from office to office. "No one wants me," she de-
clares as she sets off for still another job interview. Once employed, however, Jane flourishes, proud of her work: "The
words from the Dictaphone," she thinks to herself, "flow
through me like blood. All the noises and voices around me
disappear."

While selections also include poems about office work,
waitressing, and hatmaking, and one about selling tortillas on
a street in Texas, the bulk of contemporary portraits of women
—three prose pieces and five poems—focus on unpaid work:
mothering, housework, social activism, writing, studying
medicine. All the latter portraits, moreover, are of relatively
privileged women. They are different from other women in the
volume: they have read Betty Friedan's The Feminine Mystique (1963) and other literature of the modern women's liberation movement. Sometimes even if they precede the appearance of that book and movement by a few years, as does Lila
in Sue Davidson's "The Peace Walk," the women characters
show a new independence of spirit. The contemporary women
in this volume are aware of themselves and conscious of the
restricting nature of some of their work. The Berkeley mother
in "They Call Me Mummy," by Sheila Ballantyne, says to herself knowingly and with humor: "It's true we mothers are
understimulated. I am an individual, I think. I am, I am." These
contemporary women have an ability to analyze their relationships with their husbands and with other people around them.
Though such relationships may be far from ideal, these women

[1] Eli Ginzberg, former chairman of the National Commission on Manpower
Policy, as quoted in the New York Times, September 21, 1976.

do not feel imprisoned irrevocably by them—or by other conditions in their lives.

For several reasons selections included in this volume are least representative of the contemporary period. Partly we can blame this on our decision to concentrate on short fiction rather than on excerpts from longer works. We did not choose to include, therefore, material from such widely available excellent books as Harriette Arnow's *The Dollmaker*, Marge Piercy's *Small Changes*, or Maxine Hong Kingston's *The Woman Warrior*—all of which are about women working. Partly it is also that we have found the contemporary American short story and poem more focused on personal relationships, on individual consciousness, than on work.

In addition, much of the history of women working has not been transformed from the raw material of interviews, documents, oral histories, into the forms of stories and poems. Until accounts like the following, by Virgie Delgado, a worker at the Farah clothing plant in Texas, are assimilated into the literature of the future, anthologies like this one will necessarily be incomplete.

. . . on Monday during our break time, people started walking out at 9:30 in the morning. They said, "Come on Virgie, we're going on strike." But I didn't know why we were going on strike, even though everybody in the cutting room wanted the union. I was really confused so I didn't go with them.

I went back to my machine, but I felt so bad I couldn't work that day 'cause I knew my friends were outside. I went to a meeting of the strikers after work. For job security so we would not have to be afraid of losing our jobs all the time. And because we had been waiting for 3 years and the company wouldn't recognize our union. I decided to walk out the next day.

But I had to think about it before I walked out, because there are 9 kids in my family, and me and my sisters work at Farah to support our family. I had to go home and tell my mom what I was going to do. She said to do what I thought was right.

The next morning I got my girl friends together and said we were going to walk out. I got all their purses. We started in the very back and started calling to other workers to walk out with us. My legs were shaking the whole time. We were really scared because we didn't know what was going to happen. My 3 sisters joined us and all these guys and girls followed us. By the time we got to the front door I looked back and saw 150 people behind us.

We were about to walk out the door when the supervisor stepped in front of me and asked us where did we think we were going. So I told him he had better step out of the way or I wouldn't be responsible for what I would do. Then he said for us to punch out and I said no, we're walking out and he'd better get out of the way. He was real shocked that I talked like that so he moved out of the way and we walked outside. Then we saw all the other people outside who had left the day before and we were really happy. We started hugging each other and singing even though we didn't know each other. It was really something.[2]

Recurrent Themes in the Experience of Women's Work

Literature moves the reader not only through argument, but through images. Gestures, snatches of conversation, sometimes only a phrase, will catch the quality of a person's life. We will not easily forget the female cadaver, Ingabord, in Rikki Lights's story, "Medicine Man," or the brief exchange between the young female student and the supervising doctor who stares at "her hand, which had locked onto Ingabord's right knee." Or Aunt Georgiana's farm-worn fingers, deprived of music for thirty years, moving to the rhythms of Wagnerian music, in Willa Cather's story, "A Wagner Matinee." We will always remember the vocational guidance counselor in Anzia Yezierska's "America and I," who cannot comprehend the anguish of an immigrant girl who dreams of being a writer; "I want to work by what's in me," she tells "the college-looking counselor":

She gave me a quick, puzzled look from the corner of her eyes. "What are you doing now?"

"I'm the quickest shirtwaist hand on the floor. But my heart wastes away by such work. I think and think, and my thoughts can't come out."

"Why don't you think out your thoughts in shirtwaists?" came the reply.

And we may enjoy the humor of Mummy in Sheila Ballantyne's story, "They Call Me Mummy," who writes letters through and around her work as a mother and housekeeper.

[2] "Chicanos Strike at Farah," *United Front Press*, January 1974.

In literature by and about women working, moreover, certain images and themes recur in seemingly disparate lives. Several of them are recognizable not only in this collection, but also in a wide range of literature by and about women working.

One dominant motif of literature about working women concerns "time," the futile attempts to find enough hours in the day and night to do all that has to be done. Women feel controlled by time, as if they were endlessly operating machines. Or alternatively, they face constant interruption, the fragmentation of time. It is the latter—interruption and fragmentation—which finds expression in Rosellen Brown's poem, "The Famous Writers School Opens Its Arms in the Next Best Thing to Welcome." In the kitchen, really women's room, the mother tries to write while her children pull and tug at her. No wonder this woman with small children is writing poetry and short fiction. The short form may perhaps be perfected between naps and bottles and diapers. But the mother does conquer time, and manages to do creative work, as do others, like Aunt Mehetabel in "The Bedquilt."

In several stories and poems, survival work takes up all the time, and rules the woman's life, especially when she is working at two, sometimes three, different paid and unpaid jobs. In Tillie Olsen's "I Stand Here Ironing," after a day of work outside the home the mother's second job begins. "I would start running," the mother tells us, "as soon as I got off the street car, running . . . up the stairs. . . ." Her child greets her with tears; all day the mother has been anxious for time to begin cleaning, cooking, comforting.

Even women's "free time" is often not their own because of the special quality of most women's work. From the repetitive carrying out of small tasks which characterizes family work comes a certain habit of mind—a reviewing of and remembering about work even during leisure moments. And so Aunt Georgiana, in "A Wagner Matinee," must spend her few days of unexpected vacation worrying: Had she left instructions to give the calf skimmed milk? Had she told her daughter to use the newly opened tin of mackeral before it spoiled? Aunt Georgiana's mind is inhabited by milk and mackeral, buttons to be sewn, eggs to be brought in.

If too little time is a dominant motif in literature about women's work, this explains a recurrent image—the image of flight, and its less radical manifestation, daydreaming. The woman who stands at the door in Ellen Bryant Voigt's "Farm Wife" and the mother in "The Famous Writers School" respond to physical limitation by spiritual flight. The neighbors watch in surprise as the farmwife glides off, a "bone-white spot in the sky," until it is time to resume domesticity and serve her husband supper. In a less fantastical key, women dream and muse and think standing over the ironing board. Says the mother in "I Stand Here Ironing," thinking about her daughter, "Help her to know . . . she is more than this dress on the ironing board, helpless before the iron."

One of the most dominant themes in literature about women working grows out of the sexual division of labor: the separation of women's lives from men's, and the resulting denial of opportunities—usually to women, occasionally to men. The "sexual division of labor" describes the commonplace assumption that males and females are suited to different kinds of work: men away from home or out of doors, and paid; women in the home and unpaid, or at the bottom of the paid labor heap. But as the literature about working women's lives makes clear, the separation of the two sexes into two different work forces also accomplishes their human separation. Their interests, even within the same family, are not *shared* interests, as several stories of traditional marriages illustrate. In "The Peace Walk," for example, husband and wife do not share their daily work: he goes to an office each day, she works in the home and then at organizing a peace walk. On the Saturday of the walk, moreover, he goes off to play a game of tennis, and assumes, when his game is rained out, that her walk has been ruined. He rushes home to prepare martinis and sandwiches for his "poor baby" and looks forward to offering comfort for the lost cause he never believed in. But he is confused when she returns triumphant, having led the walk and even delivered a speech. He cannot comprehend his wife's exhilaration or her daring to say that she no longer wants or needs his support for her work: "I don't need anybody's support," she says. At the story's conclusion, much to his surprise, he finds himself troubled: "He could not recall a time when he had felt so uneasy, lost . . . uncertain of the future."

One of the stories, Sarah Orne Jewett's "Tom's Husband," illuminates the fact that it is not the nature of women but the nature of their assigned work that makes the difference in their lives, for it is Tom, not Mary, in this "ideal marriage," who complains that "he felt himself fast growing rusty and behind the times and to have somehow missed a good deal in life." Tom's experience of housekeeping for some five years while his wife runs a manufacturing business allows him to think that "his had been almost exactly the experience of most women, and he wondered if it really was any more disappointing and ignominious to him than it was to women themselves."

In "Tom's Husband," we learn that Mary's father believes "it had been a mistake that she was a girl instead of a boy," that "she was too independent and self-reliant for a wife." We see her suggest that she and her husband exchange jobs: "I believe I was made for it," she says of her wanting to direct the family business. And we hear that the (male) supervisors and millhands learn to accept and respect her. She makes enough money, moreover, to quiet the family's horror at having a woman in charge of their affairs. Characteristically, as "Tom's Husband," Mary is unprepared for Tom's housewifely dissatisfaction and subsequent small rebellion.

Quite another portrait is drawn by Willa Cather in "A Wagner Matinee," and she, too, uses a man to help us to see it. He is the nephew of Aunt Georgiana, the Nebraska farm wife who, before she married, was a well-educated music teacher in Boston. On the farm, where he worked for his keep, his aunt shared her precious evening hours, teaching him music or hearing his lessons, as she darned socks, knitted mittens, or did the farm's ironing. Thirty years later, the nephew, now a grown man, awaits his aunt's first visit to Boston. He remembers her embracing him one day as he "doggedly" practiced on her "little parlour organ," and saying: "Don't love it so well, Clark, or it may be taken from you." With this memory in mind, Clark buys tickets to a performance of Wagner, though he then grows "doubtful about her enjoyment of it." But at the concert it is through his eyes that we understand that the music "broke a silence of thirty years for her." And he continues: "There came to me an overwhelming sense of the waste and wear we are so powerless to combat; and I saw again the tall, naked house on the prairie. . . ."

At the same time, Aunt Georgiana's work—especially the mothering and teaching of Clark and her own children—is not diminished. Nor is mothering demeaned in any of the selections. It is, however, totally the province of women who live with their children in a world peopled only by other women and children. There are no views of fathering here and few anywhere in literature.

Only in one selection, in fact, do we see a woman and a man working together as equals—at any kind of work. They are María and Julián, Pueblo Indians, not fictional characters but central figures in the biographical portrait "The Whole Pot," by Alice Marriott. Together they go in search of the fine sand needed for the kind of pottery they have been asked by archeologists to replicate. On the way back, Julián also chooses some fine yucca with which to make paintbrushes. María sifts the clay and the sand, decides on the proper proportions, shapes and makes the pot; Julián finds the "paint," makes up the design, and paints it on the pot. The portrait concludes with the following dialogue between husband and wife:

María laughed. "You'd better be a potter," she said. "It's better to do something you like than something you don't like."
"Men aren't potters," said Julián, putting his brush down on the floor beside the pot of guaco, carelessly. "Is lunch ready?"

Thus, even here, in what may seem an ideal arrangement, the culture prescribes that making pottery is work appropriate only for females. If men do part of it, as Julián continues to for a while, it can only be as an avocation.

Another dominant theme in this literature is one not confined to women's work. The theme of individualism, of the solitary striving for distinction or the pleasure of achievement, is common to portraits of women and men at work in the United States. In the selections we include, the solitary work experience may be most oppressive or most satisfying; it is even, as in the case of the woman in "The Peace Walk" or Aunt

Mehetabel in "The Bedquilt," able to transform a person's life. Much rarer is the kind of work experience we have mentioned earlier in relation to teamwork. Perhaps such portraits are rare in literature about women's work because of what the young girl in Toni Cade Bambara's story, "Raymond's Run," says: "I'm thinking that girls never really smile at each other because they don't know how and don't want to know how and there's probably no one to teach us how, cause grown-up girls don't know either."

Not surprisingly, therefore, the stories of girls' and women's close friendships at work are few, though, when they occur, they are deeply moving. The girls in Mary Wilkins Freeman's "The Bound Girl," for example, defy social prejudice to be friends, as do the Jewish Sarah and the Catholic Mary in "The Triangle Fire." On the other hand, prejudice, as well as subtle manipulation, in Judith Higgins's "The Only People," illuminates some of the problems of women office workers who work in highly stratified institutions like hospitals. The doctor and his secretary talk the language of "teamwork," but what they want is a kind of competition that destroys friendships—or keeps them from ever forming. This is distinctly different from Marge Piercy's portrait of teamwork in "To Be of Use":

I want to be with people who submerge
in the task, who go into the fields to harvest
and work in a row and pass the bags along,
who stand in the line and haul in their places,
who are not parlor generals and field deserters
but move in common rhythm
when the food must come in or the fire be put out.

Piercy's poem—like others she has written and like her fiction—celebrates work itself. "The people I love the best," she writes, "jump into work head first." Her images of the swimmers who go "off with sure strokes almost out of sight"—"the black sleek heads of seals"—and of the ox and water buffalo, are not restricted by any sexual division of labor. We cannot tell whether she is writing about women or men: she is describing "people." Her poem is the closest we come in this collection to imagining a world in which work is a central and satisfying part of all our lives.

Women
Working

An Anthology of Stories and Poems

ONE:
Oppressive Work

Whose Dog Am I?

TO FEEL OPPRESSED is to feel burdened, pressed down spiritually and physically. What makes some work oppressive? Is it the cruel and unjust exercise of authority by employers, the physical danger of work? Or is oppression sometimes more subtle, a matter of attitudes of coworkers and employers? As the stories

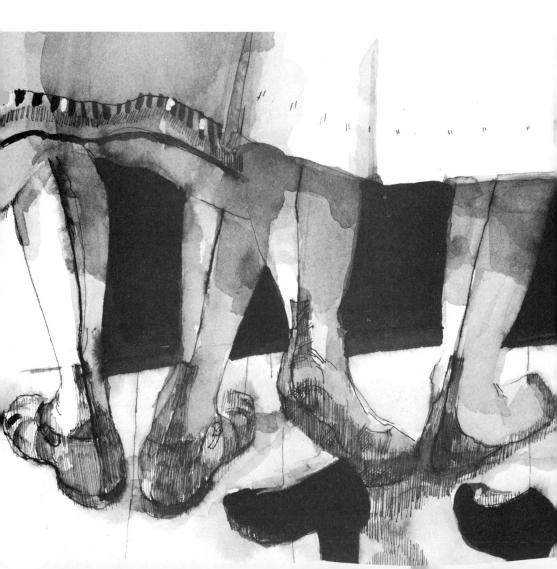

and poems in this section illustrate, work can be oppressive for all these reasons and for other ones as well. The people in these selections work at a variety of jobs in different historical periods; they may appear to have little in common. Yet on some level, all of them feel oppressed by their work.

Legal bondage, the ownership of rights to another human's labor, is the most extreme form of oppression. Slaves and indentured servants, like the child, Ann Ginnins, in "The Bound Girl," have no choice but to work on command. More commonplace today is the experience of the alienated worker who is legally "free" but who has been forced by need to work at jobs that may be oppressive in various ways. The fourteen-year-

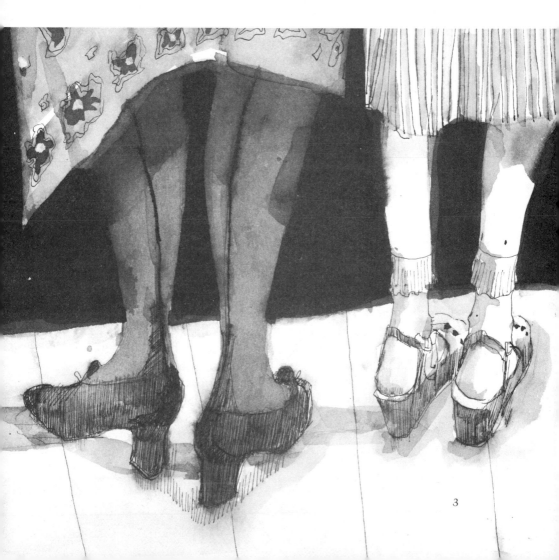

old in Charles Reznikoff's "Amelia" comes to the factory eager
for work but unprepared for its physical dangers. The speaker
in Naomi Replansky's "A Good Day's Work," who asks
"Whose dog am I?" portrays herself as a trained animal, obedient to a clock. She is "dogtired" at the end of the day she
"must go through," whatever her own desires or needs. In
Ranice Crosby's poem, the waitress feels her uniform as another skin, protective of and yet dulling to the human skin
beneath it.

The experiences of the woman in Anzia Yezierska's "America and I" are somewhat different. She seems to enjoy each day
as a domestic worker "in the sunshine" of a new country: "All
that my soul hungered to give I put into the passion with which
I scrubbed floors, scoured pots, and washed clothes." It is not
the work that oppresses her, but the attitudes of her employers
and their treatment of her. Similarly, in Nikki Giovanni's
poem, the glamor of a successful singer's work belies its oppressive qualities. Not only does no one think of her as "a
mother with four children":

nobody mentions how it feels to become a freak
because you have talent and how
no one gives a damn how you feel

Giovanni's reflections on such seemingly satisfying work
make one wonder, does all work have its oppressive aspects?
Can work be both satisfying and oppressive?

Women doing family work sometimes experience their
work as both satisfying and oppressive. For Aunt Georgiana, in
Willa Cather's "A Wagner Matinee," her work is oppressive
because it keeps her from doing other work she loves. She had
to give up her work as a music teacher for her work as wife and
mother; there was, in her day, no way to combine those jobs.
And as Cather's story suggests, a productive and compassion-
ate life on the prairie, including the education of a grateful
nephew and one's own children, does not compensate for the
suffering caused by thirty years without music.

Most of the stories and poems in this section are depressing
because the workers in them are apparently sentenced to con-

tinued oppressive labor. But they also affirm the strength of the human spirit—in small signs of resistance: humor, mischief, tears, longing, acknowledged sadness, and anger. These germs of rebellion emerge more fully in the final section of this volume, "Transforming Work."

A Good Day's Work

By Naomi Replansky

Born in the Bronx, New York, Naomi Replansky (1918–) began writing poetry when she was ten years old. When she was fifteen, Poetry *published her work.* Ring Song, *a collection of her poems, was published by Scribner's in 1952 and was nominated for a National Book Award. In 1956, Replansky earned a B.A. from the University of California/ Los Angeles, where she studied geography. These days, she works part-time in New York City as a computer programmer. Her new volume of poems, now ready for publication, is called* I Met My Solitude. *"A Good Day's Work" was written about the years Replansky worked in factories, before going to college. It appeared first in* Ring Song.

Whose dog am I?
The time clock's dog.
Whose dog are you?

Learn how to smile at foremen.
A dirty joke and time for a smoke.
Be slick, be quick, be human.

The night is small
And hard to hold,
Sinks into the spongy morning.
The day is large
And hard to pass
And I can't go over it

And can't go under it
And can't go around it
But must go through it.

And me dogtired.

The Bound Girl

By Mary Wilkins Freeman

*Mary Eleanor Wilkins (1852–1930) lived for most of her life
in the New England villages she wrote about in her fiction.
For one year, in 1870, she attended the Mount Holyoke
Female Seminary (before it had become a college). By the end
of the seventies, she had begun to earn her living through
writing poems and stories for children. She began publishing
stories for adults in the early eighties and, within that
decade, became financially independent as a writer.
Collections of her stories appeared in 1887 (*A Humble
Romance*) and 1891 (*A New England Nun*), and several
novels followed. By the midnineties, her reputation as a
writer was established. Her work was praised by such other
writers and critics as James Russell Lowell, Oliver Wendell
Holmes, William Dean Howells, and Henry James. In 1902,
she married Charles M. Freeman, and they lived for some
years in Metuchen, New Jersey, where she continued to
write until 1923. In her lifetime, she published more than 250
short stories and tales, 14 novels, 8 volumes for children,
and a play. In 1926, she received the Howells Medal of the
American Academy of Arts and Letters and she was elected
to the National Institute of Arts and Letters.*

*Successful and honored as a writer in her own day, Mary
Wilkins Freeman was "lost" to contemporary readers
until recently. She is interesting today not only because of
her control of the short story form, but also because of her
portraits of strong rural New England women. Unlike most*

*of her stories, "The Bound Girl" is set, not in the 1890s
when it was written, but some hundred and forty years
earlier, in 1753. Like Freeman's other characters, however,
the young girl in the story has spunk, and even some
humor, despite the rather joyless world she is confined in.
The legal contract and the story itself document the colonial
system of forced labor.*

This Indenture Wittnesseth, That I Margaret Burjust of Boston, in
the County of Suffolk and Province of the Massachusetts Bay in New
England. Have placed, and by these presents do place and bind out my
only Daughter whose name is Ann Ginnins to be an Apprentice unto
Samuel Wales and his wife of Braintree in the County afores:ᵈ, Black-
smith. To them and their Heirs and with them the s:ᵈ Samuel Wales,
his wife and their Heirs, after the manner of an apprentice to dwell
and Serve from the day of the date hereof for and during the full and
Just Term of Sixteen years, three months and twenty-three day's next
ensueing and fully to be Compleat, during all which term the s:ᵈ
apprentice her s:ᵈ Master and Mistress faithfully Shall Serve, Their
Secrets keep close, and Lawful and reasonable Command everywhere
gladly do and perform.

Damage to her s:ᵈ Master and Mistress she shall not willingly do.
Her s:ᵈ Master's goods she shall not waste, Embezel, purloin or lend
unto Others nor suffer the same to be wasted or purloined. But to her
power Shall discover the Same to her s:ᵈ Master. Taverns or Ailhouss
she Shall not frequent, at any unlawful game She Shall not play,
Matrimony she Shall not Contract with any persons during s:ᵈ Term.
From her master's Service She Shall not at any time unlawfully absent
herself. But in all things as a good honest and faithful Servant and
apprentice Shall bear and behave herself, During the full term afores:ᵈ
Commencing from the third day of November Anno Dom: One Thousand, Seven Hundred fifty and three. And the s:ᵈ Master for himself,
wife, and Heir's, Doth Covenant Promise Grant and Agree unto and
with the s:ᵈ apprentice and the s:ᵈ Margaret Burjust, in manner and
form following. That is to say, That they will teach the s:ᵈ apprentice
or Cause her to be taught in the Art of good housewifery, and also to
read and write well. And will find and provide for and give unto s:ᵈ
apprentice good and sufficient Meat Drink washing and lodging both
in Sickness and in health, and at the Expiration of s:ᵈ term to Dismiss
s:ᵈ apprentice with two Good Suits of Apparrel both of woolen and
linnin for all parts of her body (viz) One for Lord-days and one for
working days Suitable to her Quality. In Testimony whereof I Samuel
Wales and Margaret Burjust have Interchangably Sett their hands and

Seals this Third day of November Anno Dom: 1753, and in the twenty-Seventh year of the Reign of our Soveraig'n Lord George the Second of great Britain the King.
    Signed Sealed & Delivered.
    In presence of
    Sam Vaughan   Margaret Burgis
    Mary Vaughan   her X mark.

T his quaint document was carefully locked up, with some old deeds and other valuable papers, in his desk, by the "s:ᵈ Samuel Wales," one hundred and thirty years ago. The desk was a rude, unpainted pine affair, and it reared itself on its four stilt-like legs in a corner of his kitchen, in his house in the South Precinct of Braintree. The sharp eyes of the little "s:ᵈ apprentice" had noted it oftener and more enviously than any other article of furniture in the house. On the night of her arrival, after her journey of fourteen miles from Boston, over a rough bridle-road, on a jolting horse, clinging tremblingly to her new "Master," she peered through her little red fingers at the desk swallowing up those precious papers which Samuel Wales drew from his pocket with an important air. She was hardly five years old, but she was an acute child; and she watched her master draw forth the papers, show them to his wife, Polly, and lock them up in the desk, with the full understanding that they had something to do with her coming to this strange place; and, already, a shadowy purpose began to form itself in her mind.

She sat on a cunning little wooden stool, close to the fireplace, and kept her small chapped hands persistently over her face; she was scared, and grieved, and, withal a trifle sulky. Mrs. Polly Wales cooked some Indian meal mush for supper in an iron pot swinging from its trammel over the blazing logs, and cast scrutinizing glances at the little stranger. She had welcomed her kindly, taken off her outer garments, and established her on the little stool in the warmest corner, but the child had given a very ungracious response. She would not answer a word to Mrs. Wales' coaxing questions, but twitched herself away with all her small might, and kept her hands tightly over her eyes, only peering between her fingers when she thought no one was noticing.

She had behaved after the same fashion all the way from Boston, as Mr. Wales told his wife in a whisper. The two were a little dismayed at the whole appearance of the small apprentice; to tell the truth, she was not in the least what they had expected. They had been revolving this scheme of taking "a bound girl" for some time in their minds; and Samuel Wales' gossip in Boston, Sam Vaughan, had been requested to keep a lookout for a suitable person.

So, when word came that one had been found, Mr. Wales had started at once for the city. When he saw the child, he was dismayed. He had expected to see a girl of ten: this one was hardly five, and she had anything but the demure and decorous air which his Puritan mind esteemed becoming and appropriate in a little maiden. Her hair was black and curled tightly, instead of being brown and straight parted in the middle, and combed smoothly over her ears as his taste regulated: her eyes were black and flashing, instead of being blue, and downcast. The minute he saw the child, he felt a disapproval of her rise in his heart, and also something akin to terror. He dreaded to take this odd-looking child home to his wife Polly; he foresaw contention and mischief in their quiet household. But he felt as if his word was rather pledged to his gossip, and there was the mother, waiting and expectant. She was a red-cheeked English girl, who had been in Sam Vaughan's employ: she had recently married one Burjust, and he was unwilling to support the first husband's child, so this chance to bind her out and secure a good home for her had been eagerly caught at.

The small Ann seemed rather at Samuel Wales' mercy, and he had not the courage to disappoint his friend or her mother; so the necessary papers were made out, Sam Vaughan's and wife's signatures affixed, and Margaret Burjust's mark, and he set out on his homeward journey with the child.

The mother was coarse and illiterate, but she had some natural affection; she "took on" sadly when the little girl was about to leave her, and Ann clung to her frantically. It was a pitiful scene, and Samuel Wales, who was a very tender-hearted man, was glad when it was over, and he jogging along the bridle-path.

But he had had other troubles to encounter. All at once, as he rode through Boston streets, with his little charge behind him, after leaving his friend's house, he felt a vicious little twitch at his hair, which he wore in a queue tied with a black ribbon after the fashion of the period. Twitch, twitch, twitch! The water came into Samuel Wales' eyes, and the blood to his cheeks, while the passers-by began to hoot and laugh. His horse became alarmed at the hubbub, and started up. For a few minutes the poor man could do nothing to free himself. It was wonderful what strength the little creature had; she clinched her tiny fingers in the braid, and pulled, and pulled. Then, all at once, her grasp slackened, and off flew her master's steeple-crowned hat into the dust, and the neat black ribbon on the end of the queue followed it. Samuel Wales reined up his horse with a jerk then, and turned round, and administered a sounding box on each of his apprentice's ears. Then he dismounted, amid shouts of laughter from the spectators, and got a man to hold the horse while he went back and picked up his hat and ribbon.

He had no further trouble. The boxes seemed to have subdued Ann effectually. But he pondered uneasily all the way home on the small vessel of wrath which was perched up behind him, and there was a tingling sensation at the roots of his queue. He wondered what Polly would say. The first glance at her face, when he lifted Ann off the horse at his own door, confirmed his fears. She expressed her mind, in a womanly way, by whispering in his ear at the first opportunity, "She's as black as an Injun."

After Ann had eaten her supper, and had been tucked away between some tow sheets and homespun blankets in a trundle-bed, she heard the whole story, and lifted up her hands with horror. Then the good couple read a chapter, and prayed, solemnly vowing to do their duty by this child which they had taken under their roof, and imploring Divine assistance.

As time wore on, it became evident that they stood in sore need of it. They had never had any children of their own, and Ann Ginnins was the first child who had ever lived with them.

But she seemed to have the freaks of a dozen or more in herself, and they bade fair to have the experience of bringing up a whole troop with this one. They tried faithfully to do their duty by her, but they were not used to children, and she was a very hard child to manage. A whole legion of mischievous spirits seemed to dwell in her at times, and she became in a small and comparatively innocent way, the scandal of the staid Puritan neighborhood in which she lived. Yet, withal, she was so affectionate, and seemed to be actuated by so little real malice in any of her pranks, that people could not help having a sort of liking for the child, in spite of them.

She was quick to learn, and smart to work, too, when she chose. Sometimes she flew about with such alacrity that it seemed as if her little limbs were hung on wires, and no little girl in the neighborhood could do her daily tasks in the time she could, and they were no inconsiderable tasks, either.

Very soon after her arrival she was set to "winding quills," so many every day. Seated at Mrs. Polly's side, in her little homespun gown, winding quills through sunny forenoons— how she hated it. She liked feeding the hens and pigs better, and when she got promoted to driving the cows, a couple of years later, she was in her element. There were charming possibilities of nuts and checkerberries and sassafras and sweet flag all the way between the house and the pasture, and the chance to loiter, and have a romp.

She rarely showed any unwillingness to go for the cows; but once, when there was a quilting at her mistress's house, she demurred. It was right in the midst of the festivities; they were just preparing for supper, in fact. Ann knew all about the good things in the pantry, she was wild with delight at the unwonted stir, and anxious not to lose a minute of it. She thought some one else might go for the cows that night. She cried and sulked, but there was no help for it. Go she had to. So she tucked up her gown—it was her best Sunday one—took her stick, and trudged along. When she came to the pasture, there were her master's cows waiting at the bars. So were Neighbor Belcher's cows also, in the adjoining pasture. Ann had her hand on the topmost of her own bars, when she happened to glance over at Neighbor Belcher's, and a thought struck her. She burst into a peal of laughter, and took a step towards the other bars. Then she went back to her own. Finally, she let down the Belcher bars, and the Belcher cows crowded out, to the great astonishment of the Wales cows, who stared over their high rails and mooed uneasily.

Ann drove the Belcher cows home and ushered them into Samuel Wales' barnyard with speed. Then she went demurely into the house. The table looked beautiful. Ann was beginning to quake inwardly, though she still was hugging herself, so to speak, in secret enjoyment of her own mischief. She had one hope—that supper would be eaten before her master milked. But the hope was vain. When she saw Mr. Wales come in, glance her way, and then call his wife out, she knew at once what had happened, and begun to tremble—she knew perfectly what Mr. Wales was saying out there. It was this: "That little limb has driven home all Neighbor Belcher's cows instead of ours; what's going to be done with her?"

She knew what the answer would be, too. Mrs. Polly was a peremptory woman.

Back Ann had to go with the Belcher cows, fasten them safely in their pasture again, and drive her master's home. She was hustled off to bed, then, without any of that beautiful supper. But she had just crept into her bed in the small unfinished room upstairs where she slept, and was lying there sobbing, when she heard a slow, fumbling step on the stairs. Then the door opened, and Mrs. Deacon Thomas Wales, Samuel Wales' mother, came in. She was a good old lady, and had always taken a great fancy to her son's bound girl; and Ann, on her part, minded her better than any one else. She hid her face in the tow sheet, when she saw grandma. The old lady had on a long black silk apron. She held something concealed under it, when she came in. Presently she displayed it.

"There—child," said she, "here's a piece of sweet cake and a couple of simballs, that I managed to save out for you. Jest set right up and eat 'em, and don't ever be so dretful naughty again, or I don't know what will become of you."

This reproof, tempered with sweetness, had a salutary effect on Ann. She sat up, and ate her sweet cake and simballs, and sobbed out her contrition to grandma, and there was a marked improvement in her conduct for some days.

Mrs. Polly was a born driver. She worked hard herself, and she expected everybody about her to. The tasks which Ann had set her did not seem as much out of proportion, then, as they would now. Still, her mistress, even then, allowed her less time for play than was usual, though it was all done in good faith, and not from any intentional severity. As time went on, she grew really quite fond of the child, and she was honestly desirous of doing her whole duty by her. If she had had a daughter of her own, it is doubtful if her treatment of her would have been much different.

Still, Ann was too young to understand all this, and, sometimes, though she was strong and healthy, and not naturally averse to work, she would rebel, when her mistress set her stints so long, and kept her at work when other children were playing.

Once in a while she would confide in grandma, when Mrs. Polly sent her over there on an errand and she had felt unusually aggrieved because she had had to wind quills, or hetchel, instead of going berrying, or some like pleasant amusement.

"Poor little cosset," grandma would say, pityingly. Then she would give her a simball, and tell her she must "be a good girl, and not mind if she couldn't play jest like the others, for she'd got to airn her own livin', when she grew up, and she must learn to work."

Ann would go away comforted, but grandma would be privately indignant. She was, as is apt to be the case, rather critical with her sons' wives, and she thought "Sam'l's kept that poor little gal too stiddy at work," and wished and wished she could shelter her under her own grandmotherly wing, and feed her with simballs to her heart's content. She was too wise to say anything to influence the child against her mistress, however. She was always cautious about that, even while pitying her. Once in a while she would speak her mind to her son, but he was easy enough—Ann would not have found him a hard taskmaster.

Still, Ann did not have to work hard enough to hurt her. The worst consequences were that such a rigid rein on such a frisky little colt perhaps had more to do with her "cutting up," as her mistress phrased it, than she dreamed of. Moreover the thought of the indentures securely locked up in Mr. Wales' tall wooden desk, was forever in Ann's mind. Half by dint of questioning various people, half by her own natural logic she had settled it within herself, that at any time the possession of these papers would set her free, and she could go back to her own mother, whom she dimly remembered as being loud-voiced, but merry, and very indulgent. However, Ann never meditated in earnest, taking the indentures; indeed, the desk was always locked—it held other documents more valuable than hers—and Samuel Wales carried the key in his waistcoat-pocket.

She went to a dame's school three months every year. Samuel Wales carted half a cord of wood to pay for her schooling, and she learned to write and read in the New England Primer. Next to her, on the split log bench, sat a little girl named Hannah French. The two became fast friends. Hannah was an only child, pretty and delicate, and very much petted by her parents. No long hard tasks were set those soft little fingers, even in those old days when children worked as well as their elders. Ann admired and loved Hannah, because she had what she, herself, had not; and Hannah loved and pitied Ann because she had not what she had. It was a sweet little friendship, and would not have been, if Ann had not been free from envy and Hannah humble and pitying.

When Ann told her what a long stint she had to do before school, Hannah would shed sympathizing tears.

Ann, after a solemn promise of secrecy, told her about the indentures one day. Hannah listened with round, serious eyes; her brown hair was combed smoothly down over her ears. She was a veritable little Puritan damsel herself.

"If I could only get the papers, I wouldn't have to mind her, and work so hard," said Ann.

Hannah's eyes grew rounder. "Why, it would be sinful to take them!" said she.

Ann's cheeks blazed under her wondering gaze, and she said no more.

When she was about eleven years old, one icy January day, Hannah wanted her to go out and play on the ice after school. They had no skates, but it was rare fun to slide. Ann went home and asked Mrs. Polly's permission with a beating heart; she promised to do a double stint next day, if she would let her go. But her mistress was inexorable—work before play, she said, always; and Ann must not forget that she was to be brought up to work; it was different with her from what it was with Hannah French. Even this she meant kindly enough, but Ann saw Hannah go away, and sat down to her spinning with more fierce defiance in her heart than had ever been there before. She had been unusually good, too, lately. She always was, during the three months' schooling, with sober, gentle little Hannah French.

She had been spinning sulkily a while, and it was almost dark, when a messenger came for her master and mistress to go to Deacon Thomas Wales', who had been suddenly taken very ill.

Ann would have felt sorry if she had not been so angry. Deacon Wales was almost as much of a favorite of hers as his wife. As it was, the principal thing she thought of, after Mr. Wales and his wife had gone, was that the key was in the desk. However it had happened, there it was. She hesitated a moment. She was all alone in the kitchen, and her heart was in a tumult of anger, but she had learned her lessons from the Bible and the New England Primer, and she was afraid of the sin. But at last she opened the desk, found the indentures, and hid them in the little pocket which she wore tied about her waist, under her petticoat.

Then Ann threw her blanket over her head, and got her poppet out of the chest. The poppet was a little doll manufactured from a corn-cob, dressed in an indigo-colored gown. Grandma had made it for her, and it was her chief treasure. She clasped it tight to her bosom, and ran across lots to Hannah French's.

Hannah saw her coming, and met her at the door.

"I've brought you my poppet," whispered Ann, all breathless, "and you must keep her always, and not let her work too hard. I'm going away!"

Hannah's eyes looked like two solemn moons.

"Where are you going, Ann?"

"I'm going to Boston to find my own mother." She said nothing about the indentures to Hannah—somehow she could not.

Hannah could not say much, she was so astonished, but as soon as Ann had gone, scudding across the fields, she went in with the poppet and told her mother.

Deacon Thomas Wales was very sick. Mr. and Mrs. Samuel remained at his house all night, but Ann was not left alone, for Mr. Wales had an apprentice who slept in the house.

Ann did not sleep any that night. She got up very early, before any one was stirring, and dressed herself in her Sunday clothes. Then she tied up her working clothes in a bundle, crept softly downstairs, and out doors.

It was bright moonlight and quite cold. She ran along as fast as she could on the Boston road. Deacon Thomas Wales' house was on the way. The windows were lit up. She thought of grandma and poor grandpa, with a sob in her heart, but she sped along. Past the schoolhouse, and meeting-house, too, she had to go, with big qualms of grief and remorse. But she kept on. She was a fast traveler.

She had reached the North Precinct of Braintree by daylight. So far, she had not encountered a single person. Now she heard horse's hoofs behind her. She began to run faster, but it was of no use. Soon Captain Abraham French loomed up on his big gray horse, a few paces from her. He was Hannah's father, but he was a tithing-man, and looked quite stern, and Ann had always stood in great fear of him.

She ran on as fast as her little heels could fly, with a thumping heart. But it was not long before she felt herself seized by a strong arm and swung up behind Captain French on the gray horse. She was in a panic of terror, and would have cried and begged for mercy if she had not been in so much awe of her captor. She thought with awful apprehension of these stolen indentures in her little pocket. What if he should find that out!

Captain French whipped up his horse, however, and hastened along without saying a word. His silence, if anything, caused more dread in Ann than words would have. But his mind was occupied. Deacon Thomas Wales was dead; he was one of his most beloved and honored friends, and it was a great shock to him. Hannah had told him about Ann's premeditated escape, and he had set out on her track as soon as he had found that she was really gone, that morning. But the news which he had heard on his way, had driven all thoughts of reprimand which he might have entertained, out of his head. He only cared to get the child safely back.

So not a word spoke Captain French, but rode on in grim and sorrowful silence, with Ann clinging to him, till he reached her master's door. Then he set her down with a stern and solemn injunction never to transgress again, and rode away.

Ann went into the kitchen with a quaking heart. It was empty and still. Its very emptiness and stillness seemed to reproach her. There stood the desk—she ran across to it, pulled the indentures from her pocket, put them in their old place, and shut the lid down. There they staid till the full and just time of her servitude had expired. She never disturbed them again.

On account of the grief and confusion incident on Deacon Wales' death, she escaped with very little censure. She never made an attempt to run away again. Indeed, she had no wish to, for after Deacon Wales' death, grandma was lonely and wanted her, and she lived most of the time with her. And, whether she was in reality treated any more kindly or not, she was certainly happier.

Amelia

By Charles Reznikoff

Charles Reznikoff (1894–1976) was born in Brooklyn, New York, and made New York City his home and the scene of all his writing throughout his long life. He briefly attended the University of Missouri and, in 1915, earned a law degree at New York University, though he never practiced law. Instead, he worked as an editor and legal writer, and

*devoted his energies to writing poems, plays, and some
fiction. His early work includes* Five Groups of Verse *(1927);*
Nine Plays *(1927);* Jerusalem the Golden *(1934); and*
Inscriptions: 1944–1956 *(1959). New Directions issued* By
the Waters of Manhattan: Selected Verse *in 1962 and*
Testimony: The United States *(1885–1890) in 1965. A new
volume of his work was published posthumously.*

   *Reznikoff was not widely appreciated in his own time—
except by other poets—and his work has been rarely
anthologized. His poetry grew from his walking through New
York's streets, into its buildings, observing its people.
"Amelia" is from a group of poems called "Testimony,"
"based on cases in the law reports." It appeared first in
a volume called* Going To and Fro and Walking Up and Down
(1941) and was later reprinted in By the Waters of Manhattan.

Amelia was just fourteen and out of the orphan asylum; at
   her first job—in the bindery, and yes sir, yes ma'am, oh, so
   anxious to please.
She stood at the table, her blonde hair hanging about her shoul-
      ders, "knocking up" for Mary and Sadie, the stitchers
("knocking up" is counting books and stacking them in piles
      to be taken away).
There were twenty wire-stitching machines on the floor,
      worked by a shaft that ran under the table;
as each stitcher put her work through the machine,
she threw it on the table. The books were piling up fast
and some slid to the floor
(the forelady had said, Keep the work off the floor!);
and Amelia stooped to pick up the books—
three or four had fallen under the table
between the boards nailed against the legs.
She felt her hair caught gently;
put her hand up and felt the shaft going round and round
and her hair caught on it, wound and winding around it,
until the scalp was jerked from her head,
and the blood was coming down all over her face and waist.

America and I

By Anzia Yezierska

*In the 1920s, many had heard of Anzia Yezierska (1885–1970);
today, hardly anyone has. A "lost" woman writer for the
last forty-five years, Yezierska's first collection of ghetto
stories,* Hungry Hearts *(1920), was so well-received that, on its
reputation, she was invited to Hollywood from New York's
Lower East Side. The "rags to riches girl," as she was
called, was born in a Polish* shtetl *or small town, from which
her family emigrated to the New World in the 1880s. One
of nine children, she watched her mother take in boarders,
peddle, sew, and serve her orthodox Jewish father who
spent his time in prayer. At seventeen, against all tradition,
she left home, not to marry, but to earn money for her
education. Like the young woman in "America and I,"
Yezierska worked in laundries, sweatshops, and factories.
Finally, she attended college. After* Hungry Hearts, *she
published several novels and collections of stories, among
them* Bread Givers *(1925; newly available in paperback), and*
Children of Loneliness *(1923), from which "America and I"
is taken. After* All That I Could Never Be *(1932), she published
little except occasional journalism and* Red Ribbon on a
White Horse, *an autobiography written when she was
sixty-five.*

*Yezierska was particularly sensitive to and angry about
the domestic confinement of Jewish women. She often wrote
of the rebellious woman who must escape from the ghetto
to become "a real person." Far from being critical of American
ways, her immigrant heroes often confirm the American
success story by achieving middle-class manners and status.
Yet they, like the writer herself, suffer bitter loneliness, cut
off from the old culture and ill at ease with the new. The
emotional anguish of Yezierska's characters, their
driving energy to be free, give her deceptively simple stories
their power.*

As one of the dumb, voiceless ones I speak. One of the millions of immigrants beating, beating out their hearts at your gates for a breath of understanding.

Ach! America! From the other end of the earth where I came, America was a land of living hope, woven of dreams, aflame with longing and desire.

Choked for ages in the airless oppression of Russia, the Promised Land rose up—wings for my stifled spirit—sunlight burning through my darkness—freedom singing to me in my prison—deathless songs turning prison-bars into strings of a beautiful violin.

I arrived in America. My young, strong body, my heart and soul pregnant with the unlived lives of generations clamoring for expression.

What my mother and father and their mother and father never had a chance to give out in Russia, I would give out in America. The hidden sap of centuries would find release; colors that never saw light—songs that died unvoiced—romance that never had a chance to blossom in the black life of the Old World.

In the golden land of flowing opportunity I was to find my work that was denied me in the sterile village of my forefathers. Here I was to be free from the dead drudgery for bread that held me down in Russia. For the first time in America, I'd cease to be a slave of the belly. I'd be a creator, a giver, a human being! My work would be the living joy of fullest self-expression.

But from my high visions, my golden hopes, I had to put my feet down on earth. I had to have food and shelter. I had to have the money to pay for it.

I was in America, among the Americans, but not of them. No speech, no common language, no way to win a smile of understanding from them, only my young, strong body and my untried faith. Only my eager, empty hands, and my full heart shining from my eyes!

God from the world! Here I was with so much richness in me but my mind was not wanted without the language. And my body, unskilled, untrained, was not even wanted in the factory. Only one of two chances was left open to me: the kitchen, or minding babies.

My first job was as a servant in an Americanized family. Once, long ago, they came from the same village from where I came. But they were so well-dressed, so well-fed, so successful in America, that they were ashamed to remember their mother tongue.

"What were to be my wages?" I ventured timidly, as I looked up to the well-fed, well-dressed "American" man and woman.

They looked at me with a sudden coldness. What have I said to draw away from me their warmth? Was it so low from me to talk of wages? I shrank back into myself like a low-down bargainer. Maybe they're so high up in well-being they can't any more understand my low thoughts for money.

From his rich height the man preached down to me that I must not be so grabbing for wages. Only just landed from the ship and already thinking about money when I should be thankful to associate with "Americans."

The woman, out of her smooth, smiling fatness assured me that this was my chance for a summer vacation in the country with her two lovely children. My great chance to learn to be a civilized being, to become an American by living with them.

So, made to feel that I was in the hands of American friends, invited to share with them their home, their plenty, their happiness, I pushed out from my head the worry for wages. Here was my first chance to begin my life in the sunshine, after my long darkness. My laugh was all over my face as I said to them: "I'll trust myself to you. What I'm worth you'll give me." And I entered their house like a child by the hand.

The best of me I gave them. Their house cares were my house cares. I got up early. I worked till late. All that my soul hungered to give I put into the passion with which I scrubbed floors, scoured pots, and washed clothes. I was so grateful to mingle with the American people, to hear the music of the American language, that I never knew tiredness.

There was such a freshness in my brains and such a willingness in my heart that I could go on and on—not only with the work of the house, but work with my head—learning new words from the children, the grocer, the butcher, the iceman. I was not even afraid to ask for words from the policeman on the

street. And every new word made me see new American things
with American eyes. I felt like a Columbus, finding new worlds
through every new word.

But words alone were only for the inside of me. The outside
of me still branded me for a steerage immigrant. I had to have
clothes to forget myself that I'm a stranger yet. And so I had to
have money to buy these clothes.

The month was up. I was so happy! Now I'd have money. *My
own, earned* money. Money to buy a new shirt on my back—
shoes on my feet. Maybe yet an American dress and hat!

Ach! How high rose my dreams! How plainly I saw all that I
would do with my visionary wages shining like a light over my
head!

In my imagination I already walked in my new American
clothes. How beautiful I looked as I saw myself like a picture
before my eyes! I saw how I would throw away my immigrant
rags tied up in my immigrant shawl. With money to buy—free
money in my hands—I'd show them that I could look like an
American in a day.

Like a prisoner in his last night in prison, counting the seconds that will free him from his chains, I trembled breathlessly
for the minute I'd get the wages in my hand.

Before dawn I rose.

I shined up the house like a jewel-box.

I prepared breakfast and waited with my heart in my mouth
for my lady and gentleman to rise. At last I heard them stirring.
My eyes were jumping out of my head to them when I saw
them coming in and seating themselves by the table.

Like a hungry cat rubbing up to its boss for meat, so I edged
and simpered around them as I passed them the food. Without
my will, like a beggar, my hand reached out to them.

The breakfast was over. And no word yet from my wages.

"Gottuniu!" I thought to myself. Maybe they're so busy
with their own things they forgot it's the day for my wages.
Could they who have everything know what I was to do with
my first American dollars? How could they, soaking in plenty,
how could they feel the longing and the fierce hunger in me,
pressing up through each visionary dollar? How could they
know the gnawing ache of my avid fingers for the feel of my

own, earned dollars? *My* dollars that I could spend like a free person. *My* dollars that would make me feel with everybody alike!

Breakfast was long past.

Lunch came. Lunch past.

Oi-i weh! Not a word yet about my money.

It was near dinner. And not a word yet about my wages.

I began to set the table. But my head—it swam away from me. I broke a glass. The silver dropped from my nervous fingers. I couldn't stand it any longer. I dropped everything and rushed over to my American lady and gentleman.

"*Oi weh!* The money—my money—my wages!" I cried breathlessly.

Four cold eyes turned on me.

"Wages? Money?" The four eyes turned into hard stone as they looked me up and down. "Haven't you a comfortable bed to sleep, and three good meals a day? You're only a month here. Just came to America. And you already think about money. Wait till you're worth any money. What use are you without knowing English? You should be glad we keep you here. It's like a vacation for you. Other girls pay money yet to be in the country."

It went black for my eyes. I was so choked no words came to my lips. Even the tears went dry in my throat.

I left. Not a dollar for all my work.

For a long, long time my heart ached and ached like a sore wound. If murderers would have robbed me and killed me it wouldn't have hurt me so much. I couldn't think through my pain. The minute I'd see before me how they looked at me, the words they said to me—then everything began to bleed in me. And I was helpless.

For a long, long time the thought of ever working in an "American" family made me tremble with fear, like the fear of wild wolves. No—never again would I trust myself to an "American" family, no matter how fine their language and how sweet their smile.

It was blotted out in me all trust in friendship from "Americans." But the life in me still burned to live. The hope in me

(text continued on page 26)

Portraits
of the Authors

Ranice Henderson Crosby: 1978

Mary
Wilkins
Freeman:
circa 1880

Anzia
Yezierska:
circa 1920

Charles Reznikoff: 1974

Naomi Replansky: 1977

**Willa
Cather: 1935**

Nikki Giovanni: 1972

still craved to hope. In darkness, in dirt, in hunger and want, but only to live on!

There had been no end to my day—working for the "American" family.

Now rejecting false friendships from higher-ups in America, I turned back to the Ghetto. I worked on a hard bench with my own kind on either side of me. I knew before I began what my wages were to be. I knew what my hours were to be. And I knew the feeling of the end of the day.

From the outside my second job seemed worse than the first. It was in a sweat-shop of a Delancey Street basement, kept up by an old, wrinkled woman that looked like a black witch of greed. My work was sewing on buttons. While the morning was still dark I walked into a dark basement. And darkness met me when I turned out of the basement.

Day after day, week after week, all the contact I got with America was handling dead buttons. The money I earned was hardly enough to pay for bread and rent. I didn't have a room to myself. I didn't even have a bed. I slept on a mattress on the floor in a rat-hole of a room occupied by a dozen other immigrants. I was always hungry—oh, so hungry! The scant meals I could afford only sharpened my appetite for real food. But I felt myself better off than working in the "American" family, where I had three good meals a day and a bed to myself. With all the hunger and darkness of the sweat-shop, I had at least the evening to myself. And all night was mine. When all were asleep, I used to creep up on the roof of the tenement and talk out my heart in silence to the stars in the sky.

"Who am I? What am I? What do I want with my life? Where is America? Is there an America? What is this wilderness in which I'm lost?"

I'd hurl my questions and then think and think. And I could not tear it out of me, the feeling that America must be somewhere, somehow—only I couldn't find it—*my America*, where I would work for love and not for a living. I was like a thing following blindly after something far off in the dark!

"*Oi weh!*" I'd stretch out my hand up in the air. "My head is so lost in America! What's the use of all my working if I'm not in it? Dead buttons is not me."

Then the busy season started in the shop. The mounds of buttons grew and grew. The long day stretched out longer. I had to begin with the buttons earlier and stay with them till later in the night. The old witch turned into a huge greedy maw for wanting more and more buttons.

For a glass of tea, for a slice of herring over black bread, she would buy us up to stay another and another hour, till there seemed no end to her demands.

One day, the light of self-assertion broke into my cellar darkness.

"I don't want the tea. I don't want your herring," I said with terrible boldness. "I only want to go home. I only want the evening to myself!"

"You fresh mouth, you!" cried the old witch. "You learned already too much in America. I want no clock-watchers in my shop. Out you go!"

I was driven out to cold and hunger. I could no longer pay for my mattress on the floor. I no longer could buy the bite in the mouth. I walked the streets. I knew what it is to be alone in a strange city, among strangers.

But I laughed through my tears. So I learned too much already in America because I wanted the whole evening to myself? Well America has yet to teach me still more: how to get not only the whole evening to myself, but a whole day a week like the American workers.

That sweat-shop was a bitter memory but a good school. It fitted me for a regular factory. I could walk in boldly and say I could work at something, even if it was only sewing on buttons.

Gradually, I became a trained worker. I worked in a light, airy factory, only eight hours a day. My boss was no longer a sweater and a blood-squeezer. The first freshness of the morning was mine. And the whole evening was mine. All day Sunday was mine.

Now I had better food to eat. I slept on a better bed. Now, I even looked dressed up like the American-born. But inside of me I knew that I was not yet an American. I choked with longing when I met an American-born, and I could say nothing.

Something cried dumb in me. I couldn't help it. I didn't

know what it was I wanted. I only knew I wanted. I wanted.
Like the hunger in the heart that never gets food.

An English class for foreigners started in our factory. The
teacher had such a good, friendly face, her eyes looked so
understanding, as if she could see right into my heart. So I went
to her one day for an advice:

"I don't know what is with me the matter," I began. "I have
no rest in me. I never yet done what I want."

"What is it you want to do, child?" she asked me.

"I want to do something with my head, my feelings. All day
long, only with my hands I work."

"First you must learn English." She patted me as if I was not
yet grown up. "Put your mind on that, and then we'll see."

So for a time I learned the language. I could almost begin to
think with English words in my head. But in my heart the
emptiness still hurt. I burned to give, to give something, to do
something, to be something. The dead work with my hands
was killing me. My work left only hard stones on my heart.

Again I went to our factory teacher and cried to her: "I know
already to read and write the English language, but I can't put it
into words what I want. What is it in me so different that can't
come out?"

She smiled at me down from her calmness as if I were a little
bit out of my head. "What *do you want* to do?"

"I feel. I see. I hear. And I want to think it out. But I'm like
dumb in me. I only feel I'm different—different from everybody."

She looked at me close and said nothing for a minute. "You
ought to join one of the social clubs of the Women's Association," she advised.

"What's the Women's Association?" I implored greedily.

"A group of American women who are trying to help the
working-girl find herself. They have a special department for
immigrant girls like you."

I joined the Women's Association. On my first evening there
they announced a lecture: "The Happy Worker and His Work,"
by the Welfare director of the United Mills Corporation.

"Is there such a thing as a happy worker at his work?" I wondered. Happiness is only by working at what you love. And what poor girl can ever find it to work at what she loves? My old dreams about my America rushed through my mind. Once I thought that in America everybody works for love. Nobody has to worry for a living. Maybe this welfare man came to show me the *real* America that till now I sought in vain.

With a lot of polite words the head lady of the Women's Association introduced a higher-up that looked like the king of kings of business. Never before in my life did I ever see a man with such a sureness in his step, such power in his face, such friendly positiveness in his eye as when he smiled upon us.

"Efficiency is the new religion of business," he began. "In big business houses, even in up-to-date factories, they no longer take the first comer and give him any job that happens to stand empty. Efficiency begins at the employment office. Experts are hired for the one purpose, to find out how best to fit the worker to his work. It's economy for the boss to make the worker happy." And then he talked a lot more on efficiency in educated language that was over my head.

I didn't know exactly what it meant—efficiency—but if it was to make the worker happy at his work, then that's what I had been looking for since I came to America. I only felt from watching him that he was happy by his job. And as I looked on this clean, well-dressed, successful, one, who wasn't ashamed to say he rose from an office-boy, it made me feel that I, too, could lift myself up for a person.

He finished his lecture, telling us about the Vocational-Guidance Center that the Women's Association started.

The very next evening I was at the Vocational-Guidance Center. There I found a young, college-looking woman. Smartness and health shining from her eyes! She, too, looked as if she knew her way in America. I could tell at the first glance: here is a person that is happy by what she does.

"I feel you'll understand me," I said right away.

She leaned over with pleasure in her face: "I hope I can."

"I want to work by what's in me. Only, I don't know what's in me. I only feel I'm different."

She gave me a quick, puzzled look from the corner of her

eyes. "What are you doing now?"

"I'm the quickest shirtwaist hand on the floor. But my heart wastes away by such work. I think and think, and my thoughts can't come out."

"Why don't you think out your thoughts in shirtwaists? You could learn to be a designer. Earn more money."

"I don't want to look on waists. If my hands are sick from waists, how could my head learn to put beauty into them?"

"But you must earn your living at what you know, and rise slowly from job to job."

I looked at her office sign: "Vocational Guidance." "What's your vocational guidance?" I asked. "How to rise from job to job—how to earn more money?"

The smile went out from her eyes. But she tried to be kind yet. "What *do* you want?" she asked, with a sigh of last patience.

"I want America to want me."

She fell back in her chair, thunderstruck with my boldness. But yet, in a low voice of educated self-control, she tried to reason with me:

"You have to *show* that you have something special for America before America has need of you."

"But I never had a chance to find out what's in me, because I always had to work for a living. Only, I feel it's efficiency for America to find out what's in me so different, so I could give it out by my work."

Her eyes half closed as they bored through me. Her mouth opened to speak, but no words came from her lips. So I flamed up with all that was choking in me like a house on fire:

"America gives free bread and rent to criminals in prison. They got grand houses with sunshine, fresh air, doctors and teachers, even for the crazy ones. Why don't they have free boarding-schools for immigrants—strong people—willing people? Here you see us burning up with something different, and America turns her head away from us."

Her brows lifted and dropped down. She shrugged her shoulders away from me with the look of pity we give to cripples and hopeless lunatics.

"America is no Utopia. First you must become efficient in earning a living before you can indulge in your poetic dreams."

I went away from the vocational-guidance office with all the air out of my lungs. All the light out of my eyes. My feet dragged after me like dead wood.

Till now there had always lingered a rosy veil of hope over my emptiness, a hope that a miracle would happen. I would open my eyes some day and suddenly find the America of my dreams. As a young girl hungry for love sees always before her eyes the picture of lover's arms around her, so I saw always in my heart the vision of Utopian America.

But now I felt that the America of my dreams never was and never could be. Reality had hit me on the head as with a club. I felt that the America that I sought was nothing but a shadow—an echo—a chimera of lunatics and crazy immigrants.

Stripped of all illusion, I looked about me. The long desert of wasting days of drudgery stared me in the face. The drudgery that I had lived through, and the endless drudgery still ahead of me rose over me like a withering wilderness of sand. In vain were all my cryings, in vain were all frantic efforts of my spirit to find the living waters of understanding for my perishing lips. Sand, sand was everywhere. With every seeking, every reaching out I only lost myself deeper and deeper in a vast sea of sand.

I knew now the American language. And I knew now, if I talked to the Americans from morning till night, they could not understand what the Russian soul of me wanted. They could not understand *me* anymore than if I talked to them in Chinese. Between my soul and the American soul were worlds of difference that no words could bridge over. What was that difference? What made the Americans so far apart from me?

I began to read the American history. I found from the first pages that America started with a band of Courageous Pilgrims. They had left their native country as I had left mine. They had crossed an unknown ocean and landed in an unknown country, as I.

But the great difference between the first Pilgrims and me was that they expected to make America, build America, create their own world of liberty. I wanted to find it ready made.

I read on. I delved deeper down into the American history. I saw how the Pilgrim Fathers came to a rocky desert country, surrounded by Indian savages on all sides. But undaunted, they pressed on—through danger—through famine, pestilence, and want—they pressed on. They did not ask the Indians for sympathy, for understanding. They made no demands on anybody, but on their own indomitable spirit of persistence.

And I—I was forever begging a crumb of sympathy, a gleam of understanding from strangers who could not sympathize, who could not understand.

I, when I encountered a few savage Indian scalpers, like the old witch of the sweat-shop, like my "Americanized" countryman, who cheated me of my wages—I, when I found myself on the lonely, untrodden path through which all seekers of the new world must pass, I lost heart and said: "There is no America!"

Then came a light—a great revelation! I saw America—a big idea—a deathless hope—a world still in the making. I saw that it was the glory of America that it was not yet finished. And I, the last comer, had her share to give, small or great, to the making of America, like those Pilgrims who came in the *Mayflower*.

Fired up by this revealing light, I began to build a bridge of understanding between the American-born and myself. Since their life was shut out from such as me, I began to open up my life and the lives of my people to them. And life draws life. In only writing about the Ghetto I found America.

Great chances have come to me. But in my heart is always a deep sadness. I feel like a man who is sitting down to a secret table of plenty, while his near ones and dear ones are perishing before his eyes. My very joy in doing the work I love hurts me like secret guilt, because all about me I see so many with my longings, my burning eagerness, to do and to be, wasting their days in drudgery they hate, merely to buy bread and pay rent. And America is losing all that richness of the soul.

The Americans of to-morrow, the America that is every day nearer coming to be, will be too wise, too open-hearted, too friendly-handed, to let the least last-comer at their gates knock in vain with his gifts unwanted.

A Wagner Matinee

By Willa Cather

*Willa Cather (1873–1947) was born on a farm in Virginia into
a large family. When she was ten, the family moved to
Nebraska, where, for the first time, Cather went to school.
Before then, she had been taught at home by her grand-
mother. After her graduation from the University of
Nebraska in 1894, she worked as a journalist for much of the
next two decades, briefly in Lincoln, then in Pittsburgh, later
in New York. She taught in a high school during 1901
and was managing editor of the "muckraking" New York
magazine,* McClure's, *from 1908 to 1912. Beginning in
1912, she worked full-time at writing fiction. Her most
famous novels,* O Pioneers! *and* My Antonia, *appeared in
1913 and 1918 respectively. Cather won the Pulitzer Prize
in 1922 for a novel,* One of Ours. *She was awarded numerous
honorary degrees during her lifetime and was elected to the
National Institute of Arts and Letters in 1929 and to the
American Academy of Arts and Letters in 1938. She received
the Howells Medal of the Academy in 1930, and the Institute
medal for fiction in 1944. One of her later novels,* Shadows
on the Rock *(1931), received the first annual Prix Femina
Américaine in 1933. In all, she published twelve novels,
several volumes of stories, and a collection of essays.
Seven additional volumes of fiction, essays, travel notes, and
miscellaneous prose were published after her death.*

   *Unlike other women writers in this collection, Willa
Cather's reputation has remained relatively undimmed since
her death, though she is known mainly through a single
novel and a couple of short stories. "A Wagner Matinee,"
an early masterpiece, has rarely been anthologized. Published
first in 1904, it is based on Cather's understanding of the
lives of frontier women.*

I received one morning a letter, written in pale ink on glassy,
blue-lined note-paper, and bearing the postmark of a little

Nebraska village. This communication, worn and rubbed, looking as if it had been carried for some days in a coat pocket that was none too clean, was from my uncle Howard, and informed me that his wife had been left a small legacy by a bachelor relative, and that it would be necessary for her to go to Boston to attend to the settling of the estate. He requested me to meet her at the station and render her whatever services might be necessary. On examining the date indicated as that of her arrival, I found it to be no later than tomorrow. He had characteristically delayed writing until, had I been away from home for a day, I must have missed my aunt altogether.

The name of my Aunt Georgiana opened before me a gulf of recollection so wide and deep that, as the letter dropped from my hand, I felt suddenly a stranger to all the present conditions of my existence, wholly ill at ease and out of place amid the familiar surroundings of my study. I became in short, the gangling farmer-boy my aunt had known, scourged with chilblains and bashfulness, my hands cracked and sore from the corn husking. I sat again before her parlour organ, fumbling the scales with my stiff, red fingers, while she, beside me, made canvas mittens for the huskers.

The next morning, after preparing my landlady for the visitor, I set out for the station. When the train arrived I had some difficulty in finding my aunt. She was the last of the passengers to alight, and it was not until I got her into the carriage that she seemed really to recognize me. She had come all the way in a day coach; her linen duster had become black with soot and her black bonnet grey with dust during the journey. When we arrived at my boarding-house the landlady put her to bed at once and I did not see her again until the next morning.

Whatever shock Mrs. Springer experienced at my aunt's appearance, she considerately concealed. As for myself, I saw my aunt's battered figure with that feeling of awe and respect with which we behold explorers who have left their ears and fingers north of Franz-Joseph-Land, or their health somewhere along the Upper Congo. My Aunt Georgiana had been a music teacher at the Boston Conservatory, somewhere back in the latter sixties. One summer, while visiting in the little village

among the Green Mountains where her ancestors had dwelt for
generations, she had kindled the callow fancy of my uncle,
Howard Carpenter, then an idle, shiftless boy of twenty-one.
When she returned to her duties in Boston, Howard followed
her, and the upshot of this infatuation was that she eloped with
him, eluding the reproaches of her family and the criticism of
her friends by going with him to the Nebraska frontier. Carpenter, who, of course, had no money, took up a homestead in
Red Willow County, fifty miles from the railroad. There they
had measured off their land themselves, driving across the
prairie in a wagon, to the wheel of which they had tied a red
cotton handkerchief, and counting its revolutions. They built a
dug-out in the red hillside, one of those cave dwellings whose
inmates so often reverted to primitive conditions. Their water
they got from the lagoons where the buffalo drank, and their
slender stock of provisions was always at the mercy of bands of
roving Indians. For thirty years my aunt had not been farther
than fifty miles from the homestead.

I owed this woman most of the good that ever came my way
in my boyhood, and had a reverential affection for her. During
the years when I was riding herd for my uncle, my aunt, after
cooking the three meals—the first of which was ready at six
o'clock in the morning—and putting the six children to bed,
would often stand until midnight at her ironing-board, with me
at the kitchen table beside her, hearing me recite Latin declen-
sions and conjugations, gently shaking me when my drowsy
head sank down over a page of irregular verbs. It was to her, at
her ironing or mending, that I read my first Shakspere, and her
old text-book on mythology was the first that ever came into
my empty hands. She taught me my scales and exercises on the
little parlour organ which her husband had bought her after
fifteen years during which she had not so much as seen a musical instrument. She would sit beside me by the hour, darning
and counting, while I struggled with the "Joyous Farmer." She
seldom talked to me about music, and I understood why. Once
when I had been doggedly beating out some easy passages from
an old score of *Euryanthe* I had found among her music books,
she came up to me and, putting her hands over my eyes, gently

drew my head back upon her shoulder, saying tremulously, "Don't love it so well, Clark, or it may be taken from you."

When my aunt appeared on the morning after her arrival in Boston, she was still in a semi-somnanbulant state. She seemed not to realize that she was in the city where she had spent her youth, the place longed for hungrily half a lifetime. She had been so wretchedly trainsick throughout the journey that she had no recollection of anything but her discomfort, and to all intents and purposes, there were but a few hours of nightmare between the farm in Red Willow County and my study on Newbury Street. I had planned a little pleasure for her that afternoon, to repay her for some of the glorious moments she had given me when we used to milk together in the straw-thatched cowshed and she, because I was more than usually tired, or because her husband had spoken sharply to me, would tell me of the splendid performance of the *Huguenots* she had seen in Paris, in her youth.

At two o'clock the Symphony Orchestra was to give a Wagner program, and I intended to take my aunt; though, as I conversed with her, I grew doubtful about her enjoyment of it. I suggested our visiting the Conservatory and the Common before lunch, but she seemed altogether too timid to wish to venture out. She questioned me absently about various changes in the city, but she was chiefly concerned that she had forgotten to leave instructions about feeding half-skimmed milk to a certain weakling calf, "old Maggie's calf, you know, Clark," she explained, evidently having forgotten how long I had been away. She was further troubled because she had neglected to tell her daughter about the freshly-opened kit of mackerel in the cellar, which would spoil if it were not used directly.

I asked her whether she had ever heard any of the Wagnerian operas, and found that she had not, though she was perfectly familiar with their respective situations, and once possessed the piano score of *The Flying Dutchman*. I began to think it would be best to get her back to Red Willow County without waking her, and regretted having suggested the concert.

From the time we entered the concert hall, however, she was a trifle less passive and inert, and for the first time seemed to perceive her surroundings. I had felt some trepidation lest she might become aware of her queer, country clothes, or might experience some painful embarrassment at stepping suddenly into the world to which she had been dead for a quarter of a century. But, again, I found how superficially I had judged her. She sat looking about her with eyes as impersonal, almost as stony, as those with which the granite Rameses in a museum watches the froth and fret that ebbs and flows about his pedestal. I have seen this same aloofness in old miners who drift into the Brown hotel at Denver, their pockets full of bullion, their linen soiled, their haggard faces unshaven; standing in the thronged corridors as solitary as though they were still in a frozen camp on the Yukon.

The matinée audience was made up chiefly of women. One lost the contour of faces and figures, indeed any effect of line whatever, and there was only the colour of bodices past counting, the shimmer of fabrics soft and firm, silky and sheer; red, mauve, pink, blue, lilac, purple, ecru, rose, yellow, cream, and white, all the colours that an impressionist finds in a sunlit landscape, with here and there the dead shadow of a frock coat. My Aunt Georgiana regarded them as though they had been so many daubs of tube-paint on a palette.

When the musicians came out and took their places, she gave a little stir of anticipation, and looked with quickening interest down over the rail at that invariable grouping, perhaps the first wholly familiar thing that had greeted her eye since she had left old Maggie and her weakling calf. I could feel how all those details sank into her soul, for I had not forgotten how they had sunk into mine when I came fresh from ploughing forever and forever between green aisles of corn, where, as in a treadmill, one might walk from daybreak to dusk without perceiving a shadow of change. The clean profiles of the musicians, the gloss of their linen, the dull black of their coats, the beloved shapes of the instruments, the patches of yellow light on the smooth, varnished bellies of the 'cellos and the bass viols in the rear, the restless, wind-tossed forest of fiddle necks and bows—I recalled how, in the first orchestra I ever heard, those long bow-strokes seemed to draw the heart out of me, as a conjurer's stick reels out yards of paper ribbon from a hat.

The first number was the *Tännhauser* overture. When the horns drew out the first strain of the Pilgrim's chorus, Aunt Georgiana clutched my coat sleeve. Then it was I first realized that for her this broke a silence of thirty years. With the battle between the two motives, with the frenzy of the Venusberg theme and its ripping of strings, there came to me an overwhelming sense of the waste and wear we are so powerless to combat; and I saw again the tall, naked house on the prairie, black and grim as a wooden fortress; the black pond where I had learned to swim, its margin pitted with sun-dried cattle tracks; the rain gullied clay banks about the naked house, the four dwarf ash seedlings where the dish-cloths were always hung to dry before the kitchen door. The world there was the flat world of the ancients; to the east, a cornfield that stretched to daybreak; to the west, a corral that reached to sunset; between, the conquests of peace, dearer-bought than those of war.

The overture closed, my aunt released my coat sleeve, but she said nothing. She sat staring dully at the orchestra. What, I wondered, did she get from it? She had been a good pianist in her day, I knew, and her musical education had been broader than that of most music teachers of a quarter of a century ago. She had often told me of Mozart's operas and Meyerbeer's, and I could remember hearing her sing, years ago, certain melodies of Verdi. When I had fallen ill with a fever in her house she used to sit by my cot in the evening—when the cool, night wind blew in through the faded mosquito netting tacked over the window and I lay watching a certain bright star that burned red above the cornfield—and sing "Home to our mountains, O, let us return!" in a way fit to break the heart of a Vermont boy near dead of homesickness already.

I watched her closely through the prelude to *Tristan and Isolde,* trying vainly to conjecture what that seething turmoil of strings and winds might mean to her, but she sat mutely staring at the violin bows that drove obliquely downward, like the pelting streaks of rain in a summer shower. Had this music any message for her? Had she enough left to at all comprehend this power which had kindled the world since she had left it? I was in a fever of curiosity, but Aunt Georgiana sat silent upon her peak in Darien. She preserved this utter immobility throughout the number from *The Flying Dutchman,* though her fingers worked mechanically upon her black dress, as if, of themselves, they were recalling the piano score they had once played. Poor hands! They had been stretched and twisted into mere tentacles to hold and lift and knead with;—on one of them a thin, worn band that had once been a wedding ring. As I pressed and gently quieted one of those groping hands, I remembered with quivering eyelids their services for me in other days.

Soon after the tenor began the "Prize Song," I heard a quick drawn breath and turned to my aunt. Her eyes were closed, but the tears were glistening on her cheeks, and I think, in a moment more, they were in my eyes as well. It never really died, then—the soul which can suffer so excruciatingly and so interminably; it withers to the outward eye only; like that strange moss which can lie on a dusty shelf half a century and yet, if placed in water, grows green again. She wept so throughout the development and elaboration of the melody.

During the intermission before the second half, I questioned my aunt and found that the "Prize Song" was not new to her. Some years before there had drifted to the farm in Red Willow County a young German, a tramp cow-puncher, who had sung in the chorus at Bayreuth when he was a boy, along with the other peasant boys and girls. Of a Sunday morning he used to sit on his gingham-sheeted bed in the hands' bedroom which opened off the kitchen, cleaning the leather of his boots and saddle, singing the "Prize Song," while my aunt went about her work in the kitchen. She had hovered over him until she had prevailed upon him to join the country church, though his sole fitness for this step, in so far as I could gather, lay in his boyish face and his possession of this divine melody. Shortly afterward, he had gone to town on the Fourth of July, been drunk for several days, lost his money at a faro table, ridden a saddled Texas steer on a bet, and disappeared with a fractured collarbone. All this my aunt told me huskily, wanderingly, as though she were talking in the weak lapses of illness.

"Well, we have come to better things than the old *Trovatore* at any rate, Aunt Georgie?" I queried, with a well meant effort at jocularity.

Her lip quivered and she hastily put her handkerchief up to her mouth. From behind it she murmured, "And you have been hearing this ever since you left me, Clark?" Her question was the gentlest and saddest of reproaches.

The second half of the program consisted of four numbers from the *Ring*, and closed with Siegfried's funeral march. My aunt wept quietly, but almost continuously, as a shallow vessel overflows in a rain-storm. From time to time her dim eyes looked up at the lights, burning softly under their dull glass globes.

The deluge of sound poured on and on; I never knew what she found in the shining current of it; I never knew how far it bore her, or past what happy islands. From the trembling of her face I could well believe that before the last number she had been carried out where the myriad graves are, into the grey, nameless burying grounds of the sea; or into some world of death vaster yet, where, from the beginning of the world, hope has lain down with hope and dream with dream and, renouncing, slept.

The concert was over; the people filed out of the hall chattering and laughing, glad to relax and find the living level again, but my kinswoman made no effort to rise. The harpist slipped the green felt cover over his instrument; the flute-players shook the water from their mouthpieces; the men of the orchestra went out one by one, leaving the stage to the chairs and music stands, empty as a winter cornfield.

I spoke to my aunt. She burst into tears and sobbed pleadingly. "I don't want to go, Clark, I don't want to go!"

I understood. For her, just outside the concert hall, lay the black pond with the cattle-tracked bluffs; the tall, unpainted house, with weather-curled boards, naked as a tower; the crook-backed ash seedlings where the dishcloths hung to dry; the gaunt, moulting turkeys picking up refuse about the kitchen door.

Waitresses

By Ranice Henderson Crosby

An only child born in Baltimore and reared by a mother who always worked outside the home, Ranice Crosby (1952–) began to write poems in a creative writing class when she was a high school senior. Her first published poems—included in No More Masks: An Anthology of Poems by Women—*were written in a Goucher College freshman seminar. After a second year, she left college to work as a waitress or "in kitchens of one sort or another." She returned to finish college at the State University of New York/College at Old Westbury, and stayed on that campus with The Feminist Press, where she has worked for four years in distribution and bookkeeping.*

Ranice Crosby has been studying with the poet Jean Valentine. A small volume of her poems, Uncomplicated, *was handprinted on a press that she and three other women learned to operate. "Waitresses," she says, "grew out of an increasing awareness of the base on which the waitress system rests—both sexual and economic. Shortly after I wrote the poem, I turned in my uniform."*

I think they give us uniforms
so we remember who we are
that's what I think.

our faces are
one gigantic grin.
I don't think they even notice
when we show our teeth
and raise our hackles.
we're always smiling
and nodding
and pleasing.

as for me
my uniform feels like skin.

Poem For Aretha

By Nikki Giovanni

*Nikki Giovanni (1943–) was born in Knoxville, Tennessee,
and grew up near Cincinatti, Ohio. She graduated from
Fisk University in Nashville, Tennessee, in 1967. At Fisk, she
attended John Killens' Writers Workshop, helped to
establish a branch of the Student Nonviolent Coordinating
Committee (SNCC) on campus, and edited the literary
magazine. In the late sixties, Giovanni planned
the first Black Arts Festival in Cincinnati and worked to
found The New (Black) Theatre in that city.*

    *Her first five books of poems were published in successive
years from 1968 on:* Black Feeling, Black Talk; Black
Judgement; Re: Creation; Spin a Soft Black Song: Poems for
Children; *and* My House. *Her autobiography,* Gemini,
*was published in 1972. Since then she has continued to pub-
lish poems. Giovanni has taught at Livingston College,
Rutgers University and has lectured and read poems on
many other campuses. Currently she lives near Cincinnati,
Ohio. "Poem for Aretha" comes from* Re: Creation.

Cause nobody deals with aretha—a mother with four children—
having to hit the road
they always say "after she comes
home" but nobody ever says what it's like
to get on a plane for a three week tour
the elation of the first couple of audiences the good
feeling of exchange the running on the high
you get from singing good
and loud and long telling the world
what's on your mind

then comes the eighth show on the sixth day the beginning
to smell like the plane or bus the if-you-forget-your-toothbrush

in-one-spot-you-can't-brush-until-the-second-show   the
    strangers
pulling at you cause they love you but you having no love
to give back
the singing the same songs night after night day after day
and if you read the gossip columns the rumors that your hus-
    band
is only after your fame
the wondering if your children will be glad to see you and
    maybe
the not caring if they are the scheming to get
out of just one show and go just one place where some doe-doe-
    dupaduke
won't say "just sing one song, please"

nobody mentions how it feels to become a freak
because you have talent and how
no one gives a damn how you feel
but only cares that aretha franklin is here like maybe that'll
    stop
        chickens from frying
        eggs from being laid
        crackers from hating

and if you say you're lonely or tired how they always
just say "oh come off it" or "did you see
how they loved you did you see huh did you?"
which most likely has nothing to do with you anyway
and i'm not saying aretha shouldn't have talent and i'm cer-
    tainly
not saying she should quit
singing but as much as i love her i'd vote "yes" to her
doing four concerts a year and staying home or doing whatever
she wants and making records cause it's a shame
the way we're killing her
we eat up artists like there's going to be a famine at the end
of those three minutes when there are in fact an abundance
of talents just waiting let's put some

of the giants away for a while and deal with them like they
    have
a life to lead

aretha doesn't have to relive billie holiday's life doesn't have
to relive dinah washington's death but who will
stop the pattern

she's more important than her music—if they must be separated—
and they should be separated when she has to pass out before
anyone recognizes she needs
a rest and i say i need
aretha's music
she is undoubtedly the one person who put everyone on
notice
she revived johnny ace and remembered lil green aretha sings
"i say a little prayer" and dionne doesn't
want to hear it anymore
aretha sings "money won't change you"
but james can't sing "respect" the advent
of aretha pulled ray charles from marlboro country
and back into
the blues made nancy wilson
try one more time forced
dionne to make a choice (she opted for the movies)
and diana ross had to get an afro wig pushed every
Black singer into his Blackness and negro entertainers
into negroness you couldn't jive
when she said "you make me/feel" the blazers
had to reply "gotta let a man be/a man"
aretha said "when my show was in the lost and found/you came
along to claim it" and joplin said "maybe"
there has been no musician whom her very presence hasn't
affected when humphrey wanted her to campaign for him she
    said
"woman's only human"
and he pressured james brown

they removed otis cause the combination was too strong the
    impressions had to say "lord have mercy/we're moving
    on up"
the Black songs started coming from the singers on stage and
    the dancers
in the streets
aretha was the riot was the leader if she had said "come
let's do it" it would have been done
temptations say why don't we think about it
                         think about it
                         think about it

TWO:
Satisfying Work
Sturdiness and Singing

THE IMMIGRANT in Anzia Yezierska's "American and I," search-ing for fulfillment in her work, wonders, "Is there such a thing as a happy worker?" She answers her own question: "Happi-ness is only by working at what you love." "Working at what you love," then, is one definition of satisfying work. But what makes you love the work? What makes it satisfying?

In this section of the anthology, satisfying work comes in many shapes: from hatmaking, typing, farming, baking, to casting clay pots, running, caring for children, studying medicine, working as an anthropologist or as a manufacturer. The people who work at these diverse jobs find them satisfying for various reasons. But certain factors seem consistently important: being good at one's work; having control over one's work; overcoming isolation. Jane, in Judith Higgins's "The Only People," is an excellent typist. Working efficiently, feeling the flow of words through the dictaphone into her ears, on to her fingers at the keyboard, gives Jane much pleasure. Similarly, when the husband and wife in "Tom's Husband" exchange jobs because they are not good at the work traditionally expected of

them, Mary gets great satisfaction out of being a capable, successful manufacturer. And Squeaky, in "Raymond's Run,"
enjoys being "the fastest thing on two feet."

Most of the people in these stories and poems have a large
degree of control over their work. This control takes the form
of being able to choose work, of not being forced into a specific
job. Although the student in "Medicine Man" may be dissatis-
fied with aspects of her work, it is something she has chosen to
do. Beyond the control involved in choosing work, though,
there is the pleasure of being in daily control, of working without a supervisor or boss. María in "The Whole Pot," the woman
in "The Bowl," Zora Neale Hurston in "Mules and Men," and
other women in this section decide when and how they will
work.

Interestingly, although most of these women do not have
supervisors and hence determine their own working conditions, they all work, to some degree, with other people. Often,
in fact, they make conscious attempts to do work that is not
isolating. Zora Neale Hurston chooses to work in her home
town because, "Here in Eatonville I knew everybody was going
to help me." Sometimes, as in the case of the woman baking
bread in "The Bowl," women overcome isolation by finding
connections in their work with people of the past. The bowl
she stirs, stirs memories in her, not only of her childhood, but
of the lives of the women in her family who also "used this
bowl to mix their lives." Thus, she is connected with them in
the act of work. María's work, in "The Whole Pot," takes on
added meaning as she connects it to the past by working to
recreate a special kind of ancient Native American pottery. On
another level, some of the women in these selections do work
that is not isolating because it promises to be socially useful.
When Squeaky realizes that she can share her skills with her
retarded brother and help him feel the kind of joy she feels, her
work gives her additional pleasure.

Although the stories and poems in this section are generally
optimistic because they show women doing satisfying work,
they also—both individually and as a group of selections—
illuminate problems. The women characters here who enjoy

doing traditionally male work, like the medical student and the manufacturer, feel many tensions in their lives. They are isolated from members of their own sex and subject to criticism of their chosen work by family and friends. Men, too, are affected by the sex-stereotyping of jobs. In "The Whole Pot," it is the husband who feels confined by tradition. Although making pottery is work that gives him pleasure, he believes that "Men aren't potters."

Finally, the characters in these selections are young, far younger as a group than the characters elsewhere in the volume. Most are under thirty and many are under twenty-two. Few of them are married, and still fewer combine family work and other work harmoniously. This section of the anthology affirms women's pleasure in creative, productive, satisfying work. But it also raises disturbing questions about why more women—and men—can't do the work they love.

Lineage

By Margaret Walker

All her life, Margaret Walker (1915–) has been writing about her slave-born ancestors—her "lineage." Born in Birmingham, Alabama, her father a minister, Walker went to college at Northwestern University. In her senior year, she wrote the first version of an historical novel, Jubilee. *During the years of the depression, she worked for the WPA, taught school, and then entered the University of Iowa's Writer's Workshop. As an M.A. thesis she wrote a book of poems,* For My People, *which won the Yale University Younger Poets award in 1942. In 1944, with the aid of several fellowships, she returned to the writing of* Jubilee. *Ten years later, the novel was still unfinished, and she laid it aside for seven years more while she taught full-time at Jackson State College in Mississippi and cared for her four children. Finally,*

in two and a half months at the home of a devoted friend,
Walker pushed herself "beyond all physical endurance," and
wrote the last words of Jubilee on April 9, 1965. Through
Jubilee's main character, Walker's great-grandmother,
the novel records and illuminates the period of the Civil War.
It is based on thirty years of research into her family's history.
  Since then, Walker has written a pamphlet, "How I
Wrote Jubilee," and another volume of poems, Prophets for a
New Day (1970). She is currently the director of the Institute
for the Study of History, Life, and Culture of Black
People at Jackson State University. "Lineage" is from
Walker's first prize-winning volume of poems. It captures
the spirit and strength of working farm women and
asks a troubling question in conclusion.

My grandmothers were strong.
They followed plows and bent to toil.
They moved through fields sowing seed.
They touched earth and grain grew.
They were full of sturdiness and singing.
My grandmothers were strong.

My grandmothers are full of memories
Smelling of soap and onions and wet clay
With veins rolling roughly over quick hands
They have many clean words to say.
My grandmothers were strong.
Why am I not as they?

Tom's Husband

By Sarah Orne Jewett

Sarah Orne Jewett (1849–1909) was born and lived almost
all of her life in South Berwick, Maine, a village on the

southern boundary of the state, which was also the setting
for her writing. Her ill health was responsible for her
irregular schooling and for her spending a good deal of time
in her physician-father's company—she made "rounds" with
him to get the benefit of the air in good weather. After
his death in 1878, Jewett began a deep friendship with the
writer Annie Adams Fields that lasted until her own death
in 1909. Jewett began to publish stories before she was
twenty under the assumed name of Alice Eliot or A.C. Eliot,
because she was too shy to admit to writing. Deephaven,
her first book of short stories, was published in 1877, and
eighteen other volumes followed regularly thereafter,
including A Marsh Island *(1885),* A White Heron *(1886),*
The King of Folly Island *(1888),* A Native of Winby *(1893),*
and The Country of the Pointed Firs *(1896). She also published*
two novels, one of them, A Country Doctor *(1884), a portrait*
of her father. Because of a serious fall on her fifty-third
birthday, she wrote very little during the last seven years
of her life. She enjoyed a friendship with the young Willa
Cather that led, after Jewett's death, to Cather's two editions
of her work.

While recognized in her time as a fine "local colorist" or
"regional" writer, Jewett has not, either in her own time or
since, received the critical appreciation she merits. She is
interesting today partly because she wrote about strong
relationships between women. While "Tom's Husband" does
not reflect that thematic interest, it is an unusual story
for 1884, the year it appeared in a volume called The Mate
of the Daylight, and Friends Ashore. *The setting is Maine,*
during a period when manufacturing was still common in
the towns and villages of New England.

I shall not dwell long upon the circumstances that led to the
marriage of my hero and heroine; though their courtship was,
to them, the only one that has ever noticeably approached the
ideal, it had many aspects in which it was entirely commonplace in other people's eyes. While the world in general smiles
at lovers with kindly approval and sympathy, it refuses to be

aware of the unprecedented delight which is amazing to the lovers themselves.

But, as has been true in many other cases, when they were at last married, the most ideal of situations was found to have been changed to the most practical. Instead of having shared their original duties, and, as school-boys would say, going halves, they discovered that the cares of life had been doubled. This led to some distressing moments for both our friends; they understood suddenly that instead of dwelling in heaven they were still upon earth, and had made themselves slaves to new laws and limitations. Instead of being freer and happier than ever before, they had assumed new responsibilities; they had established a new household, and must fulfill in some way or another the obligations of it. They looked back with affection to their engagement; they had been longing to have each other to themselves, apart from the world, but it seemed that they never felt so keenly that they were still units in modern society. Since Adam and Eve were in Paradise, before the devil joined them, nobody has had a chance to imitate that unlucky couple. In some respects they told the truth when, twenty times a day, they said that life had never been so pleasant before; but there were mental reservations on either side which might have subjected them to the accusation of lying. Somehow, there was a little feeling of disappointment, and they caught themselves wondering—though they would have died sooner than confess it—whether they were quite so happy as they had expected. The truth was, they were much happier than people usually are, for they had an uncommon capacity for enjoyment. For a little while they were like a sail-boat that is beating and has to drift a few minutes before it can catch the wind and start off on the other tack. And they had the same feeling, too, that any one is likely to have who has been long pursuing some object of his ambition or desire. Whether it is a coin, or a picture, or a stray volume of some old edition of Shakespeare, or whether it is an office under government or a lover, when fairly in one's grasp there is a loss of the eagerness that was felt in pursuit. Satisfaction, even after one has dined well, is not so interesting and eager a feeling as hunger.

My hero and heroine were reasonably well established to begin with: they each had some money, though Mr. Wilson had most. His father had at one time been a rich man, but with the decline, a few years before, of manufacturing interests, he had become, mostly through the fault of others, somewhat involved; and at the time of his death his affairs were in such a condition that it was still a question whether a very large sum or a moderately large one would represent his estate. Mrs. Wilson, Tom's step-mother, was somewhat of an invalid; she suffered severely at times with asthma, but she was almost entirely relieved by living in another part of the country. While her husband lived, she had accepted her illness as inevitable, and rarely left home; but during the last few years she had lived in Philadelphia with her own people, making short and wheezing visits only from time to time, and had not undergone a voluntary period of suffering since the occasion of Tom's marriage, which she had entirely approved. She had a sufficient property of her own, and she and Tom were independent of each other in that way. Her only other step-child was a daughter, who had married a navy officer, and had at this time gone out to spend three years (or less) with her husband, who had been ordered to Japan.

It is not unfrequently noticed that in many marriages one of the persons who choose each other as partners for life is said to have thrown himself or herself away, and the relatives and friends look on with dismal forebodings and ill-concealed submission. In this case it was the wife who might have done so much better, according to public opinion. She did not think so herself, luckily, either before marriage or afterward, and I do not think it occurred to her to picture to herself the sort of career which would have been her alternative. She had been an only child, and had usually taken her own way. Some one once said that it was a great pity that she had not been obliged to work for her living, for she had inherited a most uncommon business talent, and, without being disreputably keen at a bargain, her insight into the practical working of affairs was very clear and far-reaching. Her father, who had also been a manufacturer, like Tom's, had often said it had been a mistake that

she was a girl instead of a boy. Such executive ability as hers is
often wasted in the more contracted sphere of women, and is
apt to be more a disadvantage than a help. She was too independent and self-reliant for a wife; it would seem at first
thought that she needed a wife herself more than she did a husband. Most men like best the women whose natures cling and
appeal to theirs for protection. But Tom Wilson, while he did
not wish to be protected himself, liked these very qualities in
his wife which would have displeased some other men; to tell
the truth, he was very much in love with his wife just as she
was. He was a successful collector of almost everything but
money, and during a great part of his life he had been an invalid, and he had grown, as he laughingly confessed, very old-
womanish. He had been badly lamed, when a boy, by being
caught in some machinery in his father's mill, near which he
was idling one afternoon, and though he had almost entirely
outgrown the effect of his injury, it had not been until after
many years. He had been in college, but his eyes had given out
there, and he had been obliged to leave in the middle of his
junior year, though he had kept up a pleasant intercourse with
the members of his class, with whom he had been a great favorite. He was a good deal of an idler in the world. I do not
think his ambition, except in the case of securing Mary Dunn
for his wife, had ever been distinct; he seemed to make the
most he could of each day as it came, without making all his
days' works tend toward some grand result, and go toward the
upbuilding of some grand plan and purpose. He consequently
gave no promise of being either distinguished or great. When
his eyes would allow, he was an indefatigable reader; and although he would have said that he read only for amusement,
yet he amused himself with books that were well worth the
time he spent over them.

The house where he lived nominally belonged to his step-
mother, but she had taken for granted that Tom would bring
his wife home to it, and assured him that it should be to all
intents and purposes his. Tom was deeply attached to the old
place, which was altogether the pleasantest in town. He had
kept bachelor's hall there most of the time since his father's

death, and he had taken great pleasure, before his marriage, in refitting it to some extent, though it was already comfortable and furnished in remarkably good taste. People said of him that if it had not been for his illnesses, and if he had been a poor boy, he probably would have made something of himself. As it was, he was not very well known by the townspeople, being somewhat reserved, and not taking much interest in their every-day subjects of conversation. Nobody liked him so well as they liked his wife, yet there was no reason why he should be disliked enough to have much said about him.

After our friends had been married for some time, and had outlived the first strangeness of the new order of things, and had done their duty to their neighbors with so much apparent willingness and generosity that even Tom himself was liked a great deal better than he ever had been before, they were sitting together one stormy evening in the library, before the fire. Mrs. Wilson had been reading Tom the letters which had come to him by the night's mail. There was a long one from his sister in Nagasaki, which had been written with a good deal of ill-disguised reproach. She complained of the smallness of the income of her share in her father's estate, and said that she had been assured by American friends that the smaller mills were starting up everywhere, and beginning to do well again. Since so much of their money was invested in the factory, she had been surprised and sorry to find by Tom's last letters that he had seemed to have no idea of putting in a proper person as superintendent, and going to work again. Four per cent on her other property, which she had been told she must soon expect instead of eight, would make a great difference to her. A navy captain in a foreign port was obliged to entertain a great deal, and Tom must know that it cost them much more to live than it did him, and ought to think of their interests. She hoped he would talk over what was best to be done with their mother (who had been made executor, with Tom, of his father's will).

Tom laughed a little, but looked disturbed. His wife had said something to the same effect, and his mother had spoken once or twice in her letters of the prospect of starting the mill again. He was not a bit of a business man, and he did not feel certain,

with the theories which he had arrived at of the state of the
country, that it was safe yet to spend the money which would
have to be spent in putting the mill in order. "They think that
the minute it is going again we shall be making money hand
over hand, just as father did when we were children," he said.
"It is going to cost us no end of money before we can make
anything. Before father died he meant to put in a good deal of
new machinery, I remember. I don't know anything about the
business myself, and I would have sold out long ago if I had had
an offer that came anywhere near the value. The larger mills
are the only ones that are good for anything now, and we
should have to bring a crowd of French Canadians here; the day
is past for the people who live in this part of the country to go
into the factory again. Even the Irish all go West when they
come into the country, and don't come to places like this any
more."

"But there are a good many of the old work-people down in
the village," said Mrs. Wilson. "Jack Towne asked me the
other day if you weren't going to start up in the spring."

Tom moved uneasily in his chair. "I'll put you in for superintendent, if you like," he said, half angrily, whereupon Mary
threw the newspaper at him; but by the time he had thrown it
back he was in good humor again.

"Do you know, Tom," she said, with amazing seriousness,
"that I believe I should like nothing in the world so much as to
be the head of a large business? I hate keeping house,—I always
did; and I never did so much of it in all my life put together as I
have since I have been married. I suppose it isn't womanly to
say so, but if I could escape from the whole thing I believe I
should be perfectly happy. If you get rich when the mill is going
again, I shall beg for a housekeeper, and shirk everything. I give
you fair warning. I don't believe I keep this house half so well
as you did before I came here."

Tom's eyes twinkled. "I am going to have that glory,—I
don't think you do, Polly; but you can't say that I have not been
forbearing. I certainly have not told you more than twice how
we used to have things cooked. I'm not going to be your
kitchen-colonel."

"Of course it seemed the proper thing to do," said his wife, meditatively; "but I think we should have been even happier than we have if I had been spared it. I have had some days of wretchedness that I shudder to think of. I never know what to have for breakfast; and I ought not to say it, but I don't mind the sight of dust. I look upon housekeeping as my life's great discipline"; and at this pathetic confession they both laughed heartily.

"I've a great mind to take it off your hands," said Tom. "I always rather liked it, to tell the truth, and I ought to be a better housekeeper,—I have been at it for five years; though housekeeping for one is different from what it is for two, and one of them a woman. You see you have brought a different element into my family. Luckily, the servants are pretty well drilled. I do think you upset them a good deal at first!"

Mary Wilson smiled as if she only half heard what he was saying. She drummed with her foot on the floor and looked intently at the fire, and presently gave it a vigorous poking. "Well?" said Tom, after he had waited patiently as long as he could.

"Tom! I'm going to propose something to you. I wish you would really do as you said, and take all the home affairs under your care, and let me start the mill. I am certain I could manage it. Of course I should get people who understood the thing to teach me. I believe I was made for it; I should like it above all things. And this is what I will do: I will bear the cost of starting it, myself,—I think I have money enough, or can get it; and if I have not put affairs in the right trim at the end of a year I will stop, and you may make some other arrangement. If I have, you and your mother and sister can pay me back."

"So I am going to be the wife, and you the husband," said Tom, a little indignantly; "at least, that is what people will say. It's a regular Darby and Joan affair, and you think you can do more work in a day than I can do in three. Do you know that you must go to town to buy cotton? And do you know there are a thousand things about it that you don't know?"

"And never will?" said Mary, with perfect good humor. "Why, Tom, I can learn as well as you, and a good deal better, for I like business, and you don't. You forget that I was always father's right-hand man after I was a dozen years old, and that you have let me invest my money and some of your own, and I haven't made a blunder yet."

Tom thought that his wife had never looked so handsome or so happy. "I don't care, I should rather like the fun of knowing what people will say. It is a new departure, at any rate. Women think they can do everything better than men in these days, but I'm the first man, apparently, who has wished he were a woman."

"Of course people will laugh," said Mary, "but they will say that it's just like me, and think I am fortunate to have married a man who will let me do as I choose. I don't see why it isn't sensible: you will be living exactly as you were before you married, as to home affairs; and since it was a good thing for you to know something about housekeeping then, I can't imagine why you shouldn't go on with it now, since it makes me miserable, and I am wasting a fine business talent while I do it. What do we care for people's talking about it?"

"It seems to me that it is something like women's smoking: it isn't wicked, but it isn't the custom of the country. And I don't like the idea of your going among business men. Of course I should be above going with you, and having people think I must be an idiot; they would say that you married a manufacturing interest, and I was thrown in. I can foresee that my pride is going to be humbled to the dust in every way," Tom declared in mournful tones, and began to shake with laughter. "It is one of your lovely castles in the air, dear Polly, but an old brick mill needs a better foundation than the clouds. No, I'll look around, and get an honest, experienced man for agent. I suppose it's the best thing we can do, for the machinery ought not to lie still any longer; but I mean to sell the factory as soon as I can. I devoutly wish it would take fire, for the insurance would be the best price we are likely to get. That is a famous letter from Alice! I am afraid the captain has been growling over his pay, or they have been giving too many little dinners on board ship. If we were rid of the mill, you and I might go out there this winter. It would be capital fun."

Mary smiled again in an absent-minded way. Tom had an uneasy feeling that he had not heard the end of it yet, but nothing more was said for a day or two. When Mrs. Tom Wilson announced, with no apparent thought of being contradicted, that she had entirely made up her mind, and she meant to see those men who had been overseers of the different departments, who still lived in the village, and have the mill put in order at once, Tom looked disturbed, but made no opposition; and soon after breakfast his wife formally presented him with a handful of keys, and told him there was some lamb in the house for dinner; and presently he heard the wheels of her little phaeton rattling off down the road. I should be untruthful if I tried to persuade any one that he was not provoked; he thought she would at least have waited for his formal permission, and at first he meant to take another horse, and chase her, and bring her back in disgrace, and put a stop to the whole thing. But something assured him that she knew what she was about, and he determined to let her have her own way. If she failed, it might do no harm, and this was the only ungallant thought he gave her. He was sure that she would do nothing unladylike, or be unmindful of his dignity; and he believed it would be looked upon as one of her odd, independent freaks, which always had won respect in the end, however much they had been laughed at in the beginning. "Susan," said he, as that estimable person went by the door with the dust-pan, "you may tell Catherine to come to me for orders about the house, and you may do so yourself. I am going to take charge again, as I did before I was married. It is no trouble to me, and Mrs. Wilson dislikes it. Besides, she is going into business, and will have a great deal else to think of."

"Yes, sir; very well, sir," said Susan, who was suddenly moved to ask so many questions that she was utterly silent. But her master looked very happy; there was evidently no disapproval of his wife; and she went on up the stairs, and began to sweep them down, knocking the dust-brush about excitedly, as if she were trying to kill a descending colony of insects.

Tom went out to the stable and mounted his horse, which had been waiting for him to take his customary after-breakfast ride to the post-office, and he galloped down the road in quest of the phaeton. He saw Mary talking with Jack Towne, who had been an overseer and a valued workman of his father's. He was looking much surprised and pleased.

"I wasn't caring so much about getting work, myself," he explained; "I've got what will carry me and my wife through; but it'll be better for the young folks about here to work near home. My nephews are wanting something to do; they were going to Lynn next week. I don't say but I should like to be to work in the old place again. I've sort of missed it, since we shut down."

"I'm sorry I was so long in overtaking you," said Tom, politely, to his wife. "Well, Jack, did Mrs. Wilson tell you she's going to start the mill? You must give her all the help you can."

" 'Deed I will," said Mr. Towne, gallantly, without a bit of astonishment.

"I don't know much about the business yet," said Mrs. Wilson, who had been a little overcome at Jack Towne's lingo of the different rooms and machinery, and who felt an overpowering sense of having a great deal before her in the next few weeks. "By the time the mill is ready, I will be ready, too," she said, taking heart a little; and Tom, who was quick to understand her moods, could not help laughing, as he rode alongside. "We want a new barrel of flour, Tom, dear," she said, by way of punishment for his untimely mirth.

If she lost courage in the long delay, or was disheartened at the steady call for funds, she made no sign; and after a while the mill started up, and her cares were lightened, so that she told Tom that before next pay day she would like to go to Boston for a few days, and go to the theatre, and have a frolic and a rest. She really looked pale and thin, and she said she never worked so hard in all her life; but nobody knew how happy she was, and she was so glad she had married Tom, for some men would have laughed at it.

"I laughed at it," said Tom, meekly. "All is, if I don't cry by and by, because I am a beggar, I shall be lucky." But Mary looked fearlessly serene, and said that there was no danger at present.

It would have been ridiculous to expect a dividend the first year, though the Nagasaki people were pacified with difficulty. All the business letters came to Tom's address, and everybody who was not directly concerned thought that he was the motive power of the reawakened enterprise. Sometimes business people came to the mill, and were amazed at having to confer with Mrs. Wilson, but they soon had to respect her talents and her success. She was helped by the old clerk, who had been promptly recalled and reinstated, and she certainly did capitally well. She was laughed at, as she had expected to be, and people said they should think Tom would be ashamed of himself; but it soon appeared that he was not to blame, and what reproach was offered was on the score of his wife's oddity. There was nothing about the mill that she did not understand before very long, and at the end of the second year she declared a small dividend with great pride and triumph. And she was congratulated on her success, and every one thought of her project in a different way from the way they had thought of it in the beginning. She had singularly good fortune: at the end of the third year she was making money for herself and her friends faster than most people were, and approving letters began to come from Nagasaki. The Ashtons had been ordered to stay in that region, and it was evident that they were continually being obliged to entertain more instead of less. Their children were growing fast, too, and constantly becoming more expensive. The captain and his wife had already begun to congratulate themselves secretly that their two sons would in all probability come into possession, one day, of their uncle Tom's handsome property.

For a good while Tom enjoyed life, and went on his quiet way serenely. He was anxious at first, for he thought that Mary was going to make ducks and drakes of his money and her own. And then he did not exactly like the looks of the thing, either; he feared that his wife was growing successful as a business person at the risk of losing her womanliness. But as time went on, and he found there was no fear of that, he accepted the situation philosophically. He gave up his collection of engravings, having become more interested in one of coins and

medals, which took up most of his leisure time. He often went
to the city in pursuit of such treasures, and gained much re-
nown in certain quarters as a numismatologist of great skill
and experience. But at last his house (which had almost kept
itself, and had given him little to do beside ordering the dinners, while faithful old Catherine and her niece Susan were his
aids) suddenly became a great care to him. Catherine, who had
been the main-stay of the family for many years, died after a
short illness, and Susan must needs choose that time, of all
others, for being married to one of the second hands in the mill.
There followed a long and dismal season of experimenting, and
for a time there was a procession of incapable creatures going
in at one kitchen door and out of the other. His wife would not
have liked to say so, but it seemed to her that Tom was growing fussy about the house affairs, and took more notice of those
minor details than he used. She wished more than once, when
she was tired, that he would not talk so much about the housekeeping; he seemed sometimes to have no other thought.

In the early days of Mrs. Wilson's business life, she had
made it a rule to consult her husband on every subject of importance; but it had speedily proved to be a formality. Tom
tried manfully to show a deep interest which he did not feel,
and his wife gave up, little by little, telling him much about
her affairs. She said that she liked to drop business when she
came home in the evening; and at last she fell into the habit of
taking a nap on the library sofa, while Tom, who could not use
his eyes much by lamp-light, sat smoking or in utter idleness
before the fire. When they were first married his wife had made
it a rule that she should always read him the evening papers,
and afterward they had always gone on with some book of history or philosophy, in which they were both interested. These
evenings of their early married life had been charming to both
of them, and from time to time one would say to the other that
they ought to take up again the habit of reading together. Mary
was so unaffectedly tired in the evening that Tom never liked
to propose a walk; for, though he was not a man of peculiarly
social nature, he had always been accustomed to pay an occasional evening visit to his neighbors in the village. And though

he had little interest in the business world, and still less
knowledge of it, after a while he wished that his wife would
have more to say about what she was planning and doing, or
how things were getting on. He thought that her chief aid, old
Mr. Jackson, was far more in her thoughts than he. She was
forever quoting Jackson's opinions. He did not like to find that
she took it for granted that he was not interested in the welfare of his own property; it made him feel like a sort of pensioner and dependent, though, when they had guests at the
house, which was by no means seldom, there was nothing in
her manner that would imply that she thought herself in any
way the head of the family. It was hard work to find fault with
his wife in any way, though, to give him his due, he rarely tried.

But, this being a wholly unnatural state of things, the reader
must expect to hear of its change at last, and the first blow
from the enemy was dealt by an old woman, who lived near by,
and who called to Tom one morning, as he was driving down to
the village in a great hurry (to post a letter, which ordered his
agent to secure a long-wished-for ancient copper coin, at any
price), to ask him if they had made yeast that week, and if she
could borrow a cupful, as her own had met with some misfortune. Tom was instantly in a rage, and he mentally condemned
her to some undeserved fate, but told her aloud to go and see
the cook. This slight delay, besides being killing to his dignity,
caused him to lose the mail, and in the end his much-desired
copper coin. It was a hard day for him, altogether; it was Wednesday, and the first days of the week having been stormy the
washing was very late. And Mary came home to dinner pro-
vokingly good-natured. She had met an old school-mate and
her husband driving home from the mountains, and had first
taken them over her factory, to their great amusement and
delight, and then had brought them home to dinner. Tom
greeted them cordially, and manifested his usual graceful hos-
pitality; but the minute he saw his wife alone he said in a plain-
tive tone of rebuke, "I should think you might have remembered that the servants are unusually busy to-day. I do wish
you would take a little interest in things at home. The women

have been washing, and I'm sure I don't know what sort of a dinner we can give your friends. I wish you had thought to bring home some steak. I have been busy myself, and couldn't go down to the village. I thought we would only have a lunch."

Mary was hungry, but she said nothing, except that it would be all right,—she didn't mind; and perhaps they could have some canned soup.

She often went to town to buy or look at cotton, or to see some improvement in machinery, and she brought home beautiful bits of furniture and new pictures for the house, and showed a touching thoughtfulness in remembering Tom's fancies; but somehow he had an uneasy suspicion that she could get along pretty well without him when it came to the deeper wishes and hopes of her life, and that her most important concerns were all matters in which he had no share. He seemed to himself to have merged his life in his wife's; he lost his interest in things outside the house and grounds; he felt himself fast growing rusty and behind the times, and to have somehow missed a good deal in life; he had a suspicion that he was a failure. One day the thought rushed over him that his had been almost exactly the experience of most women, and he wondered if it really was any more disappointing and ignominious to him than it was to women themselves. "Some of them may be contented with it," he said to himself, soberly. "People think women are designed for such careers by nature, but I don't know why I ever made such a fool of myself."

Having once seen his situation in life from such a standpoint, he felt it day by day to be more degrading, and he wondered what he should do about it; and once, drawn by a new, strange sympathy, he went to the little family burying-ground. It was one of the mild, dim days that come sometimes in early November, when the pale sunlight is like the pathetic smile of a sad face, and he sat for a long time on the limp, frost-bitten grass beside his mother's grave.

But when he went home in the twilight his step-mother, who just then was making them a little visit, mentioned that she had been looking through some boxes of hers that had been packed long before and stowed away in the garret. "Everything looks very nice up there," she said, in her wheezing voice (which, worse than usual that day, always made him nervous); and added, without any intentional slight to his feelings, "I do think you have always been a most excellent housekeeper."

"I'm tired of such nonsense!" he exclaimed, with surprising indignation. "Mary, I wish you to arrange your affairs so that you can leave them for six months at least. I am going to spend this winter in Europe."

"Why, Tom, dear!" said his wife, appealingly. "I couldn't leave my business any way in the"—

But she caught sight of a look on his usually placid countenance that was something more than decision, and refrained from saying anything more.

And three weeks from that day they sailed.

The Whole Pot

By Alice Lee Marriott

Alice Lee Marriott (1910–) was born in Wilmette, Illinois, and has lived all but the first sixteen years of her life in Oklahoma. She earned a B.A. in English and French at Oklahoma City University in 1930, and another B.A. in anthropology at the University of Oklahoma in 1935. Since then, she has productively combined her work as an anthropologist and a writer. She has been a consultant to the Oklahoma Indian Council since 1962, has taught anthropology at the University of Oklahoma, and has been artist-in-residence at Central State University in Edmond, Oklahoma, since 1968. Her awards and honors include the University of Oklahoma Achievement Award (1952) and membership in both the Oklahoma Hall of Fame (1958) and the Oklahoma Literary Hall of Fame (1972). Since 1945, Marriott has published more than two dozen books and innumerable essays and

stories in periodicals. Her first book, The Ten Grandmothers
*(1945), records nearly two hundred years of Kiowa history
through stories of several generations of women and men.
Her other titles include:* American Indian Mythology
(1947; 1968); Indians of the Four Corners *(1952);* Hell on
Horses and Women *(1953);* Sequoyah: Leader of the Cherokees
(1956); Oklahoma: Its Past and Its Present *(1961);* Indian
Anne: Kiowa Captive *(1965);* Plains Indian Mythology *(1975).*

A number of Marriott's books, like María: The Potter of San
Ildefonso *(1948), are biographies based on careful interviews
and extensive research. "The Whole Pot," a chapter from
María's biography, records the first effort of María and
Julián Martínez, in 1908, to reproduce the kind of pottery that
anthropologists working in New Mexico had unearthed in
the form of sherds, or pieces of broken pottery. In a subsequent chapter, the wife and husband attempt to fire the pot
and, through an accident, produce the first piece of the
"black" pottery that eventually made María Martínez's work
famous.*

W hen they got home from Frijoles in the fall, María found
that there were many things she had to do. She wanted
the house clean and neat for the winter, so the first few weeks
she spent in cleaning and plastering and calsomining the
rooms. When that work was finished, she cleaned out her storeroom and put away the vegetables and fruit and corn that
Tomás had harvested and divided with María and Julián. Then
she had to make new clothes for the little boy to wear, and after
all that she made herself two new dresses.

All the time the old potsherd was in the back of her mind.
She was thinking about it as much as she was about her other
work. Every time that she was conscious of thinking about the
pottery, she put the thought away. It was like fruit ripening on
a tree. You could go out a few times in the season and look at it
on the branches, but you could not do anything until the fruit
was really ripe. María let the thought of the potsherd ripen
slowly in her mind. When the time came and she and the
thought had ripened, she would be ready to work.

Once or twice Julián spoke about the sherd to María. He asked her once where it was, and if she would mind letting him see and handle it. Another time he asked her when she was going to start making the pot.

"When the time comes," she told him.

"It's a long time coming," said Julián.

"I'll be ready for it," María answered, and that was all that either of them said.

Soon after that, the first boy was named in English. Julián wanted to name him Adam, and María asked if it were because Adam was the first man.

"No," Julián said, "it's for Adams, that worked on the job last summer. I like that Adams, and he's got a good name. I'd like to call my boy for him."

"Why don't you call him Adams?" Tomás asked when he heard this.

"Because everybody always forgets about that extra 's' anyway," said Julián. "If we call him Adam to start with, they won't have to forget."

So there was the first new man of the family. Somehow, when she looked at him now, María knew that she was never again going to have to worry about this child. He ate and slept, and when he waked, he laughed. He needed hardly any care.

So, one morning, María awoke with all her other jobs finished and was ready to begin on the pottery. After breakfast she got out the potsherd and sat down by the fire with the fragment in her hand. She sat and looked at the sherd for a long time. The clay was so thin and hard that she had to study the broken edge for a long while to find out whether anything had been mixed with the paste. She wished that she had a little glass that folded out of a case, like one the head man had, to make small things look larger. At last, by tipping the broken edge of the sherd towards the firelight, she caught a small, bright shine on one spot in the sherd. That was it, then. There was fine sand mixed with the clay.

María went out to the storeroom and looked at her own supply of clay and sand carefully. She had good, fine clay, but no sand that was hard and small enough. She wrapped her shawl

around her and went over to Tía Nicolasa's house, taking the
piece of pottery with her.

When María showed her the sherd, Tía Nicolasa grew most
excited.

"This is beautiful," she kept saying. "I never saw pottery
like this before. It's very beautiful."

"The sand is so fine," said María. "I don't know where to get
fine sand like that."

"The blue sand bed on the way to Española has fine sand in
it," Tía Nicolasa answered. "Not everywhere, but in some
places. That's where you should go to get your fine sand."

"I could sift it and get out the finest part," said María
thoughtfully.

"That would be a good thing to do," Tía Nicolasa agreed.
"You ought to do the same thing with the clay, too. Then that
will be fine and hard and right."

Since it was winter and most of the work in the fields was
finished, Julián could take María to get the sand. The trip was
not long; about two hours each way in the wagon was all. One
day would do it. They left Adam with Desidéria, who promised
to take good care of him. María packed *tortillas* and beans and
milk for lunch, and she and Julián started out.

It was the first time they had been away from the pueblo and
alone together since they had gone to St. Louis. At first María
felt shy and almost as if she were traveling with someone she
did not know well. Then Julián began to sing, drumming with
his hand on the wagon seat beside him, and the horses started
to trot uphill, and she was happy. It was a warm day for December, with lots of sun and a little wind that picked heavy
thoughts from your heart and carried them away. Riding together and being together was good, and it seemed a short trip
to the sand bed.

María remembered what Tía Nicolasa had told her.

"The finest sand is just in certain places," she told Julián.

"We'd better hunt for a place, then," he said.

They separated, and went back and forth across the surface
of the sand dune, looking for the best place to dig. At last María
called, "Here it is. I think this is a good place to start."

"All right," said Julián. "I can't seem to find anything special. It all just looks like sand to me."

He brought the shovel from the wagon and peered doubtfully down at the place where María was standing.

"It doesn't look much different from the rest," he said.

"It is, though," María insisted. "It's finer. I can feel it with my fingers. You can dig here."

"Well," said Julián, "all right." He still looked doubtful.

María brought the two flour sacks she had packed in the wagon, and Julián began to dig up sand to fill them. María watched him closely, and when she thought he was getting near the coarser sand, she warned him about it.

"I still don't see any difference," Julián protested. "You must have good eyes to be able to tell."

"I'm watching," said María, and Julián laughed.

"You must be," he said, and finished filling the sacks, taking the sand only from the places where she told him to dig.

When they lifted the filled sacks into the wagon, though, they could both tell the difference in the sand. The sacks were heavier than they would usually be and little rings of sand sifted out through the cloth onto the floor of the wagon. These were good, new flour sacks that María had bought at the store for just this trip. There were no holes in the bags, but the sand came through the cloth as if they had been coarse bran sacks.

"That sand is the right kind," said María contentedly.

They rested and ate their lunch on the sunny side of the sand dune, where the wind could just touch the tops of their heads but not get down around their shoulders or blow sand at them to make them uncomfortable. When they had finished eating, they sat on, looking out across the valley to the river and to the rim of Pajarito Plateau beyond.

"This is good country," said Julián, and María agreed, "I never want to live anywhere else in all my life."

Julián laughed at her a little, nicely. "You won't," he said. "Pueblo Indians belong here. This is their country. They'd better like it, because it's all they have."

Going back to the pueblo, María thought about what Julián had just said. He was a man who liked to be going, to be seeing

new places and meeting new people. He was a man who had a
need for that in his life. She liked doing that herself; but if she
knew that she would never go anywhere again, she could be
happy still, with Julián and Adam and her father and mother.

Anyway, just this little trip was like going through new
country, from the first time she remembered. Things had
changed. There were houses where once there had been fields,
and fields where once there had been marshlands along the
river. Most of all, there were bare spots on the mountains,
where there had once been dense, heavy coverings of big trees.
That was the biggest change; it was because that change had
taken place that the others had come about. Maybe if there
were some way to stop the timber companies from cutting off
the big trees, the other changes would stop of themselves. That
would hold back time, so that they would all be young a long
time together, and babies would be little and soft. Then she
shook her head.

"What are you thinking about?" Julián asked.

"That maybe there might be a way to stop changes."

"There isn't any way," said Julián. "That's the way things
are. That's part of living."

"That's what I thought, too," María said.

They went along towards home then, and when they had
almost reached the pueblo, Julián said, "I want to stop here. I
need some of that yucca."

"To wash your hair? We have plenty for that at home. This
kind doesn't make very good suds."

"To wash the pot's hair, said Julián, handing her the reins.
He climbed down from the wagon, and went over to the yucca
plant. It was one of the long, tall, spindly kind with leaves like
narrow knives. Julián did not dig up the whole plant but just
cut the main stem through above the root and brought the top
of the plant back to the wagon.

"There," he said, "that ought to make me some good paint
brushes."

The next morning María had Julián bring one of the new
sacks of sand into the storeroom, where she could get at it
easily. She thought for a while, as she washed the dishes, about

how she was going to sift the sand. The flour sifter was the only real sifter that she had, and it was too coarse to use. Then she remembered how the sand had worked its way through the sacks, and she decided to use a cloth for a sifter. She stretched a piece of an old shirt over a bowl, and poured the sand on the cloth. Gently, she worked the sand back and forth with her fingers and watched the pile on the cloth grow smaller as she worked. The sand was sifting through, steadily and slowly.

After that, María started in to sift the clay. It was finer than the sand to begin with, so she began by sifting it through a piece of flour sack. She needed much more clay than sand and it went through the cloth very slowly, but by noon she had a pile in the bottom of a dishpan. She thought it would be enough. Julián came in for dinner, and found her cooking and smiling.

"What's the joke?" he asked her. He was a man who always loved jokes.

"I was remembering," María replied. "I was remembering when Desidéria and I were little girls and made ourselves toy dishes. Tía Nicolasa made us sift the clay and sand for them then. I wouldn't think anything about it any more, but then it was just as hard work as sifting these things was this morning."

"Well," said Julián, helping himself to the beans, "if you keep on making fine pottery, maybe you'll get so this won't be anything to think about, either."

"Maybe," said María, and sat down beside him to eat her own lunch.

After they had eaten, Julián got out his new clump of yucca. He sat and looked at it for quite a while. Then he cut off a piece about six inches long from one of the heaviest leaves. He trimmed the blade of the leaf back to the stem, so that all that was left was a narrow, three-sided little stick.

"It looks like the quill of a feather," Julián said, holding the stick out on the palm of his hand, and studying it.

"Miss Grimes told us once that the white people used to write letters with feather quills," said María. She was sitting on the opposite side of the fireplace, mixing sand and clay together, getting ready to add the water to them.

"Maybe they were smart," said Julián. "I'll have to try a feather quill for this some time." He put the yucca quill in his mouth, and began to chew its thicker end, so that bits of the hard, stiff part came away from the long fibres. When he had his mouth full of the scraps he looked at María suddenly, startled.

"Spit it in the fireplace," she said. "You can't go running to the door every time you get a mouthful. Next time you'd better do it outdoors, where you can spit as much as you like."

"Thanks," said Julián, when his mouth was empty and he could speak. "I'll remember about that," he went on. "This stuff doesn't have much taste, but it's puckery."

María brought some water and began to mix it with her clay and sand. The stuff was so fine that it made only a small ball in the bottom of the mixing pan, instead of the big pile she had expected.

"I can make just one pot this time," she said, looking at the mixture.

"That's all they want of this kind," said Julián. "They didn't tell you to go on making a lot of these pots. Just one was all."

"Well," said María, "I thought as long as we were at it we could make four or five. Then maybe they could sell the extra ones, the way they said."

"Maybe," said Julián. "I think we ought to wait and see how the first one turns out. Are you going to start now?"

"Not this afternoon," María answered. "Good clay is better if it rests overnight. I'll start in the morning, and then the pot will have all day to dry."

She went ahead with the work that she had to do in the house, while Julián sat and looked at the potsherd and tried to draw its designs on a clean board with his new brush. Finally he put the brush away and shook his head. "I can't make it come out right," he said. "Besides, how can I know what kind of design to make till I see the pot?"

María started in shaping the pot the next morning. From the way that the sherd curved, she thought it must have come from a big bowl, although she could not be sure. Besides, she did not have enough fine clay ready to make a very big piece of pottery. She patted out a clay *tortilla* for the base, and then pinched off a small piece of the clay, punched it thoroughly to get out the air bubbles, and began rolling it between her hands to make the first coil.

The fine mixture rolled and worked more easily than any clay she ever remembered handling. She was surprised at how quickly she could build the bowl, and how thin she could make it. Before noon the shaping and polishing were finished, and she set the bowl on the kitchen table to dry. It was round and firm and lighter than any piece of pottery she had seen made in San Ildefonso.

When Julián came in, he stood and looked at the bowl for a long time. "Is it dry enough to paint?" he asked.

"I don't think so," María answered. "It ought to dry overnight, I believe."

"That's all right anyway," Julián said. "I've got to figure out what to paint it with."

"What did they use on the old pots?" María inquired.

"Jack said probably guaco," answered Julián. "He said they made a syrup out of guaco, like sugar syrup, and boiled it down till it got thick. Then when the pot was fired, the guaco burned and made a black design."

"We haven't got any guaco," María said.

"I guess I'll have to go out and look for some this afternoon," replied Julián.

"It's pretty late in the year to find any growing," María reminded him. "It all dries up in the fall."

"Well, I'll ask around," said Julián. "Maybe somebody will have some syrup made up to use for tea, or something."

When he came back late in the afternoon, he had a little jar in his hand.

"Where did you get it?" María demanded.

"Your Tía Nicolasa had it," Julián answered with a grin. "When you want to know anything about pottery, you go to your Tía Nicolasa. So did I. She said she made it up a long time ago, to decorate a storage jar. Then she put it away and forgot about it, so it dried out. She says if we grind the dry syrup up fine and boil it down again with lots of water, it will be just as good as ever."

"Well, we can try," said María. She put the hard little black cake that she found in the bottom of the jar on the fine *metate*, and ground it until it was a powder she could have sifted through a cloth like the clay. Then she put the powder, mixed with water, in a bowl by the fireplace, and let it cook slowly. There was a faint, plantlike smell all through the house in a little while and by bedtime they could smell nothing else.

While María ground and cooked the guaco, Julián sat by the fire. Sometimes he looked at the bowl, and sometimes he looked at the potsherd in his hand. He was studying them both together, one with the other, and he never moved or spoke until María gave him a bowl of *atole* for supper. Then he ate it, and said, "That was good. What was it?"

"Coffee," María told him.

"I'd like another cup, please," said Julián. This time she did give him coffee, and he drank it and never knew the difference. At bedtime he got up, stretched, and said, "It will fit," and they went to bed without another word.

The next morning Julián took his bowl of guaco and his yucca brush into the living room as soon as he had finished his outdoor work. Then he took the new bowl from the kitchen table. Last of all, he got the potsherd and set it beside the bowl on a stool. Then he sat down on the floor, with the pot of guaco beside him, dipped the brush into the paint, and went to work. María went away and left him. She wanted to sift some more sand and clay and get ready to begin another bowl.

When María went to call him to lunch, Julián had finished his part of the work. He was still sitting on the floor in front of the stool, and before him was the bowl, covered with fine gray lines. They made a pattern of a water snake, with square, even designs for the pueblo and the fields around it. María had never seen a bowl like this before.

"It's beautiful," she said, when she had looked and looked.

"It's all right," said Julián. "It came out all right. The lines matched."

"It looks as if the design grew on the bowl," María said.

"It's all right," Julián repeated. "I like it. I like this sort of work. It's like making saddles. You think what you're doing, and that makes your hands do it. It's good. Everything goes with you. Not like plowing, when everything can go against you."

María laughed. "You'd better be a potter," she said. "It's better to do something you like than something you don't like."

"Men aren't potters," said Julián, putting his brush down on the floor beside the pot of guaco, carelessly. "Is lunch ready?"

Mules and Men

By Zora Neale Hurston

Zora Neale Hurston (1901–1960) was born in Eatonville, Florida, into the family of poor tenant farmers. After her mother died in 1910, she attended school only irregularly, and at sixteen, she ran away from her brother's home. In Baltimore, where she did domestic work, she also began to attend Morgan Academy (now Morgan State College) and to write. The following year, at Howard University, she met Alain Locke, editor of Opportunity: Journal of Negro Life, *who entered a story of hers in a contest. "Spunk" won second prize in 1925. Hurston traveled to New York and met Fannie Hurst, one of the judges, who offered her a place to live, a job as her secretary, and eventually helped her to get a scholarship to Barnard College. At Barnard, Hurston studied anthropology under Franz Boas and was encouraged to go back to Eatonville as an anthropologist, to investigate and record the folklore of the people with whom she grew up.*

In the thirties, she published three novels, Jonah's Gourd Vine *(1934),* Their Eyes Were Watching God *(1937), and* Moses, Man of the Mountain *(1939), as well as* Mules and Men *(1935), the result of her trip to Eatonville. In 1936 and 1937, she was awarded Guggenheim Fellowships to study folklore in Haiti. Following that, she published another volume of folklore,* Tell My Horse *(1938); her autobiography,*

Dust Tracks on a Road (1942), which won the Anisfield Wolf Award; and Seraph on the Suwanee (1948). Through this period, Hurston was one of the best known and most highly regarded writers of what has come to be known as the Harlem Renaissance, in a group that included Langston Hughes and Richard Wright. In 1950, Hurston dropped out of sight; she died in Florida a decade later, penniless, alone, and out of touch even with other writers.

Rediscovered by black feminists who consider Hurston the single most important black woman writer of her generation, Hurston's work is beginning to receive the critical attention it deserves. Many regard Mules and Men as her most significant work, the key to all her other writing, and a source book for writers of her generation and ours. This selection from the introductory pages is particularly appealing, for it combines two themes: the college-educated daughter returning to her hometown, and the awakening of interest in small-town culture and folklore. Hurston has the skill of a consummate participant-observer; she fits in among the people she is observing, and, thus, they lovingly "show" her their ways. She is not only an anthropologist, but an artist who turns folklore into stories that ring with the truth of life.

I was glad when someone told me, "You may go and collect Negro folk-lore."

In a way it would not be a new experience for me. When I pitched headforemost into the world I landed in the crib of negroism. From the earliest rocking of my cradle, I had known about the capers Brer Rabbit is apt to cut and what the Squinch Owl says from the house top. But it was fitting me like a tight chemise. I couldn't see it for wearing it. It was only when I was off in college, away from my native surroundings, that I could see myself like somebody else and stand off and look at my garment. Then I had to have the spy-glass of Anthropology to look through at that.

Dr. Boas asked me where I wanted to work and I said, "Florida," and gave, as my big reason, that "Florida is a place

that draws people—white people from all over the world, and
Negroes from every Southern state surely and some from the
North and West." So I knew that it was possible for me to get
a cross section of the Negro South in the one state. And then
I realized that I was new myself, so it looked sensible for me
to choose familiar ground.

First place I aimed to stop to collect material was Eatonville, Florida.

And now, I'm going to tell you why I decided to go to my
native village first. I didn't go back there so that the home
folks could make admiration over me because I had been up
North to college and come back with a diploma and a Chevrolet. I knew they were not going to pay either one of these items
too much mind. I was just Lucy Hurston's daughter, Zora, and
even if I had —to use one of our down-home expressions—had
a Kaiser baby,[1] and that's something that hasn't been done in
this Country yet, I'd still be just Zora to the neighbors. If I had
exalted myself to impress the town, somebody would have
sent me word in a match-box that I had been up North there
and had rubbed the hair off of my head against some college
wall, and then come back there with a lot of form and fashion,
and outside show to the world. But they'd stand flat-footed
and tell me that they didn't have me, neither my shampolish,
to study 'bout. And that would have been that.

I hurried back to Eatonville because I knew that the town
was full of material and that I could get it without hurt, harm
or danger. As early as I could remember it was the habit of the
men folks particularly to gather on the store porch of evenings
and swap stories. Even the women folks would stop and break
a breath with them at times. As a child when I was sent down
to Joe Clarke's store, I'd drag out my leaving as long as possible
in order to hear more.

Folk-lore is not as easy to collect as it sounds. The best
source is where there are the least outside influences and these
people, being usually under-privileged, are the shyest. They
are most reluctant at times to reveal that which the soul lives

---

[1] Have a child by the Kaiser.

by. And the Negro, in spite of his open-faced laughter, his seeming acquiescence, is particularly evasive. You see we are a polite people and we do not say to our questioner, "Get out of here!" We smile and tell him or her something that satisfies the white person because, knowing so little about us, he doesn't know what he is missing. The Indian resists curiosity by a stony silence. The Negro offers a feather-bed resistance. That is, we let the probe enter, but it never comes out. It gets smothered under a lot of laughter and pleasantries.

The theory behind our tactics: "The white man is always trying to know into somebody else's business. All right, I'll set something outside the door of my mind for him to play with and handle. He can read my writing but he sho' can't read my mind. I'll put this play toy in his hand, and he will seize it and go away. Then I'll say my say and sing my song."

I knew that even *I* was going to have some hindrance among strangers. But here in Eatonville I knew everybody was going to help me. So below Palatka I began to feel eager to be there and I kicked the little Chevrolet right along.

I thought about the tales I had heard as a child. How even the Bible was made over to suit our vivid imagination. How the devil always outsmarted God and how that over-noble hero Jack or John—not *John Henry*, who occupies the same place in Negro folk-lore that Casey Jones does in white lore and if anything is more recent—outsmarted the devil. Brer Fox, Brer Deer, Brer 'Gator, Brer Dawg, Brer Rabbit, Ole Massa and his wife were walking the earth like natural men way back in the days when God himself was on the ground and men could talk with him. Way back there before God weighed up the dirt to make the mountains. When I was rounding Lily Lake I was remembering how God had made the world and the elements and people. He made souls for people, but he didn't give them out because he said:

"Folks ain't ready for souls yet. De clay ain't dry. It's de strongest thing Ah ever made. Don't aim to waste none thru loose cracks. And then men got to grow strong enough to stand it. De way things is now, if Ah give it out it would rear them shackly bodies to pieces. Bimeby, Ah give it out."

So folks went round thousands of years without no souls. All de time de soul-piece, it was setting 'round covered up wid God's loose raiment. Every now and then de wind would blow and hist up de cover and then de elements would be full of lightning and de winds would talk. So people told one 'nother that God was talking in de mountains.

De white man passed by it way off and he looked but he wouldn't go close enough to touch. De Indian and de Negro, they tipped by cautious too, and all of 'em seen de light of diamonds when de winds shook de cover, and de wind dat passed over it sung songs. De Jew come past and heard de song from de soul-piece then he kept on passin' and all of a sudden he grabbed up de soul-piece and hid it under his clothes, and run off down de road. It burnt him and tore him and throwed him down and lifted him up and toted him across de mountain and he tried to break loose but he couldn't do it. He kept on hollerin' for help but de rest of 'em run hid 'way from him. Way after while they come out of holes and corners and picked up little chips and pieces that fell back on de ground. So God mixed it up wid feelings and give it out to 'em. 'Way after while when He ketch dat Jew, He's goin' to 'vide things up more ekal'.

So I rounded Park Lake and came speeding down the straight stretch into Eatonville, the city of five lakes, three croquet courts, three hundred brown skins, three hundred good swimmers, plenty guavas, two schools, and no jail-house.

Before I enter the township, I wish to make acknowledgments to Mrs. R. Osgood Mason of New York City. She backed my falling in a hearty way, in a spiritual way, and in addition, financed the whole expedition in the manner of the Great Soul that she is. The world's most gallant woman.

As I crossed the Maitland-Eatonville township line I could see a group on the store porch. I was delighted. The town had not changed. Same love of talk and song. So I drove on down there before I stopped. Yes, there was George Thomas, Calvin Daniels, Jack and Charlie Jones, Gene Brazzle, B. Moseley and "Seaboard." Deep in a game of Florida-flip. All of those who were not actually playing were giving advice—"bet straightening" they call it.

"Hello, boys," I hailed them as I went into neutral.

They looked up from the game and for a moment it looked

as if they had forgotten me. Then B. Moseley said, "Well, if it ain't Zora Hurston!" Then everybody crowded around the car to help greet me.

"You gointer stay awhile, Zora?"

"Yep. Several months."

"Where you gointer stay, Zora?"

"With Mett and Ellis, I reckon."

"Mett" was Mrs. Armetta Jones, an intimate friend of mine since childhood and Ellis was her husband. Their house stands under the huge camphor tree on the front street.

"Hello, heart-string," Mayor Hiram Lester yelled as he hurried up the street. "We heard all about you up North. You back home for good, I hope."

"Nope, Ah come to collect some old stories and tales and Ah know y'all know a plenty of 'em and that's why Ah headed straight for home."

"What you mean, Zora, them big old lies we tell when we're jes' sittin' around here on the store porch doin' nothin'?" asked B. Moseley.

"Yeah, those same ones about Ole Massa, and colored folks in heaven, and—oh, y'all know the kind I mean."

"Aw shucks," exclaimed George Thomas doubtfully. "Zora, don't you come here and tell de biggest lie first thing. Who you reckon want to read all them old-time tales about Brer Rabbit and Brer Bear?"

"Plenty of people, George. They are a lot more valuable than you might think. We want to set them down before it's too late."

"Too late for what?"

"Before everybody forgets all of 'em."

"No danger of that. That's all some people is good for—set 'round and lie and murder groceries."

"Ah know one right now," Calvin Daniels announced cheerfully. "It's a tale 'bout John and de frog."

"Wait till she get out her car, Calvin. Let her get settled at 'Met's' and cook a pan of ginger bread then we'll all go down and tell lies and eat ginger bread. Dat's de way to do. She's tired now from all dat drivin'."

"All right, boys," I agreed. "But Ah'll be rested by night. Be lookin' for everybody."

So I unloaded the car and crowded it into Ellis' garage and got settled. Armetta made me lie down and rest while she cooked a big pan of ginger bread for the company we expected.

Calvin Daniels and James Moseley were the first to show up.

"Calvin, Ah sure am glad that you got here. Ah'm crazy to hear about John and dat frog," I said.

"That's why Ah come so early so Ah could tell it to you and go. Ah got to go over to Wood Bridge a little later on."

"Ah'm glad you remembered me first, Calvin."

"Ah always like to be good as my word, and Ah just heard about a toe-party over to Wood Bridge tonight and Ah decided to make it."

"A toe-party! What on earth is that?"

"Come go with me and James and you'll see!"

"But, everybody will be here lookin' for me. They'll think Ah'm crazy—tellin' them to come and then gettin' out and goin' to Wood Bridge myself. But Ah certainly would like to go to that toe-party."

"Aw, come on. They kin come back another night. You gointer like this party."

"Well, you tell me the story first, and by that time, Ah'll know what to do."

"Ah, come on, Zora," James urged. "Git de car out. Calvin kin tell you dat one while we're on de way. Come on, let's go to de toe-party."

"No, let 'im tell me this one first, then, if Ah go he can tell me some more on de way over."

James motioned to his friend. "Hurry up and tell it, Calvin, so we kin go before somebody else come."

"Aw, most of 'em ain't comin' nohow. They all 'bout goin' to Wood Bridge, too. Lemme tell you 'bout John and dis frog:

It was night and Ole Massa sent John,[2] his favorite slave, down to the spring to get him a cool drink of water. He called John to him.

"John!"

[2] Negro story-hero name.

"What you want, Massa?"

"John, I'm thirsty. Ah wants a cool drink of water, and Ah wants you to go down to de spring and dip me up a nice cool pitcher of water."

John didn't like to be sent nowhere at night, but he always tried to do everything Ole Massa told him to do, so he said, "Yessuh, Massa, Ah'll go git you some!"

Ole Massa said: "Hurry up, John. Ah'm mighty thirsty."

John took de pitcher and went on down to de spring. There was a great big ole bull frog settin' right on de edge of de spring, and when John dipped up de water de noise skeered de frog and he hollered and jumped over in de spring.

John dropped de water pitcher and tore out for de big house, hollerin' "Massa! Massa! A big ole booger[3] done got after me!"

Ole Massa told him, "Why, John there's no such thing as a booger."

"Oh, yes it is, Massa. He down at dat Spring."

"Don't tell me, John. Youse just excited. Furthermore, you go git me dat water Ah sent you after."

"No, indeed, Massa, you and nobody else can't send me back there so dat booger kin get me."

Ole Massa begin to figger dat John musta seen somethin' sho nuff because John never had disobeyed him before, so he ast: "John, you say you seen a booger. What did it look like?"

John tole him, "Massa, he had two great big eyes lak balls of fire, and when he was standin' up he was sittin' down and when he moved, he moved by jerks, and he had most no tail."

Long before Calvin had ended his story James had lost his air of impatience.

"Now, Ah'll tell one," he said. "That is, if you so desire."

"Sure, Ah want to hear you tell 'em till daybreak if you will," I said eagerly.

"But where's the ginger bread?" James stopped to ask.

"It's out in the kitchen," I said. "Ah'm waiting for de others to come."

"Aw, naw, give us ours now. Them others may not get here before forty o'clock and Ah'll be done et mine and be in Wood Bridge. Anyhow Ah want a corner piece and some of them others will beat me to it."

So I served them with ginger bread and buttermilk.

[3] A bogey man.

"You sure going to Wood Bridge with us after Ah git thru tellin' this one?" James asked.

"Yeah, if the others don't show up by then," I conceded.

So James told the story about the man who went to Heaven from Johnstown.

You know, when it lightnings, de angels is peepin' in de lookin' glass; when it thunders, they's rollin' out de rainbarrels; and when it rains, somebody done dropped a barrel or two and bust it.

One time, you know, there was going to be big doin's in Glory and all de angels had brand new clothes to wear and so they was all peepin' in the lookin' glasses, and therefore it got to lightning all over de sky. God tole some of de angels to roll in all de full rain barrels and they was in such a hurry that it was thunderin' from the east to the west and the zigzag lightning went to join the mutterin' thunder and, next thing you know, some of them angels got careless and dropped a whole heap of them rain barrels, and didn't it rain!

In one place they call Johnstown they had a great flood. And so many folks got drownded that it looked jus' like Judgment day.

So some of de folks that got drownded in that flood went one place and some went another. You know, everything that happen, they got to be a nigger in it—and so one of de brothers in black went up to Heben from de flood.

When he got to the gate, Ole Peter let 'im in and made 'im welcome. De colored man was named John, so John ast Peter, says, "Is it dry in dere?"

Ole Peter tole 'im, "Why, yes it's dry in here. How come you ast that?"

"Well, you know Ah jus' come out of one flood, and Ah don't want to run into no mo'. Ooh, man! You ain't *seen* no water. You just oughter seen dat flood we had at Johnstown."

Peter says, "Yeah, we know all about it. Jus' go wid Gabriel and let him give you some new clothes."

So John went on off wid Gabriel and come back all dressed up in brand new clothes and all de time he was changin' his clothes he was tellin' Ole Gabriel all about dat flood, jus' like he didn't know already.

So when he come back from changin' his clothes, they give him a brand new gold harp and handed him to a gold bench and made him welcome. They was so tired of hearing about dat flood they was glad to see him wid his harp 'cause they figured he'd get to playin' and forget all about it. So Peter tole him, "Now you jus' make yo'self at home and play all de music you please."

John went and took a seat on de bench and commenced to tune up his harp. By dat time, two angels come walkin' by where John was settin' so he throwed down his harp and tackled 'em.

"Say," he hollered, "Y'all want to hear 'bout de big flood Ah was in down on earth? Lawd, Lawd! It sho rained, and talkin' 'bout water!"

Dem two angels hurried on off from 'im jus' as quick as they could. He started to tellin' another one and he took to flyin'. Gab'ull went over to 'im and tried to get 'im to take it easy, but John kept right on stoppin' every angel dat he could find to tell 'im about dat flood of water.

Way after while he went over to Ole Peter and said: "Thought you said everybody would be nice and polite?"

Peter said, "Yeah, Ah said it. Ain't everybody treatin' you right?"

John said, "Naw. Ah jus' walked up to a man as nice and friendly as Ah could be and started to tell 'im 'bout all dat water Ah left back there in Johnstown and instead of him turnin' me a friendly answer he said, 'Shucks! You ain't seen no water!' and walked off and left me standin' by myself."

"Was he a *ole* man wid a crooked walkin' stick?" Peter ask John. "Yeah."

"Did he have whiskers down to here?" Peter measured down to his waist.

"He sho did," John tol' 'im.

"Aw shucks," Peter tol' 'im. "Dat was Ole Nora.[4] You can't tell *him* nothin' 'bout no flood."

There was a lot of horn-honking outside and I went to the door. The crowd drew up under the mothering camphor tree in four old cars. Everybody in boisterous spirits.

"Come on, Zora! Le's go to Wood Bridge. Great toe-party goin' on. All kinds of 'freshments. We kin tell you some lies most any ole time. We never run outer lies and lovin'. Tell 'em tomorrow night. Come on if you comin'—le's go if you gwine."

So I loaded up my car with neighbors and we all went to Wood Bridge. It is a Negro community joining Maitland on the north as Eatonville does on the west, but no enterprising souls have ever organized it. They have no schoolhouse, no post office, no mayor. It is lacking in Eatonville's feeling of unity. In fact, a white woman lives there.

While we rolled along Florida No. 3, I asked Armetta where was the shindig going to be in Wood Bridge. "At Edna Pitts'

[4] Noah.

house," she told me. "But she ain't givin' it by herself; it's for the lodge."

"Think it's gointer be lively?"

"Oh, yeah. Ah heard that a lot of folks from Altamonte and Longwood is comin'. Maybe from Winter Park too."

We were the tail end of the line and as we turned off the highway we could hear the boys in the first car doing what Ellis Jones called bookooing[5] before they even hit the ground. Charlie Jones was woofing[6] louder than anybody else. "Don't y'all sell off all dem pretty li'l pink toes befo' Ah git dere."

Peter Stagg: "Save me de best one!"

Soddy Sewell: "Hey, you mullet heads! Get out de way there and let a real man smoke them toes over."

Gene Brazzle: "Come to my pick, gimme a vaseline brown!"

Big Willie Sewell: "Gimme any kind so long as you gimme more'n one."

Babe Brown, riding a running-board, guitar in hand, said, "Ah want a toe, but if it ain't got a good looking face on to it, don't bring de mess up."

When we got there the party was young. The house was swept and garnished, the refreshments on display, several people sitting around; but the spot needed some social juices to mix the ingredients. In other words, they had the carcass of a party lying around up until the minute Eatonville burst in on it. Then it woke up.

"Y'all done sold off any toes yet?" George Brown wanted to know.

Willie Mae Clarke gave him a certain look and asked him, "What's dat got to do with you, George Brown?" And he shut up. Everybody knows that Willie Mae's got the business with George Brown.

"Nope. We ain't had enough crowd, but I reckon we kin start now," Edna said. Edna and a sort of committee went inside and hung up a sheet across one end of the room. Then she came outside and called all of the young women inside. She had to coax and drag some of the girls.

[5] Loud talking, bullying, woofing. From French *beaucoup*.
[6] Aimless talking.

"Oh, Ah'm shame-face-ted!" some of them said.

"Nobody don't want to buy *mah* ole rusty toe." Others fished around for denials from the male side.

I went on in with the rest and was herded behind the curtain.

"Say, what *is* this toe-party business?" I asked one of the girls.

"Good gracious, Zora! Ain't you never been to a toe-party before?"

"Nope. They don't have 'em up North where Ah been and Ah just got back today."

"Well, they hides all de girls behind a curtain and you stick out yo' toe. Some places you take off yo' shoes and some places you keep 'em on, but most all de time you keep 'em on. When all de toes is in a line, sticking out from behind de sheet they let de men folks in and they looks over all de toes and buys de ones they want for a dime. Then they got to treat de lady dat owns dat toe to everything she want. Sometime they play it so's you keep de same partner for de whole thing and some-time they fix it so they put de girls back every hour or so and sell de toes agin."

Well, my toe went on the line with the rest and it was sold five times during the party. Everytime a toe was sold there was a great flurry before the curtain. Each man eager to see what he had got, and whether the other men would envy him or ridicule him. One or two fellows ungallantly ran out of the door rather than treat the girls whose toe they had bought sight unseen.

Babe Brown got off on his guitar and the dancing was hilarious. There was plenty of chicken perleau and baked chicken and fried chicken and rabbit. Pig feet and chitterlings[7] and hot peanuts and drinkables. Everybody was treating wildly.

"Come on, Zora, and have a treat on me!" Charlie Jones insisted. "You done et chicken-ham and chicken-bosom wid every shag-leg in Orange County *but* me. Come on and spend some of *my* money."

"Thanks, Charlie, but Ah got five helpin's of chicken inside already. Ah either got to get another stomach or quit eatin'."

---

[7] Hog intestines.

"Quit eatin' then and go to thinking. Quit thinkin' and start to drinkin'. What you want?"

"Coca-Cola right off de ice, Charlie, and put some salt in it. Ah got a slight headache."

Big Willie Sewell said, "Come on, heart-string, and have some gospel-bird[8] on me. My money spends too." His Honor, Hiram Lester, the Mayor, heard him and said, "There's no mo' chicken left, Willie. Why don't you offer her something she can get?"

"Well there *was* some chicken there when Ah passed the table a little while ago."

"Oh, so you offerin' her some chicken *was*. She can't eat that. What she want is some chicken *is*."

"Aw shut up, Hiram. Come on, Zora, le's go inside and make out we dancin'." We went on inside but it wasn't a party any more. Just some people herded together. The high spirits were simmering down and nobody had a dime left to cry so the toe-business suffered a slump. The heaped-up tables of refreshments had become shambles of chicken bones and empty platters anyway so that there was no longer any point in getting your toe sold, so when Columbus Montgomery said, "Le's go to Eatonville," Soddy Sewell jumped up and grabbed his hat and said, "I heard you, buddy."

Eatonville began to move back home right then. Nearly everybody was packed in one of the five cars when the delegation from Altamonte arrived. Johnny Barton and Georgia Burke. Everybody piled out again.

"Got yo' guitar wid you, Johnnie?"

"Man, you know Ah don't go nowhere unless Ah take my box wid me," said Johnnie in his starched blue shirt, collar pin with heart bangles hanging on each end and his cream pants with the black stripe. "And what make it so cool, Ah don't go nowhere unless I play it."

"And when you git to strowin' yo' mess and Georgy gits to singin' her alto, man it's hot as seven hells. Man, play dat 'Palm Beach'."

[8] Chicken. Preachers are supposed to be fond of them.

Babe Brown took the guitar and Johnnie Barton grabbed the piano stool. He sung. Georgia Burke and George Thomas singing about Polk County where the water taste like wine.

My heart struck sorrow, tears come running down.

At about the thirty-seventh verse, something about:

Ah'd ruther be in Tampa with the Whip-poor-will,
Ruther be in Tampa with the Whip-poor-will
Than to be 'round here—
Honey with a hundred dollar bill,

I staggered sleepily forth to the little Chevrolet for Eatonville. The car was overflowing with passengers but I was so dull from lack of sleep that I didn't know who they were. All I knew is they belonged in Eatonville.

Somebody was woofing in my car about love and I asked him about his buddy—I don't know why now. He said, "Ah ain't got no buddy. They kilt my buddy so they could raise me. Jus' so Ah be yo' man Ah don't want no damn buddy. Ah hope they kill every man dat ever cried, " 'mamma' but me. Lemme be yo' kid."

Some voice from somewhere else in the car commented, "You sho' Lawd is gointer have a lot of hindrance."

Then somehow I got home and to bed and Armetta had Georgia syrup and waffles for breakfast.

The Only People

By Judith Higgins

Judith Higgins (1936–) grew up in New Jersey, graduated from Pembroke College of Brown University in Rhode Island, and then earned an M.A. degree at Trinity College, Dublin. Her stories have appeared in Southern Review, Quarterly Review, *and* Texas Quarterly. *She lives in Princeton, New*

*Jersey, with her husband and child, and she is now writing
a novel.*

*Like the women in "The Only People," Judith Higgins has
been a clerical worker in a pathology laboratory. She has
always interspersed writing and editing with what she
calls "sociable work"—selling, factory work, and, currently,
teaching art in a hospital. "The Only People," her first
published story, was selected for inclusion in the* Best Short
Stories of 1968, *edited by Martha Foley and David Burnett.*

Mommy made me answer the ad for a medical typist. I
wanted to stay home and watch *I Love Lucy* and *The Edge
of Night.* I was tired of job-hunting, and I thought my leg
needed a rest.

I had polio when I was a child, and I wear a brace on my
right leg. It is attached to my black oxford and runs up to my
knee, where it ends in a padded circle of steel. The leg seems
boneless, and its pinkish-purple hue shows through my nylon.
In fact, it looks like a rag doll's leg.

I know other people would hate to have such a leg, and
looking at it they thank God it is I who have it and not they.
But what they don't know is that I don't always detest my
leg. I've had to favor this rag leg for eighteen years, so I'm
quite attached to it. At night when I take off the brace and sit
in my bath or when I first get between the sheets of my bed,
I think of my leg rather tenderly. It seems so vulnerable, how
could I wish it further harm? I rub it gently with my hands
or my good foot. I hop from tub to bed, holding it carefully in
the air.

But I sympathize fully with others' disgust and wish to spare
them the sight of such a leg. That was another reason for my
wanting to stay at home. Let Boston employers have a day off
from the sight of me. But Mommy would not listen to my
reasons. "You've had a hard time, but so have I! You're twenty-
seven. Get a job—and keep it for once!"

"No one wants me—" I said. But she was already pushing
me out the door.

My mother and I live in the South End. My father left us

when I was three, when I had two nice normal legs and no limp. I wonder what he would think if he saw what happened to me. Mother says he would probably take one look and leave on the next train. He never could, she says, stand any kind of responsibility or trouble. Mother and I both work, or I do most of the time, and on weekends we go to the laundromat and wash our hair and cook pot roast, and on Sundays we go to High Mass and watch Ed Sullivan. Looking at TV is what I always put down under "hobbies" on the job applications—and I list my programs.

The trip to Downtown Hospital was very hot, and I got lost once on the MTA. I wanted to turn back, but I was afraid Mommy would pull out the plug of the TV. She had done that twice before.

"Eighty words a minute. That's very impressive," said the personnel manager at the hospital. "And you've used a Dictaphone?"

"Yes."

"Well, we certainly need somebody. We were without a chief pathologist for four months when our former one retired, and there's a backlog of autopsies to be typed up. Would you be interested?"

"Oh, yes." I hate talking to people. I mean, where are you supposed to look—in their eyes the whole time? I think that annoys them, and I know I ought to look away every few seconds. But my eyes *stick.*

"You'd be working in the pathology lab, near the operating room. How would you feel about that?"

"OK."

"It wouldn't upset you?"

"No."

"Good. I'll take you up to Surgery to meet Doctor Wiles. He's our new pathologist."

G. Wilbur Wiles, in his forties I guessed, had red hair, a crewcut, and a starched white coat. He was much better looking than anyone on *General Hospital* or *Doctor Kildare.* His secretary stood beside his desk.

"This is Miss Murphy," said the personnel man. "She's

come to help us out on the autopsies. Types eighty words a minute."

"It's true," I said, then blushed. I felt like a racehorse that had suddenly spoken.

"Great!" exclaimed Doctor Wiles. He jumped up and shook my hand. "What's your first name? I hate this formal business."

I looked around for the personnel man, but he had gone. "Jane," I said.

"Well, Jane, this is Marsha Polanski, my secretary."

"Hi, Jane!" She came forward and shook my hand, just as heartily as Doctor Wiles had. "We're glad to have you aboard." Then she returned to her place beside Doctor Wiles's desk. She was younger than I was, blond and pretty. Her eyes took in my brace in the most discreet way, and then she never looked down again.

"Well, little one," said Doctor Wiles, "let's get Miz Jane started. Eighty words a minute—gee whiskers, are we lucky!"

They looked at each other and smiled. Marsha said, "Yes. She's made our day."

Facing me, they seemed to present a united front, so at ease. I knew then that they were Only People. Only People are handsome, successful, relaxed, and above all they are paid attention to and taken seriously. In fact, Only People are *the* only people. The rest of the population are either Grays or Janes. Grays are harmless but not very interesting. I suppose Mommy is a Gray; I know she is not an Only Person or she would not be living in two rooms in the South End with me. Janes are the creeps of the universe. They have everything possible the matter with them, and no one would dream of taking them seriously. Naturally, Only People don't like to have to look at Janes, but sometimes they tolerate the Janes when they prove themselves good workers. I pride myself on being a good worker and therefore possibly useful to Only People. That is my one hope, because everyone stays the way he is. Grays stay gray, and Only People reign forever. It took me a long time to *make* myself understand that I would

(text continued on page 94)

Portraits
of the Authors

Barbara Smith: 1977

Sarah Orne
Jewett:
circa 1890

Rikki Lights: 1977

Jean Pedrick: 1976

Alice Lee Marriott: 1977

Zora Neale Hurston: 1934

Margaret Walker: 1942

Toni Cade Bambara: 1972

Judith Higgins: 1978

always be a Jane. I had to put a sign on the wall of my room:
Live Without Hope.

Marsha led me down the hall to the office where I would
be typing. People stared at me as I passed, but I kept my eyes
on Marsha's strapped high heels. That's one more thing I hate
about starting a new job—the spurt of curiosity I stir up.

My gray steel desk touched another: from behind it a heavy
older woman looked up, rather startled. She pulled the Dictaphone apparatus from her ears and tried to smile at me.

"Miss Lupowitz," said Marsha, "this is Jane Murphy. She'll
be typing the autopsies. Miss Lupowitz enters the specimens
in the surgical book and types our gross surgical descriptions.
A gross is the pathologist's rough description of the tissue
removed during an operation—its measurements, appearance,
how it feels to the touch. I type the microscopic description
of the same tissue—how it looks on a slide—and the diagnoses.
The surgical report on a patient consists of gross, then micro,
then diagnosis. And of course I am Doctor Wiles's secretary."

"How do you do?" said Miss Lupowitz to me.

Marsha addressed me, smiling. "Sit down, sit down." She
pulled out my typewriter for me (a manual one), got out paper,
and inserted a belt in my Dictaphone. No one except Mommy
had ever waited on me like this.

"Everything all right now?"

"Oh, yes, fine. Thank you."

"If you have any questions, just ask me. Or ask Miss
Lupowitz. She's been here twenty years."

"Oh, thank you, I will."

Miss Lupowitz spoke up. She had an accent of some sort.
"Miss Polanski, here is a belt of micros. Doctor Hendrix
handed them to me a little while ago."

"Oh. Well, what about it?"

"Well, don't you want to take it?" The tape fluttered in her
outstretched hand. Marsha did not take it.

"You start them, Miss Lupowitz. I'd like the surgical reports
to go out today."

"Of course. If I would have known that you wanted *me* to do
the micros, I would have started them already. But yesterday
you said that *you—*"

"Do the best you can, Miss Lupowitz." With a smile at me, she was gone through the swinging door that led from this office into the lab.

Miss Lupowitz was staring at me with wide eyes. Her cheeks had turned red. "She's twenty years old," she said to me. I didn't know what she wanted, but I couldn't take time out to ponder it. I had my work laid out before me.

I am proud of one thing, and that is my typing. If your legs don't work, I guess you have to concentrate on the hands. And that's what I have done. I knit and I sketch a little and I type. When all is going well, words go in my ears and come out my fingertips without any mental interference in between. The thing that has to be right is the atmosphere. I have to have peace. Then I get into a kind of dream, and the words from the Dictaphone flow through me like blood. All the noises and voices around me disappear. My eyes stare only at the letters falling onto the paper, line after line, as steadily as rain.

The body is that of an emaciated white female, weighing an estimated 98 pounds and measuring 5 feet 5 inches in length. The body is opened in the usual Y-shaped ventral incision. . . .

When the door of our office was open, you could see the patients being rolled by from the operating room to the recovery room. In their little plastic caps and with the I.V. bottles dripping into their arms, they never spoke. The only noises were the grinding wheels on the beds and the orderlies saying, "Watch it, watch it." All day there was a sound like trains going by our door.

The left lung is surgically absent. The right lung weighs 550 grams. Its pleura is opaque gray and diffusely thickened.

I could scarcely wait to tell Mommy what a good job I had found and with what nice people. I knew she had not believed that I would ever get it.

When I took in some mail to him the next morning, Doctor Wiles made me sit down and have coffee with him. I watched while he measured coffee into two cups and poured water from an electric pot. A doctor in a white coat was making *me* coffee—I could scarcely believe it. "How many sugars?" he asked.

"Oh, that's all right."

He laughed. "Miss Murphy, you're a very agreeable young lady. I'll assume you take two lumps." He handed me my cup and sat down at his desk. He smiled. "Isn't this heat brutal?"

"Yes, it certainly is."

"I'm from Little Rock, but this has me beat." He touched his white coat (I realized I had been staring at it) and said, "These damn things don't help either, but a doctor doesn't look like a doctor unless he has one on. I envy this little fella his outfit." And pulling out his wallet, he showed me a snapshot of a smiling baby in a diaper.

"Ah," I said.

"He's my new son. Daddies aren't supposed to praise their offspring, I know, but I think this guy's pretty great."

"Oh, he is. He's beautiful." But not a tenth as good-looking as you, I thought. Oh, Mommy, if you could see me now—

I had to make myself concentrate on what he was saying. He was explaining that he was in charge not only of the pathology lab, where they examined tissue, but of the chemistry lab, where they examined blood and urine, and the blood bank as well. He wanted no splits between the three departments or any of the people in them. "I hate pigeonholes, job roles," he said. "At the risk of sounding like a country bumpkin, Miz Jane, when my Boy Scout troop back in Arkansas went on a camping trip, we all pitched in. Nobody said, 'I get to do that because I'm older than you or smarter than you or because my Dad's richer than yours.' And we all cooperated with the leader. Here people have gotten solidified into categories, everybody pulling in his own direction. It's not their fault they're lazy. Nobody has ever supervised them properly before. We can double our output here, and if we double our output, we double our business. It's as simple as that."

We finished our coffee. "Those letters you've got, are they for me, Ma'am?"

"Yes." I laid them on his desk.

"Thank you kindly, Ma'am." And he smiled at me again.

I went away realizing that this was the best job I had ever had.

There were three doctors besides Doctor Wiles who worked in the pathology laboratory, and often they came out to our office to use their new Dictaphones or to receive specimens wrapped in green surgical cloth.

One nurse was very loud and would always call out the organ. "Stomach! Sign, please." And Miss Lupowitz would get up, enter the information in the surgical book, and then bring the organ into the lab for the doctors to dissect. For her recording she used a ballpoint pen called a NOBLOT Thinrite #2435. I would have liked one, but she had the only one.

She also had the IBM typewriter. I had to go very carefully on my manual, because the k and y stuck each time. There were also the accents to contend with. Doctor Duval and Doctor Chang both had accents: "The you-nayree bla-drees deestanded and cohntens a-boon-dant torr-beed youreen."

Marsha came in, put her hand on my shoulder, and said to Miss Lupowitz: "Are you finished with the grosses yet, Miss Lupowitz?"

"No. I am going as fast as I can, Miss Polanski. You used to want them by twelve o'clock. Now it is only ten o'clock, and already you are asking for them."

Her cheeks had turned red again. I felt so comfortable with Marsha's hand on my shoulder. How wonderful that she would want to touch me. It made me want to laugh at Miss Lupowitz.

It was Marsha who laughed. "Ruth doesn't like Dictaphones," she said to me. "She's used to taking down the doctors' reports in longhand."

"No, no, that's not the point. I could get used to it if it would work right. I don't ask that you should get a new machine for me, but could you call the repairman? Please. This has been broken already one week."

Marsha pushed a stray blond hair behind one ear. Yesterday she had worn her hair down, and today she wore it up in a bun and had horn-rimmed spectacles on. It almost seemed that she could be two different people. "I'll try to call him again, Miss Lupowitz. That's not the only thing I have to do."

A doctor walked in just then carrying a raincoat and a brief-
case. Marsha brightened. In fact, she shone. She pulled her
hand from my shoulder and thrust it at him. "Doctor Norton,
hul-lo! It's delightful to see you again. Doctor Wiles will be
delighted also, I am sure. Won't you follow me to his office?
Here, let me carry your coat."

"No, no, that's all right, honey."

"Doctor Norton, I insist. You've come so far for us. You
must tell us, did you have a good flight?"

And away he went, following that little heart-shaped behind. I was sure that men must find her very attractive. I'm not
much to look at from the back because I'm not symmetrical;
on the right side, where I had polio, my buttock is much
smaller; because of this I never wear tight skirts.

"Stroggling along with these broken machines—it's terrible," Miss Lupowitz muttered. "And then the deadlines. I
never know when they want something."

I did not answer her.

"Hi, ladies." Doctor Wiles stood in the doorway, his hands
on the frame. " 'Lo," I mumbled, smiling, and Miss Lupowitz
twisted her face into a smile. I was sure he had heard her; it
served her right if she got into trouble, for being such a poor
sport. "Good morning, sir," she said, and put the Dictaphone
apparatus back into her ears.

Later on, when he came back into the room—and this is the
truth—he put his arm around my shoulders. First Marsha's
hand and now Doctor Wiles's arm—this was really my day.

After what seemed five minutes (and I was afraid my shoulders were sweating), he said: "Miss Murphy?"

"Yes, yes?"

"Could you type this address on a label, please Ma'am?"

"Oh, yes, Doctor Wiles, I'll do it right away." I took the slip
of paper from him, and my hand was shaking. It was, I thought,
just like a scene from *The Nurses*, everyone working together,
the sultry midday city beyond the window looking like a paper
set.

He straightened and withdrew his arm, and said, "Thank
you, Ma'am," and winked at me.

Oh, God, God, God, I thought, isn't he wonderful. I was too happy to be jealous when he said, "Miss Lupowitz?"

She removed her earphones. "Yes, sir?"

"I'm hungry, and I'm going to lunch. *Ich wolle haben Mitta-gessen. Ich habe ein grossen Hunger!*"

He smiled and waited until she gave a small chuckle (adding that she did not know much German), and then he departed, his white coat swirling.

"The cafeteria for the lab help, clerical help, and laundry staff is located in the sub-basement," Marsha explained, as Willie the Negro operator rode us down.

"Oh, I see," I said, trying to concentrate. I was so happy— she had made Miss Lupowitz wait her turn and had asked *me* to lunch with her.

"Let's sit by ourselves," she said, laughing and tickling me in the ribs. "I want to talk to you!"

She signed for both our meals and brought them to the table. "Now, if you will spread these things out while I get our milk and coffee." Mommy had not been this nice to me since I was sick.

"Doctor Wiles likes people to feel they're working *with* him, not *for* him." As she spoke, her eyes studied my face so eagerly that I felt it would be wrong to look down at my plate. "You just don't say 'no' to a doctor. Doctors are special people. You have to show them you know they're the boss. Doctor Wiles gets irritated with people who don't like him. He gives them every opportunity to show their goodwill, and then if they don't come across, well . . ."

Her eyes are beautiful, I thought. A pale gray, the color of my steel desk.

"I worked for him a year at Camden Hospital," she went on, never picking up her fork. "I guess you know, he brought me here with him. At Camden I used to have the grosses on his desk by noon, so that he could come right back from lunch and dictate the micros. Then in the afternoon I'd type those up and knock off four belts of letters."

She had a piece of bread in her left hand, but had taken only one bite out of it and had not touched the food on her plate. I was terribly hungry, but I felt it would be wrong to chew while she was talking to me, her face held only a few inches from mine.

"That's why I become so irritated when people here don't meet the deadlines we set up. Miss Lupowitz says this hospital is three times the size of Camden and has three times as many operations per day, but she will grab, I have found, at any excuse for slow production.

"All our jobs depend on one another's, you see. We're like a conveyor belt of work. If one person along the way is late, then everybody after him is late, and the doctors don't get their reports on time. The reports should be mailed out to the surgeons the same day the operation was performed. So far they haven't been, but I intend to see that they are. Doctor Wiles is counting on it."

She took a bite of her food, and I took three quick bits of mine.

"The former pathologist was a nice man, but all he was interested in was pathology. He'd come in, give everyone an encouraging word, and then go about his business. He never checked up on people. Doctor Wiles and I have had to do that. And we've found, just as you'd expect, that people have been getting away with murder. The girls in hematology and blood bank have been having a ball. They're never at their desks, which annoys me no end. Betty and Harold in the chemistry lab will get away with as little work as they can. We're watching them closely."

She looked at me thoughtfully. "We must think of something else for you to do so that you won't be typing all day."

"Answering the telephone?"

"No, I'd better do that. There's a way of doing it, you see. You have to be very polite with doctors—always refer to them as 'Doctor.' They're very sensitive about that. How about making out the lab bills? Perhaps you could do that. I've been doing it, but I'm helping Doctor Wiles with research on the book he's writing—"

"Oh, are you? How exciting!"

"Yes, it is exciting. Interesting. But in any case, it entails visits to the library, so I may give you the lab bills to do—"

"Oh, I'd love to!"

"Good." She laughed. "There, I've done it again! Talked shop the whole time. But I can't help it, it's so interesting." She stood up, running her fingers up my arm. "Finish that slop, if you want it. I'll bus our dishes and ring for the elevator."

I took only one huge bite of rice, so that I could ride back up with her.

One day shortly thereafter, Doctor Wiles introduced a sign-in, sign-out book, which he placed in our office. Marsha explained it to me at lunch. "We're going to cut down on people slacking off. Mike in chemistry is always making trips to the supply room—*he* says—but we suspect he's secretly sunning himself in the solarium. He's just too tan. And Lilly's a smart cookie. She comes in at nine-thirty. Because she's been here five years she thinks she can get away with it. But Doctor Wiles will fire everybody here if he has to."

I choked on my Welsh rarebit.

She laid a hand on my arm. "Not you. We're very pleased with you so far. Doctor Wiles just wants to be sure that people are putting in their eight hours and that they're on legitimate errands when they're away from their desks." She sighed. "So far, Miss Lupowitz hasn't signed the book. We're giving her another day. That woman just won't cooperate."

Later that day Doctor Wiles explained the book in a much less alarming way. "This is the sign-out book, Miss Lupowitz." (Of course, it had been sitting on the corner of her desk all day.) "I'm signing myself out to chemistry and blood bank. See how useful this is, Ma'am? If anyone asks for me, why you just have to look at the book to tell them where I am. Now doesn't this make a lot of sense? I know it sure makes sense to me."

"Yes, sir," said Miss Lupowitz. Without looking up from my work, I knew that her cheeks would be flaming red.

Yet despite his special plea, an hour later she was still resisting. She lingered in the doorway of our office until I looked up. "I'm just going to the bathroom, Miss Murphy. If *he* asks." She laughed. "Just to urinate, so it won't be long." She looked

as though she were about to cry. I realized that Marsha was
right: Miss Lupowitz just could not adjust.

"Hey." Someone was touching me on the shoulder. "I don't
believe I know your name."

It was a fat young man in a white lab coat. "Dick Nalban-
dian. . . . Well, you still won't tell me?"

"Jane Murphy." My fingers remained arched over the keys;
he had interrupted me in the middle of a sentence.

"Gee," he went on, "I've been trying to introduce myself for
two days, but you never look up from that machine. I'll be
assisting the doctors now in your lab. Used to be at New Bank
Memorial."

I looked down at the paper in my typewriter; I did not type,
but I would not talk to him, either. What if Marsha should
come in and find me not working? Besides, I wanted to finish
Autopsy 8759 before noon.

"Dick!" called one of the doctors. "Did you get that tray of
slides yet?"

"Not yet, Doc. I'm on my way now, Doc. Well," he said to
me, "take it easy. I'll be seeing you around."

Good riddance, I thought. But I had thought too soon. At
noon he brought his food over to the table where Marsha and I
were sitting. What nerve, butting in on our conversation. I
hated the way black hairs crawled out over the collar of his lab
coat, and I kept my eyes on my tuna casserole.

"So tell me about Doctor Wiles," he said to Marsha. "No,
don't look at me that way—I'm serious. He's my new boss, and
I don't wanna do anything to upset the applecart. What's he
like? He must fly off the handle *some*time. I'd like to know
what sets him off so as I don't do it."

"Doctor Wiles is always just as you see him. He doesn't 'fly
off the handle,' as you put it."

"You mean, he's always that jolly and good-natured with
everybody?"

"Yes. I've been asked this question before—what's the real
Doctor Wiles like? But there is no real Doctor Wiles. I mean,
what you see on the surface is the real Doctor Wiles. He's a
very unusual man. He likes people, and he wants them to like

him as much as he likes them." She waved her hand. "But I'm not giving out any more information. You'll find out for yourself. If you do your job well, if you cooperate, you have nothing to worry about."

He laughed. "Well, thanks."

On the way up, Marsha confided to me that Dick, who was thirty-seven, was really nothing more than Lilly's lab maid, and that she and Doctor Wiles were watching his performance closely.

"I knew he was only a Jane!"

"A what?"

"Nothing," I said blushing.

The afternoon confirmed my suspicions. Dick was in and out of our office and the lab, spanked on his fat bottom by the swinging door. I'll do that right away, Doctor . . . . Certainly Doctor . . . . Let me clean that spot out of your jacket Doctor . . . . Can I sweeten your coffee, Doctor?" Oh, he was a Jane all right. I detested him for it.

Marsha had an IBM Selectric typewriter and the only new Dictaphone. Again this was proof, if I had needed any, of what she was: Only People work with only the best materials. Like Miss Lupowitz, I was having trouble with my Dictaphone, but I didn't say anything to Marsha. The repairman had not yet come to fix Miss Lupowitz's, and I could see how her complaints were annoying Marsha.

Typing on a manual typewriter all day tied my shoulders, especially the right one, in knots. In the evenings Mommy had been rubbing them with Ben-Gay. Afterward I would sit with the right one over the back of a chair as I watched TV. I was missing all the good shows now because I had to go to bed by nine o'clock. Otherwise I would not be fresh enough for my work. In addition to five autopsies a day (I used to do two), I was now doing the lab bills, addressing envelopes, typing and filing cards on the day's operations, and typing over anything that Marsha had made a mistake on and did not feel like redoing. I think Marsha was surprised at how much work I was turning out, although she never said anything.

I did not regret missing *Doctor Kildare* and *Run for Your*

Life, however. Today Doctor Wiles had put his hand on my shoulder: "Jane, my girl?"

"Yes?"

"Can we make this in triplicate?"

Before I had had a chance to reply, Marsha came in and put her hand on Doctor Wiles's shoulder: "Mrs. Wiles called." "Thank you, little one," he said. For a moment we had remained linked together, the three of us, and for that moment I was not Jane but one of the Only People. I had never been so happy.

"They are like a couple of Arabs, aren't they?" Miss Lupowitz had remarked after Marsha and the doctor had gone back to their office. "Always pawing a person."

I was shocked at her. Then I realized that she was jealous— not only of Marsha (everyone is jealous of Only People)—but of *me.* Imagine.

The next evening Marsha offered to drive me home.

"Oh, you don't *have* to," I murmured, astonished.

She pulled down the hem of my skirt (I guess my slip was showing). "Don't be silly. I'd like to. I have my car with me today." And she hopped off to tell Doctor Wiles that we were leaving together.

Don't let this go to your head, I kept telling myself as I followed her out to the parking lot, or you'll be punished. But it was almost impossible to hold down my happiness. How do you like this, leg, I said to it as I pulled it in after me into Marsha's car, no subway for you tonight.

"Oh, there's Doctor Wiles!" cried Marsha, and began beeping her horn. Sure enough, I could see his fuzzy-topped head in a little car that nosed us over and passed us. When he was ahead, he winked his left light. She honked three short bursts and flashed her headlights.

"He's off to suburbia tonight," she explained to me. "About three nights a week he works late and stays in town. It's a long drive to Minnisocket" (here she drew in her cheeks and talked very soberly), "but when you bring children into the world, you owe it to them to give them the best possible environment in which to grow up. And after all, the wife and children are the ones who have to be home most of the day. For the man, what goes on at his job is more important than where he puts his family down."

She went on talking about Doctor Wiles. He had been the youngest ever to graduate from the University of Pennsylvania Medical School and had had one of the largest scholarships. He used to be a gynecologist and obstetrician. But delivering babies was really the easiest kind of medicine, and much as Doctor Wiles loved dealing with people directly, he was too brilliant to be satisfied staying with the "carriage trade." And so he had gone into pathology.

There was a lot more that she said, but I was too nervous to concentrate: it had gradually dawned on me—what if she expected to be invited in? If Marsha were to see those two rooms we lived in, I would never get a ride from her again. I was sure of it. And Mommy had gotten so fat. Worse yet, it was very possible that she would fail to see that Marsha was an Only Person and ought to be treated the right way; Grays can be stupid like that.

My worries were suddenly dispelled when, parking in front of the house where we lived, Marsha said, "I won't come in."

"Oh," I said with relief. "I mean—"

"Before you go, there is one thing I want to mention."

"Yes?"

She sighed and traced a circle around the steering wheel with her fingertips. "As you may have guessed, we're having our problems with Miss Lupowitz. She won't cooperate. It's very sad. She can't learn our ways of doing things, and nothing is ever finished when we ask for it. I'm not saying that I'm any more qualified than she is just because I went to medical secretarial school and she never had the slightest formal training, not the slightest! And yet she can be so *sure* of herself!"

She lowered her voice. "Anyway, the point is, leaving Miss Lupowitz out of it, we want to be sure you're on our side. Will you work with us? If we all work together, we can get out of the hole. It will take a lot of time, but we can do it. How about it?"

"Oh, yes," I said. "Oh, yes. I'll do anything I can."

She smiled and patted my thigh. "That's what I thought you'd say. OK, run in now."

She revised that when she saw my hand darting from my

brace to the door handle and back to my leg again. "Take your time," she said, stretching. "I'm in no rush tonight."

First thing the next morning, I was summoned into Doctor Wiles's office.

"Thank you for the ride," I said to Marsha. She smiled and closed the partition between Doctor Wiles's desk and hers, leaving me alone with him.

"Sit down, Ma'am," he said. "Miss Murphy, you look apprehensive. Don't."

"Don't what?"

"Don't look worried."

I tried not to.

"That's better." He lay back in his chair and brushed a hand back over his crew cut. He had on a short-sleeved shirt (his medical coat was hanging on the chair), and I couldn't help noticing how white the flesh of the underside of his arm was. Shocked at myself, I switched my eyes at once to his face.

"When I came here three months ago," he said, folding his hands across his stomach, "I found a laboratory that would have been modern about ten years back. The equipment was outdated. People were using methods of doing things that were twice as slow as they need be. Well, by now I think—I *think*—we may be coming out of the Middle Ages. At least I hope so. Some of the new lab machinery I've ordered has already been installed. I've gotten the doctors to use Dictaphones, instead of having Miss Lupowitz sit in there like a scribe taking it all down. I'm also waiting on the new multiplex snap-out forms for our surgical reports; they have *built-in* carbon paper, which will save you gals in the office one heck of a lot of time."

He leaned on the desk with his elbows. "It's the human end of things that's our problem number one. You know, Miz Jane, it's almost easier to requisition another radiation unit than it is to get people to work *with* you. I have one person I can count on, and that's Marsha. She's been coming in evenings and on weekends while we get organized. I need someone like her.

"But Marsha and I can't straighten out this place alone. We need the cooperation of everyone here. We can't have people coming in here and sealing themselves into their own little slots. We're not a bunch of artists. We have to work as a team. And if I don't get the cooperation I want, there's going to be a shake-up here that people won't forget, and I'm the guy to do it."

He leaned back in his chair and lit a cigarette. "I guess you're aware that we have a problem child in the lab."

"Miss Lupowitz!" I said promptly.

He smiled. "The kindest interpretation of her behavior is that she is finding it hard to adjust to our ways of doing things. The former pathologist was an awfully nice man who just wanted to be left in peace so he could look through his microscope all day. And he evidently didn't share my antipathy to rigid ladies who treat men, doctors at that, like foolish little boys. The result was, we had this DP running the administrative end of things when I got here. I have nothing personal against Jews, you understand. They can be fine people. We just ran into the stereotype in Miss Lupowitz.

"She came in here yesterday morning and told me about a mistake I had made—and I sure am glad she caught it, but I didn't like the *way* she told me about it. Sort of triumphant. It's incidents like these that make me suspect she's not just an old fossil that can't adjust—I think she really has it in for me.

"Which brings me to why I asked you in here this morning. I don't want to fire the good lady. She's been here twenty years, and before we came I'm told that she *did* get the surgical reports out on time. But starting right now I'd like to bypass this Rumanian lady as much as possible. So Jane, my girl, we're going to give *you* the surgical reports to type—Marsha will do the microscopies in the afternoon—and confine Miss Lupowitz to the autopsies. The time element isn't as important on autopsies. She can fool around with them all day and collect her ninety dollars a week, but she won't be undermining me. How about it, Miz Jane? Will you work with us?"

"Oh, yes, I will. But—"

"What is it?"

"Well, who's going to tell her? I don't want to be the one."

"You won't have to be. It'll be my pleasure. She'll balk at

the switch, but I'll write up a new job description for her. That
Old World compulsiveness, you know; they have to see everything in writing."

When Miss Lupowitz came back from Doctor Wiles's office, I
knew she had been told. Her eyes were very bright and her
mouth pinched. "May I have please the autopsies that you have
not done?"

I handed them to her and went on with my grosses.

While I typed, I was aware every so often of noises from Miss
Lupowitz like "Och!" and "What, what?" And I could hear the
click of her foot again and again on the "repeat" pedal of her
Dictaphone. "Doctor Duval," she said at one point, "could it
be 'the bowel spaces are gaping'? You are talking about the
kidneys." "Bowman's spaces," he called back. Later, "I am
sorry to bother you again, Doctor Duval. I am afraid you will
have to come and listen to this one. It sounds like 'apple water.'
I can't make it out at all."

He came over in his baggy surgical suit and put the earphones on. "The ampulla of Vater," he said. "The mehn pan-
creatic duct em-teez into the am-*pulla* of Vater jointly weeth
the chole*do*cus."

"Thank you very much, sir. I am sorry to have to keep
bothering you. I was so familiar with the vocabulary of the
surgical reports. This I have to learn all over again. And they
have never fixed my machine."

"I know, I know," he said. "Believe me, I have never lived
through such disorganization. I am getting the migraine—I can
feel it coming over my right eye."

The truth was, I was having just as much trouble with the
surgical reports as Miss Lupowitz was with the autopsies.
Every third word was a new one to me, and I had to play it over
many times. But I did not want to ask the doctors to help me
because *she* was doing that.

When the telephone rang and Marsha was not in her office
to pick it up, Miss Lupowitz would answer it. Snatches of her
replies occasionally reached me: "You'd better ask Doctor
Wiles. I don't know how they are planning to handle that, sir.

I can only tell you the way we used to do it, and of course that may all be changed now ... Sir, I would not know anything about that now. I believe Doctor Wiles's secretary is handling that from now on."

I guess this was an example of what Doctor Wiles meant by her "rigidity." Really, she was very foreign-looking, too. She had heavy hips, and she wore men's sweaters and black oxfords like mine, although she didn't have to. I honestly disliked her now.

I became all the more desirous of proving that I could do the grosses faster than she could after twenty years. Marsha would not find *me* missing her deadlines. By eleven-thirty I was ready for another belt of grosses. "Doctor Chang," I called. "I can do your grosses if you have them dictated."

He had just come out of the lab and was pulling off his rubber gloves. "A twenty-one-year-old girl," he said, to no one in particular. "Married, and four months pregnant, and this is definitely carcinoma."

I waited, my fingers arched over the keys. He went on and on, that the husband was hysterical and that the girl lay in a kind of happy dream state. "They'll have to take that baby from her. Boyoboy, I feel like crying myself."

He paused, whereupon I said eagerly: "Doctor Chang, do you have any grosses for me to type?"

"Such a pretty girl, too. What was that, Miss Murphy?"

I had to ask him a third time. I was very annoyed; it was now eleven-forty.

Marsha seemed rather strange at lunch. Her gray eyes stared past my shoulder. I missed her talking to me about the progress we were making and about who was still not pulling his weight. At the other lab table were two girls from chemistry. "Are those the girls you and Doctor Wiles are watching?" I asked.

"Two of the ones, yes. Maybe I'm not very sociable," she remarked, spreading out our food, "but I just don't enjoy sitting with them. All they talk about is their husbands and their children. It's very boring." She had a beautiful sweater around her shoulders. The flesh on her arm was a lovely tan. She seemed so fresh and clean-looking; almost everyone else down here was either Puerto Rican or Negro. "I come from a big family myself," she added, "so I've heard my fill."

"Oh, do you?"

"Yes—seven children."

It turned out that she came from Roxbury, a neighborhood as bad as mine. I was shocked. It did not fit. "You don't still live there, do you?"

"Oh, no. I have an apartment by myself on Beacon Hill."

"How nice!" I was so glad she was out of Roxbury.

"Yes, it is nice. I wake up in the morning, with the sun streaming in my window, and I say to myself, 'Marsha, my girl, this is the life. Be glad you're footloose and fancy-free. Would you really want a brood of screaming brats at your heels?'"

"That's such a beautiful sweater."

"Why thank you. I used to wear a uniform when we were at Camden, but Doctor Wiles hates women to wear uniforms. I couldn't agree more." She sighed and fell silent.

I had thought she would be in a good mood. Tomorrow began the Fourth of July weekend, and it meant that we would be off for three days. I had been imagining her as part of a "gay crowd": boys and a convertible, transistors and lying in the sand in a dotted bikini, kicking up perfect tan legs. But seeing her gloom, I began to worry that she thought me not fast enough on the grosses. We were still getting them out a day late to the surgeons. "Maybe I could come in on Monday," I suggested, "and do the surgical reports that are left over."

Her eyes focused on me slowly. "What?"

I repeated my offer.

"Don't be silly. Monday's a holiday."

"I know, but I wouldn't mind. I have nothing else to do."

"Well, thanks, but they won't be doing any operations except emergencies on Monday. I think Doctor Chang will be on, but no one else." She sighed. "I had thought Doctor Wiles would ask for the Fourth so that we could get a number of things straightened out, but he won't be coming in. I can't say that I blame him. He has five acres and a perfectly delightful house. Boston will be hot as Hades this weekend."

"You've been to his house!"

"Don't shriek. Of course I've been to his house." She frowned suddenly. "I'm thirsty and fat around the middle. Two of the seventeen symptoms I have that I'm about to get my period." She grimaced. "The 'curse.' I'll never understand why women dread the menopause. I can't wait." She lapsed into silence again. When she looked up, her eyes were much brighter: "What has Miss Lupowitz been doing all morning?"

"An autopsy, I guess."

"Just one?"

"I guess so." Something was in the wind. I felt excited, the way you do at school when the principal has sent for someone —not you. "Is there something wrong?"

"Yes," she said firmly. "Yes, I believe there is." She broke off, seized at that point by a cramp.

The long weekend of the Fourth seemed interminable. On Monday, the holiday, Mommy went to the beach with her sister. I didn't go because I didn't want to get sand in my brace. I stayed home by the fan, fiddling with the TV dial. It was quiet and depressing. None of my programs were on. I thought about how I would try to beat the speed record I had set last week. And then I thought about Miss Lupowitz and how Marsha had seemed especially displeased with her. That cheered me up: something was brewing, I was sure.

My suspicions were confirmed on Tuesday morning. Every so often Marsha would come in, stand in our doorway, and survey Miss Lupowitz and me. Sometimes she would say, "How's it coming, ladies?" She frightened me. She wore her horn-rimmed glasses, and her hair was drawn back so tightly that her cheekbones and nose were like three sharp points. I would offer to tell her about my progress or hand her a sheaf of finished reports, but she would only nod at me and pass on to Miss Lupowitz's desk. There she would stand going through papers on the woman's desk. I could see Miss Lupowitz's eyes dart sideways while she tried to keep on typing. At last she pulled the Dictaphone apparatus from her ears and said, "Miss Polanski, what is it you are looking for? If you would tell me, I could find it for you."

"No, no, go on with what you're doing."

"It's just that you are getting everything out of order."

"Oh, am I? That's too bad, Ma'am. I'm looking for finished autopsies, and I seem to find only four."

"I'm on my fifth one now—"

"But so far you've completed only four since we started you on them. Is that right?"

"Miss Polanski, I am doing my best. You and Doctor Wiles knew I would have to become familiar with this vocabulary all over again. It's you who are after me all the time for the autopsies; the doctors aren't asking for them."

At this Marsha turned on her heel and walked out.

Two nurses who had been in the office the whole time watched her go. One was the loud nurse. "*She's* in a great mood today," she said. "I guess he went home to his wife last night."

"What future does that kid have?" said the other one.

"No future, none at all."

"He'll have a coronary. Look at the difference in their ages."

"Yeah, and don't forget, he has to do two."

"Pat, you think of everything."

I felt like bursting into tears. Oh, *please* stop talking. I can't hear my Dictabelt.

Marsha did not come in anymore that morning. I grew hungry and began waiting for her buzz-buzz, meaning wash your hands, sign us out, and meet me by the service elevator to go down to lunch. But the signal never came. At last, screwing up my courage, I called her on the interoffice phone. I tried to sound funny about it: "I'm hon-greee." It was a failure: she did not understand me. "I thought—um, whu-well, do you want to go down to lunch yet?"

"Why don't you go ahead," she said. "I want to speak to Doctor Wiles about something. *I'm* sorry—I should have let you know. Can you manage?"

"Sure, I guess so."

I would have been very sad and uneasy about going down without her, except that in the hall I passed a man with a tray of sandwiches and coffee, and he asked me to direct him to Doctor Wiles's office. That changed everything: Marsha and

Doctor Wiles were dining together in his office. What a wonderful idea! The hard-working doctor and his secretary grabbing a fast bite together: it was better than anything I had seen on *Doctor Kildare*. I felt so proud of them for thinking of it.

I brought my lunch to the table where the other lab workers sat. After a moment they went on talking among themselves, for which I was thankful. I kept my eyes on my lunch.

Finally one of them asked me, "How's 'little one'?"

"I don't understand," I replied.

"Miss Polanski."

"She's fine. I—I think she's eating sandwiches with Doctor Wiles."

"Oh, that's nice. Isn't that nice, Barbara? She's smart. This ravioli is murder on your figure"—she knocked her girl friend's elbow and smirked—"for them that has to eat it."

I didn't understand them and did not care to try. I hurried with my lunch, bussed my dishes, and rode up with a carful of nurses. I can walk very quietly if I swing my leg out in a wide arc and step down on it very slowly. I got to the door of Doctor Wiles's office without making a sound. There on the chair outside the door was the tray, the food gone. There were two sandwich plates, two coffee cups, and on one of the cups was a smear of lipstick. Smiling, I took a napkin for a souvenir, and then swung and stepped slowly, swung and stepped slowly, back to my desk.

I found Miss Lupowitz blotting her face with a wet paper towel. "I am not feeling so good," she explained. I did not wonder that she was nervous, having been so rude to Marsha. I stacked the reports that I had finished that morning in a neat pile (they rose much higher than Miss Lupowitz's completed work, I was sure) and went on to the next one. It would not be good, I felt, for me to be seen speaking to her.

Toward the end of the afternoon Miss Lupowitz was summoned by buzzer to go into Doctor Wiles's office.

"Well, here it is," she said to Doctor Hendrix. "A dressing down." She pronounced it "drrressink."

"Don't take it to heart, Ruth," he said. "In a year those two won't be here."

When she came back she began at once to dispose of things

in her drawers and lockers. Doctor Chang and Doctor Hendrix were watching her. Finally Chang came over to her desk and asked her what had happened. She murmured something. "Really?" he said, "I don't believe it." She simply stared back at him with wet eyes. "Boyoboy, they're crazy," he said, shaking his head and walking away.

Of course I was dying to know what had been said in Doctor Wiles's office, but I did not let on. It was exciting, having all this discord eddying around you but not involving you—the typing went much faster.

When I arrived at work the next morning there was already a belt of grosses on my desk, and on the table with the surgical book there were several specimens in jars or in green cloth waiting to be entered. "Would you do it," Doctor Hendrix asked me, "since Ruth's not here?"

I didn't have time to wonder where she was. "Keep calm, keep calm, you fool," I told myself as I wrote in the surgical book. "If you don't, you'll make an error." But I kept mislaying my pencil, and then every time I got myself seated at the typewriter, thinking that perhaps I could get another report done, in would come a nurse: "Gallbladder. Sign, please." And I would get up again.

"I told Marsha she could come in a little late this morning," said Doctor Wiles to Hendrix and me when he signed in. "She was here until ten-thirty last night filing slides for me." He said nothing about Miss Lupowitz.

It was almost noon hour before Marsha came rushing in. Her long blond hair hung down to her shoulders, and she had on a violet dress I had never seen before. "Oh, you look so beautiful!" I told her.

"Why, thank you, Miss Jane," she said, signing in. She looked like her old happy self again. "How is it coming? Have you finished the grosses?"

"No, but I came in at eight-thirty so I could get a head start, and I've been entering all the specimens, too. Is it OK? Is it all right that I haven't finished all of them yet?"

She gave me a smile. "It's all right."

A half-hour later, when I still had a number of reports to do, she reappeared. "Turn off that machine!" she said gaily. "I'm hungry."

"Lunch? Can I eat after you today? Then I can have these reports for Doctor Chang when he comes back from his lunch."

"Oh, the heck with *him*." She stamped her foot playfully. "Come now. I don't want to eat alone."

"OK."

Marsha and I were midway through our lunch when she said to me, "Miss Lupowitz is leaving, you know."

"What!" I said.

"It was coming for a long time. We kept giving her more work, and she just wasn't getting it done. And she couldn't adjust to the Dictaphone."

"But it was broken—"

"Yes, that was her excuse. She had lots of them." She sighed. Her voice was very soft. "Doctor Wiles was going to think it over a little longer—what to do about her. But yesterday I told him some of the things she has done and about how uncooperative she's been with me, and he just realized it would never work. I would get *worn out* fighting her stubbornness, and he wouldn't want that. He's so kind, it breaks his heart to have to fire somebody. I'm the same way—I hated telling him about her, but it was my duty, and he was glad I did." Her voice tightened. "I gather the old fossil was a little surprised to get the ax, but that's her problem. She had no right—no right!—to think she was indispensable. Why, the agencies are crawling with people who can't be anything but typists."

I was staring at her. The food I had eaten had knotted in my stomach. I didn't know why I should feel so apprehensive. They were Only People, and Only People got to fire nonpeople. As long as they were pleased with *my* work, they would keep me. But I felt frightened nonetheless.

"She wasn't fired, you know," Marsha said. "Doctor Wiles simply asked her to resign. He told her that he was afraid if she stayed, they'd only lock horns, and he didn't want that to happen because she was such a nice lady and he was fond of her. By the way," she added, "we're very pleased with the way you're working out."

At that I began to feel better, and the piece of bread that was stuck slid the rest of the way down my esophageal tract.

When we got upstairs, Marsha asked me to sign her back in. I guess that she did not want to encounter Miss Lupowitz, who had come in while we were eating. I found her rolling up her calendar with the picture of Bucharest on it. She put it in a large box of other papers, little jars of medicine, and wax flowers. Then she came over to me. My shoulders tensed: Now what?

"Goodbye, Miss Murphy. I am sorry that I had so little time to talk to you." She paused, adjusting the box under her arm. "I must think about where I shall go now. I've always worked close to doctors, you see. My father was one, in Rumania"—she laughed—"before the Germans decided suddenly he doesn't know anything about medicine anymore. I don't know what I'll do now. I've sometimes thought if I wouldn't be working in this hospital, I would die. I suppose that's a foolish idea, isn't it?"

I looked up at her, my fingers remaining poised over the keys. She seemed to be waiting for me to reply. I could think of nothing to say but "Well, goodbye."

When she had gone, I took her NOBLOT Thinrite. I had wanted it for weeks, and I needed it now. The nurses were coming in constantly with specimens, and it was I, now, who had to enter the patients' names in the surgical book.

The next day I acquired something bigger. Marsha said, "Why don't you sit at the IBM now? There's no reason why you shouldn't have it. It must be tiring typing on a manual all day."

How kind she was to me! I felt shy but happy. "Yes, but what if she comes back or something?"

Marsha tweaked my hair. "Miss Lupowitz isn't coming back," she said, smiling.

Well, I thought, settling myself in, Miss Lupowitz certainly disappeared fast. But that's Life. You have to adjust to change or go under.

"They fired that Rumanian woman," I told Mommy that night. I had saved the news until after supper. "I have her IBM now, and my shoulders don't hurt a bit. They had to let her go. She just wasn't meeting the deadlines."

Raymond's Run

By Toni Cade Bambara

*Toni Cade Bambara was born and grew up in New York
City. She earned a B.A. at Queens College/City University
of New York, and during the next several years, continued
to study drama, mime, and dance in Florence, Italy; in
Paris; and in New York. She earned an M.A. in 1964 at
City College/CUNY. Through the sixties and into the
seventies, she worked at many different jobs: free-lance
writer, social investigator for the New York State
Department of Social Welfare, director of recreation, and
teacher of English in various precollege and college programs. Beginning in 1969, she was an assistant professor
at Livingston College, Rutgers University. Since 1970
and the publication of her timely and enormously useful
anthology called* The Black Woman–*the first black feminist collection of stories, essays, poems, and polemics–
she has published three volumes of short stories:* Tales
and Stories for Black Folks *(1971);* Gorilla, My Love
(1972); and The Sea Birds Are Still Alive *(1977). Currently,
she lives in Atlanta where she is working on a novel.*

Like other stories in Gorilla, My Love, *"Raymond's Run"
is told through the consciousness of a young black girl,
wise beyond her years, and blessed, like the author,
with the gifts of humor and compassion.*

I don't have much work to do around the house like some
girls. My mother does that. And I don't have to earn my
pocket money by hustling; George runs errands for the big
boys and sells Christmas cards. And anything else that's got to
get done, my father does. All I have to do in life is mind my
brother Raymond, which is enough.

Sometimes I slip and say my little brother Raymond. But as
any fool can see he's much bigger and he's older too. But a
lot of people call him my little brother cause he needs looking
after cause he's not quite right. And a lot of smart mouths got
lots to say about that too, especially when George was minding

him. But now, if anybody has anything to say to Raymond, anything to say about his big head, they have to come by me. And I don't play the dozens or believe in standing around with somebody in my face doing a lot of talking. I much rather just knock you down and take my chances even if I am a little girl with skinny arms and a squeaky voice, which is how I got the name Squeaky. And if things get too rough, I run. And as anybody can tell you, I'm the fastest thing on two feet.

There is no track meet that I don't win the first place medal. I used to win the twenty-yard dash when I was a little kid in kindergarten. Nowadays, it's the fifty-yard dash. And tomorrow I'm subject to run the quarter-meter relay all by myself and come in first, second, and third. The big kids call me Mercury cause I'm the swiftest thing in the neighborhood. Everybody knows that—except two people who know better, my father and me. He can beat me to Amsterdam Avenue with me having a two fire-hydrant headstart and him running with his hands in his pockets and whistling. But that's private information. Cause can you imagine some thirty-five-year-old man stuffing himself into PAL shorts to race little kids? So as far as everyone's concerned, I'm the fastest and that goes for Gretchen, too, who has put out the tale that she is going to win the first-place medal this year. Ridiculous. In the second place, she's got short legs. In the third place, she's got freckles. In the first place, no one can beat me and that's all there is to it.

I'm standing on the corner admiring the weather and about to take a stroll down Broadway so I can practice my breathing exercises, and I've got Raymond walking on the inside close to the buildings, cause he's subject to fits of fantasy and starts thinking he's a circus performer and that the curb is a tightrope strung high in the air. And sometimes after a rain he likes to step down off his tightrope right into the gutter and slosh around getting his shoes and cuffs wet. Then I get hit when I get home. Or sometimes if you don't watch him he'll dash across traffic to the island in the middle of Broadway and give the pigeons a fit. Then I have to go behind him apologizing to all the old people sitting around trying to get some sun and getting all upset with the pigeons fluttering around them, scattering their newspapers and upsetting the wax-paper lunches in their laps. So I keep Raymond on the inside of me, and he plays like he's driving a stage coach which is O.K. by me so long as he doesn't run me over or interrupt my breathing exercises, which I have to do on account of I'm serious about my running, and I don't care who knows it.

Now some people like to act like things come easy to them, won't let on that they practice. Not me. I'll high-prance down 34th Street like a rodeo pony to keep my knees strong even if it does get my mother uptight so that she walks ahead like she's not with me, don't know me, is all by herself on a shopping trip, and I am somebody else's crazy child. Now you take Cynthia Procter for instance. She's just the opposite. If there's a test tomorrow, she'll say something like, "Oh, I guess I'll play handball this afternoon and watch television tonight," just to let you know she ain't thinking about the test. Or like last week when she won the spelling bee for the millionth time, "A good thing you got 'receive,' Squeaky, cause I would have got it wrong. I completely forgot about the spelling bee." And she'll clutch the lace on her blouse like it was a narrow escape. Oh, brother. But of course when I pass her house on my early morning trots around the block, she is practicing the scales on the piano over and over and over and over. Then in music class she always lets herself get bumped around so she falls accidently on purpose onto the piano stool and is so surprised to find herself sitting there that she decides just for fun to try out the ole keys. And what do you know— Chopin's waltzes just spring out of her fingertips and she's the most surprised thing in the world. A regular prodigy. I could kill people like that. I stay up all night studying the words for the spelling bee. And you can see me any time of the day practicing running. I never walk if I can trot, and shame on Raymond if he can't keep up. But of course he does, cause if he hangs back someone's liable to walk up to him and get smart, or take his allowance from him, or ask him where he got that great big pumpkin head. People are so stupid sometimes.

So I'm strolling down Broadway breathing out and breathing in on counts of seven, which is my lucky number, and here comes Gretchen and her sidekicks: Mary Louise, who used to be a friend of mine when she first moved to Harlem from Baltimore and got beat up by everybody till I took up for her on account of her mother and my mother used to sing in the same choir when they were young girls, but people ain't grateful, so now she hangs out with the new girl Gretchen and talks about me like a dog; and Rosie, who is as fat as I am skinny and has a big mouth where Raymond is concerned and is too stupid to know that there is not a big deal of difference between herself and Raymond and that she can't afford to throw stones. So they are steady coming up Broadway and I see right away that it's going to be one of those Dodge City scenes cause the street ain't that big and they're close to the buildings just as we are. First I think I'll step into the candy store and look over the new comics and let them pass. But that's chicken and I've got a reputation to consider. So then I think I'll just walk straight on through them or even over them if necessary. But as they get to me, they slow down. I'm ready to fight, cause like I said I don't feature a whole lot of chit-chat, I much prefer to just knock you down right from the jump and save everybody a lotta precious time.

"You signing up for the May Day races?" smiled Mary Louise, only it's not a smile at all. A dumb question like that doesn't deserve an answer. Besides, there's just me and Gretchen standing there really, so no use wasting my breath talking to shadows.

"I don't think you're going to win this time," says Rosie, trying to signify with her hands on her hips all salty, completely forgetting that I have whupped her behind many times for less salt than that.

"I always win cause I'm the best," I say straight at Gretchen who is, as far as I'm concerned, the only one talking in this ventriloquist-dummy routine. Gretchen smiles, but it's not a smile, and I'm thinking that girls never really smile at each other because they don't know how and don't want to know how and there's probably no one to teach us how, cause grown-up girls don't know either. Then they all look at Raymond who has just brought his mule team to a standstill. And they're about to see what trouble they can get into through him.

"What grade you in now, Raymond?"

"You got anything to say to my brother, you say it to me, Mary Louise Williams of Raggedy Town, Baltimore."

"What are you, his mother?" sasses Rosie.

"That's right, Fatso. And the next word out of anybody and I'll be *their* mother too." So they just stand there and Gretchen shifts from one leg to the other and so do they. Then Gretchen puts her hands on her hips and is about to say something with her freckle-face self but doesn't. Then she walks around me looking me up and down but keeps walking up Broadway, and her sidekicks follow her. So me and Raymond smile at each other and he says "Gidyap" to his team and I continue with my breathing exercises, strolling down Broadway toward the ice man on 145th with not a care in the world cause I am Miss Quicksilver herself.

I take my time getting to the park on May Day because the track meet is the last thing on the program. The biggest thing on the program is the May Pole dancing, which I can do without, thank you, even if my mother thinks it's a shame I don't take part and act like a girl for a change. You'd think my mother'd be grateful not to have to make me a white organdy dress with a big satin sash and buy me new white baby-doll shoes that can't be taken out of the box till the big day. You'd think she'd be glad her daughter ain't out there prancing around a May Pole getting the new clothes all dirty and sweaty and trying to act like a fairy or a flower or whatever you're supposed to be when you should be trying to be yourself, whatever that is, which is, as far as I am concerned, a poor Black girl who really can't afford to buy shoes and a new dress you only wear once a lifetime cause it won't fit next year.

I was once a strawberry in a Hansel and Gretel pageant when I was in nursery school and didn't have no better sense than to dance on tiptoe with my arms in a circle over my head doing umbrella steps and being a perfect fool just so my mother and father could come dressed up and clap. You'd think they'd know better than to encourage that kind of nonsense. I am not a strawberry. I do not dance on my toes. I run. That is what I am all about. So I always come late to the May Day program, just in time to get my number pinned on and lay in the grass till they announce the fifty-yard dash.

I put Raymond in the little swings, which is a tight squeeze this year and will be impossible next year. Then I look around for Mr. Pearson, who pins the numbers on. I'm really looking for Gretchen if you want to know the truth, but she's not around. The park is jam-packed. Parents in hats and corsages and breast-pocket handkerchiefs peeking up. Kids in white dresses and light-blue suits. The parkees unfolding chairs and chasing the rowdy kids from Lenox as if they had no right to be there. The big guys with their caps on backwards, leaning against the fence swirling the basketballs on the tips of their fingers, waiting for all these crazy people to clear out the park so they can play. Most of the kids in my class are carrying bass drums and glockenspiels and flutes. You'd think they'd put in a few bongos or something for real like that.

Then here comes Mr. Pearson with his clipboard and his cards and pencils and whistles and safety pins and fifty million other things he's always dropping all over the place with his clumsy self. He sticks out in a crowd because he's on stilts. We used to call him Jack and the Beanstalk to get him mad. But I'm the only one that can outrun him and get away, and I'm too grown for that silliness now.

"Well, Squeaky," he says, checking my name off the list and handing me number seven and two pins. And I'm thinking he's got no right to call me Squeaky, if I can't call him Beanstalk.

"Hazel Elizabeth Deborah Parker," I correct him and tell him to write it down on his board.

"Well, Hazel Elizabeth Deborah Parker, going to give someone else a break this year?" I squint at him real hard to see if he is seriously thinking I should lose the race on purpose just to give someone else a break. "Only six girls running this time," he continues, shaking his head sadly like it's my fault all of New York didn't turn out in sneakers. "That new girl should give you a run for your money." He looks around the park for

Gretchen like a periscope in a submarine movie. "Wouldn't it be a nice gesture if you were . . . to ahhh . . ."

I give him such a look he couldn't finish putting that idea into words. Grownups got a lot of nerve sometimes. I pin number seven to myself and stomp away, I'm so burnt. And I go straight for the track and stretch out on the grass while the band winds up with "Oh, the Monkey Wrapped His Tail Around the Flag Pole," which my teacher calls by some other name. The man on the loudspeaker is calling everyone over to the track and I'm on my back looking at the sky, trying to pretend I'm in the country, but I can't, because even grass in the city feels hard as sidewalk, and there's just no pretending you are anywhere but in a "concrete jungle" as my grandfather says.

The twenty-yard dash takes all of two minutes cause most of the little kids don't know no better than to run off the track or run the wrong way or run smack into the fence and fall down and cry. One little kid, though, has got the good sense to run straight for the white ribbon up ahead so he wins. Then the second-graders line up for the thirty-yard dash and I don't even bother to turn my head to watch cause Raphael Perez always wins. He wins before he even begins by psyching the runners, telling them they're going to trip on their shoelaces and fall on their faces or lose their shorts or something, which he doesn't really have to do since he is very fast, almost as fast as I am. After that is the forty-yard dash which I used to run when I was in first grade. Raymond is hollering from the swings cause he knows I'm about to do my thing cause the man on the loudspeaker has just announced the fifty-yard dash, although he might just as well be giving a recipe for angel food cake cause you can hardly make out what he's sayin for the static. I get up and slip off my sweat pants and then I see Gretchen standing at the starting line, kicking her legs out like a pro. Then as I get into place I see that ole Raymond is on line on the other side of the fence, bending down with his fingers on the ground just like he knew what he was doing. I was going to yell at him but then I didn't. It burns up your energy to holler.

Every time just before I take off in a race, I always feel like I'm in a dream, the kind of dream you have when you're sick with fever and feel all hot and weightless. I dream I'm flying over a sandy beach in the early morning sun, kissing the leaves of the trees as I fly by. And there's always the smell of apples, just like in the country when I was little and used to think I was a choo-choo train, running through the fields of corn and chugging up the hill to the orchard. And all the time I'm dreaming this, I get lighter and lighter until I'm flying over the beach again, getting blown through the sky like a feather that weighs nothing at all. But once I spread my fingers in the dirt and crouch over the Get on Your Mark, the dream goes and I am solid again and am telling myself, Squeaky you must win, you must win, you are the fastest thing in the world, you can even beat your father up Amsterdam if you really try. And then I feel my weight coming back just behind my knees then down to my feet then into the earth and the pistol shot explodes in my blood and I am off and weightless again, flying past the other runners, my arms pumping up and down and the whole world is quiet except for the crunch as I zoom over the gravel in the track. I glance to my left and there is no one. To the right, a blurred Gretchen, who's got her chin jutting out as if it would win the race all by itself. And on the other side of the fence is Raymond with his arms down to his side and the palms tucked up behind him, running in his very own style, and it's the first time I ever saw that and I almost stop to watch my brother Raymond on his first run. But the white ribbon is bouncing toward me and I tear past it, racing into the distance till my feet with a mind of their own start digging up footfuls of dirt and brake me short. Then all the kids standing on the side pile on me, banging me on the back and slapping my head with their May Day programs, for I have won again and everybody on 151st Street can walk tall for another year.

"In first place . . ." the man on the loudspeaker is clear as a bell now. But then he pauses and the loudspeaker starts to whine. Then static. And I lean down to catch my breath and here comes Gretchen walking back, for she's overshot the finish line too, huffing and puffing with her hands on her hips

taking it slow, breathing in steady time like a real pro and I sort
of like her a little for the first time. "In first place . . ." and then
three or four voices get all mixed up on the loudspeaker and I
dig my sneaker into the grass and stare at Gretchen who's
staring back, we both wondering just who did win. I can hear
old Beanstalk arguing with the man on the loudspeaker and
then a few others running their mouths about what the stop-
watches say. Then I hear Raymond yanking at the fence to call
me and I wave to shush him, but he keeps rattling the fence
like a gorilla in a cage like in them gorilla movies, but then
like a dancer or something he starts climbing up nice and easy
but very fast. And it occurs to me, watching how smoothly
he climbs hand over hand and remembering how he looked
running with his arms down to his side and with the wind pulling his mouth back and his teeth showing and all, it occurred
to me that Raymond would make a very fine runner. Doesn't
he always keep up with me on my trots? And he surely knows
how to breathe in counts of seven cause he's always doing it at
the dinner table, which drives my brother George up the wall.
And I'm smiling to beat the band cause if I've lost this race,
or if me and Gretchen tied, or even if I've won, I can always
retire as a runner and begin a whole new career as a coach with
Raymond as my champion. After all, with a little more study
I can beat Cynthia and her phony self at the spelling bee. And
if I bugged my mother, I could get piano lessons and become a
star. And I have a big rep as the baddest thing around. And I've
got a roomful of ribbons and medals and awards. But what has
Raymond got to call his own?

So I stand there with my new plans, laughing out loud by
this time as Raymond jumps down from the fence and runs
over with his teeth showing and his arms down to the side,
which no one before him has quite mastered as a running
style. And by the time he comes over I'm jumping up and down
so glad to see him—my brother Raymond, a great runner in the
family tradition. But of course everyone thinks I'm jumping up
and down because the men on the loudspeaker have finally
gotten themselves together and compared notes and are an-
nouncing "In first place—Miss Hazel Elizabeth Deborah

Parker." (Dig that.) "In second place—Miss Gretchen P. Lewis." And I look over at Gretchen wondering what the "P" stands for. And I smile. Cause she's good, no doubt about it. Maybe she'd like to help me coach Raymond; she obviously is serious about running, as any fool can see. And she nods to congratulate me and then she smiles. And I smile. We stand there with this big smile of respect between us. It's about as real a smile as girls can do for each other, considering we don't practice real smiling every day, you know, cause maybe we too busy being flowers or fairies or strawberries instead of something honest and worthy of respect ... you know ... like being people.

Medicine Man

By Rikki Lights

One of seven children, Rikki Lights (1952–) grew up in a black family on the South Carolina Sea Islands and spoke English and the African dialect Gullah. Until the age of sixteen, she suffered from incapacitating asthma, and so, although her family was poor, she did not work. By the age of three, Rikki Lights had already decided on her two loves— she would be a writer and a doctor—and she had constructed the plot of a novel by the time she was ten. A recent medical school graduate, Lights is now an intern in obstetrics and gynecology. She is a performing poet as well and reads her work with the jazz band of her husband, drummer Ronald Gilliam. She has written a libretto for a rock opera called "Divine Sugar" and a book of poems, Dog Moon, *published by Sunbury Press in 1976. Her writing has also appeared in* HooDoo, Essence, Painted Bride Quarterly, *and in an anthology,* Women Surviving Massacres and Men.*

"Medicine Man" was published in 1974 when Lights was a senior at Bryn Mawr College. When she entered the University of Pennsylvania Medical School the next fall,*

she—like the fictional character she had already *created—*
demanded a female cadaver and dissected it at a table
with ten male medical students.

September 6, 1974: Stayed up all night last night. I've stopped smoking and I need something to do with my hands, so I plugged in the iron and starched my white tunic to perfection. The angry roar of automobile horns and motors blocked my entrance to sleep, so I ate, polished my shoes, washed clothes, pressed my plaid skirt and matching red blouse, curled my hair, took another bath in warm water (Father says it's good for the nerves) talked to my sister in Atlanta for two hours on the telephone. All this began at eight and ended at six in the morning. Dozed for two hours. Classes begin at nine.

My starched white coat made me feel conspicuous, and the stiffness of my collar irritated my neck as I sat in lecture. Today I had my first glimpse of God. Dr. P—— came striding into the lecture room stooped over as if a truck driver had assembled his spinal column. His legs moved as if they were independent of his body, and his writing looked like the early manifestations of my three-year-old nephew's art, which my sis guards with the jealousy and pride of a war bird. Boys with red faces punctuated with fresh pimples and old acne scars sat behind their pencils writing notes as they fell from the lips of the grand giver. He teaches us anatomy with kindly condescension, while he walks, talks, and gesticulates as if every muscle in his body is trying to strain the other. There is no harmony of motion in his body. There are two women in my class: myself and a young woman from Texas named Carlotta who speaks to my shoes when she says Hello. She has this throbbing hypnotic gaze which she fixes into the strangest points in space, like the floor, the ceiling, a corner. Anything that she can see that's already defined for her.

The walls on the sixth floor of the Myers building are a dull gray, the kind of gray that floods the sky and swallows the sun. The kind of gray that hides snow in warm weather when everyone's expecting spring; yet the rank pungency of the formaldehyde reminds you that you might be the only living thing on the floor. I call it the catacombs, because it houses the dead, who sleep in rigid contraction inside the aluminum belly of their containers. As we waited in the dissection room, the dead remained with their gazes frozen into other dimensions. One student received a male body that was known for its advanced case of lung cancer. Nobody knows any names, the dead have no identity here, and only their deformities make them stand out. My eyes must have been stretched wide as I waited for the lab instructor (Ms. Miller, who has a habit of flaring up like a king cobra whenever "the boys ask silly questions") to announce which body belonged to whom. My wish to have a female cadaver was granted. The name Ingabord Stearns was typed neatly on a slim plastic bracelet, like the ones they put on the wrists of newborn babies. I asked in astonishment why Ingabord had been so honored as to have a name tag. "She willed her body to science, dear." I didn't like the way Ms. Miller said that—so cold and indifferent, as if the dead have no place in heaven or hell or earth.

At first I was afraid to touch Ingabord. I poked at her with my living brown eyes and felt my throat begin to close when I noticed the wads of cotton and gauze that were jammed down her throat. What is it that they didn't want her to say? Her mouth was wide open, and the stiffened muscles of her face broke the peaceful stillness of death with a silent scream. All of her teeth were missing except the one at the very front of her mouth. The mouth had dried and stretched the once-full lips to the consistency of catgut, exposing one tiny white tooth. I felt like crying when I remembered how proud my father was when my baby brother's first tooth broke its angry way through his gums.

"Having problems, now?" Dr. P—— seemed pleased at my distress. I could have traced the faint smile that stretched across his face with my carefully manicured index finger. The smile made me feel strange, as if I had been caught by God eating the forbidden fruit that would doom all women to the pains of childbirth and male domination: "I will increase your labor and your groaning, and in labor you shall bear children. . . ." I wanted to run. My thighs felt like they were sink-ing over my knees into the floor. My hands grabbed onto something very cold. "I'm not afraid," I whispered. "Of course you're not." The faint smile appeared again and froze my apology inside my brain. I followed the bloodshot path from his eyes to my hand, which had locked onto Ingabord's right knee.

The cold moisture of her flesh spread up my arm, ending in a tingle at the base of my spine and the back of my neck. I'm sure my hair must have stood on end as well, for by then the entire class was staring at me as though I was some kind of raving idiot. My stomach started a slow crawl toward my throat. Ms. Miller's shoes squeaked against the floor in rapid steps which halted at my back. "Those who are unaccustomed to the feel of death use rubber gloves. It also keeps the fingernail polish on your nails." The back of my neck felt her smile as she whipped around to my side and gently lifted my hand off the cadaver. A ring of sophisticated giggles spread across the room. I pulled my white coat around me as if to cover my nakedness, washed my hands, and carefully put my hands into the rubber gloves. Ms. Miller was right after all—the rubber gloves did buffer the sensation of death.

Our first incision was to be made in the chest region. Ingabord's arms were cramped across her chest as if she had struggled with the angel of death. I tried to unfold her arms, but they were too stiff. I hesitated to apply more pressure, for I felt as though I was violating her in some way. I grabbed her by the wrist and upper arm while slowly trying to pull the arm into a more relaxed position. I couldn't take my eyes off her face; I couldn't get over feeling as though she was watching me from some point in space. The eye sockets had long since dried out and the stubbly remains of her eyelashes gave them a rough texture. The eyeball itself was difficult to see. The round orbits had long since collapsed into a thin moist sheet of faded blue made wet by the sting of formaldehyde. The old women back home would make big juju off those eyes; and if the eyes didn't work they'd take the tooth.

The struggle of my life force to comprehend the absence of life made me feel as though I was fighting a dream. It was as if her soul were watching me from behind a moist film of air, or from the bottom of a shallow pool of fresh pond water. She was so close, my hands were touching her, fighting her flesh so that I could probe every inch of her gut and hold her heart in the palm of my hand. I knew her name, and in one year's time I will know more about her than she could ever have known in all her eighty-three years on this round green ball which goes hurtling through space on God's time.

When I heard the wet cracking sound I knew that the arm was broken. Fortunately it broke in the right place—at the elbow. Both professors were pleased at the clean breakage, and for a second I felt vindicated in my clumsiness. Ingabord's arm limped like a dying plant and danced like a feather in a wind gust as I let it fall to her side. Breaking the other arm was much simpler. Now her chest lay exposed and her weak limbs lay helplessly at her sides like a puppet whose strings have been cut by some malicious child.

December 20, 1974: I must muster up all my strength just to hold onto the rapid pace at which my senses rip through hundreds of pages of cold scientific texts and regimented learning. No one wants to know what I think, and only my ability to repeat what the texts say tells them that I am learning. I constantly repeat facts to myself. Sometimes it is the only life sign I have outside of the fragile rhythm of my breath and the determined beating of my heart. My mind and my body have been honed down to a functional fine point which resembles more the cold steel of my scalpel than the rounded fruitlike quality that my flesh used to have. My fingernails have been shed, and a manicure is now unthinkable. I am wholly consumed within the belly of my schedule which raises me up at six and lays me down with swollen eyes at two.

It is now four. I am due at the hospital for observation at seven but I cannot sleep. I look in the closet and I realize the peacocklike quality and feminine arrogance I must have had one year ago. All sorts of soft and lacy frilly things hang from padded hangers. Shoes that now look like they must have been worn by a country cousin on a night on the town crowd the floor of the closet. The bright reds and aquamarine blues and Bahamian yellows still bloom in velvet from the large cushions in the living room—which gives shelter to nothing but the past: tête-à-têtes with soft-voiced men in pinstriped Pierre Cardins. Myself staring through a thick sheet of ennui induced by the thick sweetness of Southern Comfort, or glasses of Chivas. Now a winter draft blows a song from the Chinese wind chimes across the hushed blue carpet. I am all alone. The large Chinese vases and the hanging green plants with their cool green leaves still demand my attention. Only my rubber tree, Quanzaa, seems to thrive even when I forget the water and the plant food. The canary's cage is now empty. Yesterday was one snow too many, and the temporary drop in heat put poor Omeiyya to sleep. I wanted to go back home. Home to Port-au-Prince, to lay my head in Maman's lap and listen to the raucous stories of Man Waharah.

Today in the O.B. ward, I accidently saw myself in one of the mirrors. It was like looking at a stranger. My face now calls out to the masks on the wall. But then the loss of thirty pounds would do that to anyone. I never realized how long and heavy my limbs are. My eyes have the vacant porcelain look of an antique Chinese doll which a shopkeeper once tried to sell me. The inward curvature of my abdomen leaves a wrinkled space in the front of my dress. In a word, I looked like a lost Watusi in the early stages of starvation.

It is almost Christmas, and the snow is falling. I decorated my potted pine with a few locks of tinsel and angel hair; but then I took it off because angel hair is scratchy and I didn't want to hurt the plant. Christmas day I think I'll bake a turkey and take it over to the kids in Pediatrics, or maybe I'll bake a cake. We'll see. . . .

April 3, 1976: Put my pet Aji in the vet hospital. When I first bought her she was so round and soft with her coat of jet and her wild crossed eyes and kinky tail. Usually she is so tame, but today she was a rogue. She kept running in mad circles around my feet whenever I walked across the room. She growled like a panther and jumped up on the window ledge, knocking over the plants. Then she ran from me when I tried to catch her. I sat on the sofa and watched her lying there rubbing herself against the bright yellow pillow, rolling over and

over and miauling as though she were in pain. Usually the
yellow in the pillows calms her, but now it seemed to drive her
crazy. I kept still, trying to spread my calm to her. I felt her
eyes blink inside my own as I lowered myself onto the rug.
Slowly I approached her on all fours, yet as I drew closer, the
angry sound boiling over in her throat echoed inside my own.
She sprang up from the pillow and I chased her around the
room until I caught her. I held her up to look in her face and
talk to her, but she pulled out her claws and raked me across
my cheek. In my anger, I threw her across the room against the
wall. I wrapped her body in what used to be my favorite hand-
knit blue Italian shawl. By the time I got her to the vets, it was
soaked with blood where her nose and mouth had bled. What
will I do with her body if she dies?

May 6, 1976: I want to be reckless. I want to dash headlong into
life or just sit in quiet protest and let myself be washed of the
city by the rain.

   Dozed for about two hours and woke up in chills from a
dream I was having. There I was, lost in the midst of a lush
green jungle. I was surrounded by large prehistoric fronds with
wet leaves that seemed to touch me all over the naked top of
my body. I was trying to run away from something, but the
cool greenness of the forest floor made me want to slow down.
The long violet skirt which flew in every direction as I ran
frightened me because it could make me lose my balance. The
large wooded root of a vine tripped me up and I fell headlong
into a mass of soft green foliage. What I saw fascinated me. I
could see each leaf and stem as if it were under a microscope.
I pulled myself closer to them, trying to merge my belly with
the ground. The protoplasm shone as it streamed in circles
around the tiny nuclei, which radiated light most intensely.
Suddenly the ground began to undulate softly, slowly, like the
oceans. I rolled over on my back. My spine tingled with an intense energy which was transferred to it by the moving protoplasm of the grass. I began to feel the rounded space marked
out by my arms, which were placed close to my body. Slowly
my left hand began to rise from its own energy, pulling the rest

of my arm slowly with it. I saw that it, too, was green like the plants, and my protoplasm moved and shone like the particles of golden light which spin off from the surface of the sun. The slight rustle of leaves above my head made me look up. The leaves parted, and from the opening emerged a delicate yellow-and-pink flower. My breathing increased and the energy of my spine began to increase and build up. The stem of the flower grew longer and it bent toward my face. A thick wine-colored fluid that sparkled inside began to flow out. I flicked out my tongue and tilted back my head to receive each cool drop as it melted into my senses. The earth began to spin around slowly, and past the pink edge of the flower I saw heaven break open, and song sprang from all existence. Within the instants at the end of the dream I knew what it was like to house the knowledge of infinite unity within the finite sensations of flesh and memory.

July 19, 1976: "People are Hell!" says Jean Paul Sartre. But I cannot afford the wordy selfishness of his philosophy. Maybe people do cause you to bury your senses alive—I don't know. But I'm not alone, not really alone. Today I was sitting in my window seat watching the heavy droplets of transparent rain wash the comet tail of summer into the drains. Then the rain ceased and the sun came up, making the asphalt steam. One by one the doors of the houses along the street began to open, and the young men poured into the street to play football. The sound of their laughter flew like spirits in the air. It echoed around the treetops, shaking the leaves with breath and wind. I could almost reach my hand out of the window and touch it. I put down my midday gin and tonic to watch them and my head felt warm and full. Their happiness made me feel good. But the plumpness of their youth made me feel hard and dry by comparison. Someone looked up and called me: "Hey, Moma. Hey, Babe!" I waved faintly, for I knew that they were addressing me. They had seen me in a way that I hadn't been seen in months. Their eyes had transformed me into a beautiful giraffe floating within an entire herd of giraffes doing a liquid feather dance across the American savannah. I had forgotten that feeling of the herd, of being just one of many proud and strutting females with a flaming red chest—a mute sign for all virile males.

The laughter cajoled me into a pair of blue jeans, down the stairs, and out the front door.

"Can I play?" My announcement made everyone get quiet.

"Oh man looka hah, Oh my ain't she the big one! Whew!"

"What's the matter, am I too tall for you?"

"Naw but almost. How tall are you anyway?"

"Six, one." I put my hands in my pockets.

"Can you play?"

"Sure I know how to play. I have seven brothers." Everyone laughed.

"All right then, Moma, play ball."

The ball came spiraling toward me and I grabbed it with ease. The grunts and hollers whizzed past my ears as I flew over their attempts to stop me. The rustle of the tennis shoes against the pavement sounded like an elephant stampede. We laughed, greased, sweated, and sprawled across each other, making a heap of human laughter in the middle of the street. One woman came outside to sweep her porch, looked at me, and shook her head. At sunset I was too tired to continue. As I leaned against the car to catch my breath, Jocko (the short one with the dimple in his chin) offered me a cigarette. I accepted and inhaled deeply. Sahn (plaid shirt, fast runner) said, "Hey, man, I'm hip you smell like likker. You got some booze in your pad?" "Yes, I got booze in my pad, but you're too young to get any. I can, however, give you young men something to eat and plenty iced tea to drink." Despite the groans, they were too hungry to turn me down, so we went inside.

As soon as we opened the door, Cinque (mynah bird) yelled: "Oh Cha-Cha run away come again some other day, Ahhhhhhhh-k." She scared everyone half to death, but someone got rid of the chill bumps quick enough to ask what she meant. I explained that Cha-Cha was my cat, and that she had run away to live with the old lady across the street. "Cinque started teasing me because she thinks that I love Cha-Cha more than her." "Maybe you do," someone responded while taking a seat on the sofa. Yes, maybe I do.

I fixed a big bowl of spaghetti, sipped on a glass of Southern Comfort, and sneaked a little bit of wine into the punch. I answered a barrage of questions the whole time. Someone said I talked funny and why did I sound like that. I told him that I was born and raised in Haiti, and that the only reason I was in the United States was because I was being trained to be a doctor. And that started something altogether different. So I chilled them with a few horror stories about hospital life and cadavers—which made some one choke on a meatball. Manno (the Puerto Rican) discovered my scalpels in the bathroom. He did all kinds of flourishes with his feet and jumped around like a madman, swirling the sterling blade over his head. "Hey, man, look what I found." Everyone gathered around him. One by one they stroked the blade as if it were a child. "Man I sure like to have one of these in a gang war, wouldn't you?" With that I interrupted by taking the blade away. "This instrument is to heal, not to bring death," I told them softly. There was no more laughter in my voice and they all sat down quietly as if they were waiting for the teacher to begin class.

The laughter was broken and we limped toward the end of our togetherness. One by one they laid down their punch glasses and swapped glances. Manno was the first to cut the cord: "O.K., doc, time for you to go to bed." "Me, what about you young things?" I tried to laugh. Jocko stood up and offered me another cigarette. He lit a match, took a puff on his own and said, "Who us? We got all day tomorrow, and the day after, and the day after that. We got all the time in the world to go to bed. But you, you're a doctor, and doctors have bedtimes. Come on, ya'll, lessgo." They all stood up at the same time, mumbled something which sounded like thanks, and in a moment they were all gone.

I finished the night with my drinks, loaded the dishwasher, set the controls. Went down the corner for some cigarettes and smoked and sipped my way to sleep, while listening to Billie Holiday sing "God Bless the Child."

August 15, 1976: Went to a meeting this morning to help make plans for the first-year students. Everyone was so starched and stiff and self-centered. God forbid that anyone should disagree with the actual committee members (i.e., the real M.D.s. We students are just token representatives whose opinions are swatted down like flies whenever the buzzing gets too loud or too close).

I had the misfortune to have the guts to argue with Alva Workman, M.D. ("Mad Dog"), who made some slick remark about women in medicine. He had the nerve to propose a cutback in female admissions. That same little baldheaded fatlipped man with the cold fleshy fingers with hairy knuckles who couldn't keep his hand off my knee when I was his assistant. The nerve of that DOG! That really galled me and I boiled over like a berserk teapot.

Went to the market after the meeting and cussed everybody that got in my way. Came home and found a note on my door. The words "Medicine Man" were printed (and misspelled) on the envelope. I took the note off the door and maneuvered my keys into the locks. In between the baguettes and the celery leaves, I opened the envelope. It contained a short poem by Langston Hughes which said:

Folks.
Birthin is hard and
dyin is mean
so get yourself a little lovin'
in between.

love, us.

I reread the note, sat down on the sofa, and cried.

The Bowl

By Barbara Smith

Barbara Smith (1946–) was born in Cleveland, Ohio, graduated from Mount Holyoke College in 1969, and was awarded an M.A. degree from the University of Pittsburgh in 1971. Her essays and reviews, almost all about black women in life and in literature, have appeared in Ms., New Republic, Freedomways, The Radical Teacher, The Second Wave, *and* Conditions. *Since 1974, she has lived and worked in Boston's black community. With her twin sister Beverly, she started a black feminist collective.*

Smith is writing a Ph.D. dissertation on four black women writers—Zora Neale Hurston, Frances E. W. Harper, Ann Petry, and Alice Walker. "The Bowl" is Smith's second published poem. The first, "Poem for My Sister, I; Birmingham, 1963," appeared in Southern Voices.

Today
I'm making for my friends
a rich dark dough,
coarse with a million seeds,
a smell as deep as dreaming.
What do I have to hold it?

I search and find a
crockery bowl,
leftover from my childhood.

Suddenly work is ritual.

This empty bowl,
bright-sky-blue-striped,
is full of pictures,
Everything.
Rolls and cake and sweet potato pie,
stuffing, cream,
my mouth and eyes fill up.

My people used this bowl to mix their lives.
It's where I learned
a way of giving
caring
with a cake.

I see them mixing now:
Beating,

Stirring,
Keeping time.
(My fingers slyly dipping in.)

If women's lives were fables
and kitchen feats adventures,
this bowl would be a talisman,
tell tales
and even fly.

But now it is an ordinary bowl.

The place those first women in my world
taught me to shape more
than necessary bread
my life.

Hats

By Jean Pedrick

*Born in Salem, Massachusetts, Jean Pedrick (1922–)
graduated from Wheaton College in 1943. She has been a
full-time writer since she was eight, with the exception
of a single year as a parts inspector at Sylvania Company
during World War II. Her only novel,* The Fascination,
*was published by Houghton Mifflin in 1947. Her poems
have appeared in* The New Yorker, Antioch Review,
Little Magazine, Michigan Quarterly, *and elsewhere,
and she has received awards from the New England Poetry
Club. In the early seventies, Pedrick was cofounder of
a cooperative press, Alice James Books, devoted especially
to the publication of poetry by women.* Wolf Moon *(1974)
and* Pride and Splendor *(1976)—two volumes of her poems—
were published by that press. "Hats" comes from the
second volume. Jean Pedrick lives in Boston with her
husband and two sons. A new volume of her poems,* The
Gaudy Book, *will be published by The Juniper Press.*

S he went out making hats when she was young
for *gnädige* ladies living in rich houses.
She knew just how—the knack—to tilt,
follow the eyebrow, follow the color of iris
in the ribbon, in the veil mist. Had
a silk sack of feathers.

Sometimes stayed and dined at mile-long
tables. Sometimes ate in the kitchen
thrown with peddlers.

         Always felt
superior. Any woman should know
how to confect it, how to set it on,
how to sail forth.

THREE:
Family Work

And When Is There Time

UNLIKE ALL OTHER WORK, family work has traditionally belonged to women. Perhaps the most important idea in this collection is the recognition of family work as dignified and essential human labor, worthy of definition, examination, and analysis. A significant proportion of the prose and poetry in all

sections of this collection contains portraits of women working as wives and mothers, sometimes in addition to other jobs. Their work may be both satisfying and oppressive, depending on the particular tasks and the conditions under which they must be done. It is, however, almost exclusively theirs; that is, it is rarely shared by male family members.

From one perspective, the rearing of children and the nurturing of a loving relationship between two adults might be considered the most desirable and rewarding work in any society. But from another perspective, the work involved in caring for spouse, children, and home is both difficult and often unrewarding. There are constant pressures on women—to be al-

ways there, to be entirely giving without concern for their "own" selves. In addition, such repetitive tasks as washing diapers, dishes, floors, hands, and faces, especially when done in isolation from other adults, can dull the spirit. When the wife and mother also works in the paid labor force she may find herself less or more satisfied, depending on her job, her economic status, and her family's attitudes. Almost always though, she is clearly more burdened by having two jobs—one paid, one unpaid.

In general, the literature that takes family work as its subject separates housework and the relationships between wife and husband from caring for children and relationships between mothers and children. Unpaid housework alone is never satisfying work, whether performed by women, men, or by both together in some shared arrangement. In Wilma Shore's "The Butcher," for example, the boredom of housework, often attributed to middle-class women, overcomes a working-class woman who has gladly given up secretarial work to become a housewife.

When child care is added to women's housework, the possibilities for satisfying work increase, but so do the complications and conflicts. The work of parenting is consistently portrayed as sex-specific—women's work—and literary portraits of fathers caring for children are not yet available. August Strindberg, in "An Attempt at Reform," depicts an effort to share housework equitably between husband and wife, both of whom also hold paid jobs. When the wife discovers she is pregnant, she weeps. What will become of their sharing, of her independent income? The "attempt at reform" that worked so well would seem to have vanished. Several selections illustrate attempts to combine child care with other work, as in Rosellen Brown's poem, "The Famous Writers School Opens Its Arms in the Next Best Thing to Welcome." Though often difficult, such combinations can be satisfying.

Even when their lives are filled with conflicting demands, mothers find the work of caring for children ultimately meaningful: children are both a source of delight and a hope for the future. One story in the collection, Tillie Olsen's "I Stand Here

Ironing," allows a working-class mother to reflect on her struggles, two decades earlier, to love and provide support for her first daughter. "What did I gather together, to try and make coherent?" she asks in the story. And although, in one response to herself, she says, "I will never total it all," the story offers a complex portrait of a mother's anguish and pleasure, as well as her view of a daughter's growth to maturity.

Quite a different picture of family work emerges in Alice Marriott's "An Indian Trader." In this nineteenth-century family, part of the work of mothering includes teaching a daughter about family work, and the work shown here is deeply gratifying. María, even at age five, has some choice about the jobs she wants to do and understands that work is required of all members of the family—female and male—for their survival. For María, family work is a serious and shared responsibility.

The stories and poems in this volume do not gloss over the tensions and frustrations of women's family work. But they also point to the importance of that work and provide glimpses of the possibilities for satisfaction.

Farm Wife

By Ellen Bryant Voigt

Born in Chatham, Virginia, Ellen Bryant Voigt (1943–)
earned a Bachelor of Arts degree at Converse College in South
Carolina and a Master of Fine Arts from the University
of Iowa's Writer's Workshop. She has played piano in a bar,
worked as a technical writer at Iowa Wesleyan University's
School of Pharmacy, and now earns her living as a teacher.
Currently, she directs the Master of Fine Arts program at
Goddard College in Vermont, where she lives with her
husband and two children. Her poems have appeared in
the New Yorker, *the* Atlantic, American Poetry Review, *and*

elsewhere. Claiming Kin *(1973),* in which *"Farm Wife"*
appears, is her first volume of poems.

Dark as the spring river, the earth
opens each damp row as the farmer
swings the far side of the field.
The blackbirds flash their red
wing patches and wheel in his wake,
down to the black dirt; the windmill
grinds in its chain rig and tower.

In the kitchen, his wife is baking.
She stands in the door in her long white
gloves of flour. She cocks her head and
tries to remember, turns like the moon
toward the sea-black field. Her belly
is rising, her apron fills like a sail.
She is gliding now, the windmill churns
beneath her, she passes the farmer,
the fine map of the furrows.
The neighbors point to the bone-white
spot in the sky.

        Let her float
like a flat gull that swoops and circles,
before her husband comes in for supper,
before her children grow up and leave her,
before the pulley cranks her down
the dark shaft, and the church blesses
her stone bed, and the earth seals
its black mouth like a scar.

Midsummer

By Patricia Cumming

Patricia Cumming (1932–) earned a B.A. at Radcliffe College
in 1954 and an M.A. at Middlebury College in 1956. Her

*husband died when her two daughters were very young, and
she supported them and herself by teaching in the writing
program at the Massachusetts Institute of Technology and
at the University of Massachusetts/Boston, and by doing
other kinds of work. She coordinated publicity for* Daedalus,
*a scholarly quarterly; she worked as co-producer and
assistant to the director of the Theatre Company of Boston,
of which she was also a founder. Early in the seventies, she
was a founding member of Alice James Books, a cooperative
publishing house with an emphasis on publishing poetry
by women. Alice James Books has published two volumes
of her poems,* Afterwards *(1974) and* Letter from an Outlying
Province *(1976). "Midsummer" comes from the most recent
volume.*

(for Julie, Sue, Sarah, and Beka)

Rain in torrents has washed out the road
already, out-of-season, a hurricane

is predicted. The sun shines, but the wind
strengthens, the waves

reflect grey. The children
are restless, they've been shouting

all day: winter tore us to rags, it was not
well spent; now the nights will lengthen

again, and the fireflies will blink
out. The children, relentless, insist

on the beach; I take them, they fling themselves in
to the water before I can stop them: the tides

shift, the waves
rise. I cry out, "Come back, come

back!" and call over and over their names
lost in the wind; they've gone

all the way to the rock, slippery with seaweed and spray,
they climb to the shoulder, dance

at the edge and throw out their arms to the sky;
hesitate, balance, and plummet

into high waves trumpeting, charging like elephants.
I count

heads and can't find two in the grey
sea. No one

is nearby, I can't do
anything. I wait, hating

myself, forever, on the dry, empty beach, miles away.
Then I see them rise on the crest of a wave,

one, then the others: they all come
to shore, breathless, wild-haired, in triumph.

Later. The clouds have lifted, they blow
across a full moon. The children fight over supper,

their stretched voices rise, they're at war
with themselves, with each other, they want

justice—"Go out!"
I tell them, "It's Midsummer's Night!"

Now they dance, arms wide to the white, stormy moon.
I chase

them off the roof, from the edge
of the well, and out of the poison ivy;

it's the longest day of the year, the wind
has blown me to tatters, forewarns me of more

disorder, but the children sing
at the fireflies, leap on the edges

of shadows, lunatic, wild: they are breaking
the tomatoes, trampling the iris

and dahlias, they are bruising their feet
on branches, they are dancing,

dancing.

Allí por la calle San Luis

By Carmen Tafolla

*Carmen Tafolla (1951–) was born in San Antonio, Texas, and
earned her B.A. and M.A. degrees at Austin College in 1972
and 1973. Presently, she is working on a Ph.D. in bilingual
education at the University of Texas. She has taught high
school French in Sherman, Texas, and she has been director
of the Mexican American Studies Center at Texas Lutheran
College. Her poems have appeared in a number of anthologies.
Currently, she is preparing for publication a volume of poems
accompanied by prose sketches of Chicanas in history.
Her prose writing includes a chapter on Hispanic women
to be published in* The Emergent Ethnic Woman Confronting
Racism and Sexism, *and a program on parenting written for
the Southwest Educational Development Laboratories.*

*In the summer of 1972, as part of a church-related project
called "Creative Arts of San Antonio," Tafolla collected
folklore by walking door-to-door in the* barrio *or ghetto
community, asking elderly residents if she could interview
them. Two people she interviewed were the mother and
daughter in "Allí por la calle San Luis." The poem appeared
originally in* Hembra, *a publication that emerged from a
course called "La Chicana," taught by Inez Hernandez
Tovar in the Center for Mexican American Studies at the
University of Texas.*

West Side—corn tortillas for a penny each
Made by an aged woman
   and her mother.
   Cooked on the homeblack of a flat stove,
   Flipped to slap the birth awake,
   Wrapped by corn hands.
Roasted morning light and dancing history—
   earth gives birth to corn gives birth to man
   gives birth to earth.
Corn tortillas—penny each.
   No tax.

The Indian Trader

By Alice Lee Marriott

See page 65 for biographical information on Alice Marriott. "The Indian Trader" is an early chapter in María: The Potter of San Ildefonso *(1948), the biography of María Montoya Martínez, who was born in 1881 in a small village in New Mexico. Marriott's artistry turns each chapter in the biography into a self-contained "story."*

It was Tuesday, and on Tuesday Mother made cheese. She started early in the morning, using milk that had clabbered overnight, and worked quickly so that the cheese would be finished before the heat of the day set in. Her wooden molds stood in a row on the table beside the fire, three big molds and six little ones. When the cheese was set, she turned it out of the molds on a clean board. Usually there was more cheese than the family could use before she made more, on Friday.

There was never any doubt in Mother's mind about what she would do with the extra cheese. She went to the door of the house and called to her second daughter, "María, come here. I need you."

María was a good little girl. She came quickly from her play place by the irrigation ditch, and stood before her mother. "What is it, Mother? The cheese?"

"Yes, the cheese. I have four big ones and three little ones to sell."

Together they went through the short hallway and back to the kitchen. Mother took a basket down from the rafters, where it hung by its handle, and lined it with a clean cloth. She folded other freshly laundered cloths about the cheeses, and put the packages in the basket.

"Here you are, María. Ten cents for the little ones and twenty-five cents for the big ones."

"A shirt size for the little ones and a skirt size for the big ones." The child nodded gravely, and took the basket. Quietly, she left the house.

Going down the hill from the house to the village seemed like a long walk for a little girl five years old. The slope of the ground was irregular, in long and short steps, and María walked slowly, balancing her basket in her arms. This was her second trip with the cheeses. The first had been a week ago, after her sister Ana had announced that she would rather help her father in the alfalfa field than go around to people's houses with things to sell. Ana liked outdoor things better than she did people.

Thus it had been María's turn to help her mother. Selling had been fun the first time, and María did not see why Ana minded it. This time, when María knew just what she was doing, she walked very straight and held her head like a grown-up lady's. She would have liked to balance the basket on her head like a water jar, but since it was too wide and flat for that, she held it firmly in her arms before her. When she tried to carry the basket by its handle, it dragged at her arm and hurt her.

Down the hill, across the cleared space where the round kiva stood alone, and through the Gonzales family's fields she went, to the south wall of the pueblo. Here there was a passageway from the kiva to the plaza. During dance times the passage was closed to all but the dancers, but on other days people walked through it freely. María went through the coolness of its shade and came out into the plaza before the big cottonwood tree that had always been there. She turned to the right, and knocked on the door of the first house.

The woman who answered her knock smiled when she saw the child. "There is the Indian trader," she said, and held the door open. "Come in."

"My mother sent me to sell these," said María, opening the cloth that covered one of the cheeses.

"They look nice," said the woman. "Reyes always makes good cheese. How much are they?"

"A shirt size for the little ones and a skirt size for the big ones," María answered.

The woman frowned a little, and shook her head. "That's too bad," she said. "I have no money in the house to pay you. Perhaps your mother would trade with me?"

"I don't know," said María doubtfully. Her mother had said nothing about trading, and when she had gone out before, the people had had their money ready to give her.

"I have some corn meal that I just ground," said the woman, thoughtfully. "Perhaps Reyes would like to have that in exchange for a cheese."

"Maybe," said María. "I don't know."

"I'll tell you what," said the woman. "I'll give you the corn meal. Then if Reyes doesn't want it, she can send you back with it; and when my husband comes in from the fields this evening, I'll get some money from him to pay her."

"Well, all right," María agreed. "I'll tell my mother what you say."

The woman went into her kitchen and came back in a moment with a measure of corn meal and a clean cloth. She laid the cloth on the floor of her house and poured the meal on the cloth. María watched the woman doubtfully. The measure of meal was larger than the measure of cheese, but she was not sure that it was as big as the meal measure she had seen the Spanish man use in his store. She was still thinking about this when the woman tied the corners of the cloth tightly together and handed the bundle to her.

"There," said the woman. "Now I'll take one of these nice little cheeses, and that will be all right."

María felt better when the woman said that she would take one of the little cheeses. She was quite sure that there was not enough meal in the cloth to pay for a big cheese.

"Don't forget," said the woman, as she opened the door for the child to go, "if your mother isn't satisfied, she can send the meal back this evening."

"All right," answered María. "Good-bye."

"Good-bye," said the woman, and closed the door.

At the next house the people did not want any cheese and at the one beyond it there seemed to be nobody at home. María knocked and knocked at the door, but no one came. The basket of cheese was slippery and hard to hold, especially now that she had to carry the bag of corn meal too. She tried slipping the knotted corners of the cloth over her arm, and that made carrying it a little easier, but then she had to hold the basket with the other arm. The basket slipped and slid, and before she got to the door of the fourth house she almost dropped her load. Her arms were so full that she had to kick on the door with her toe instead of knocking with her hands in the polite way. The door was opened so fast that she was afraid the woman of the house must have seen her kick instead of knock.

"Good morning," said this woman. "Come in. What have you today?"

"My mother made some cheese to sell," said María. She was relieved because the woman had not called her a trader, so maybe she would not want to trade. The child set down the bag of corn meal and opened the cloth over the basket again.

"I think I'd like a big one," said the woman, looking at the cheese carefully. "Are they the regular price?"

"The big ones are twenty-five cents," María told her. This time she did not say anything about the shirt-sized and the skirt-sized coins. They called the money that at home because for ten cents one could buy enough material at the store for a blouse, but the cloth for a skirt cost twenty-five cents. Maybe other people had not heard money talked about in that way.

"That's the regular price," said the woman. "Here, I'll take this one." She lifted a cheese out of the basket and laid it on a plate. Then she folded the cloth carefully and put it back in the basket. María was glad the woman did that. The first woman had kept the cloth. Now that she thought about it, María wondered if she should have asked to have the wrapping back.

This woman reached inside the folds of her blouse and took out a cloth package. She unwrapped it carefully, and from its folds she took a coin purse. She saw María watching her, and smiled.

"Always wrap your purse up, child," she said. "Cloth sticks to cloth, but leather will slip. If you wrap your purse, you'll always be sure you have it."

María nodded gravely and watched the woman open the purse and take out a coin. It was a whole twenty-five cents.

"I'll tie it in the cloth that was around the cheese," the woman said. "Then, when you get home, you can count your

cloths and your coins, and you'll know that you have something to show your mother for each cheese."

Again María nodded. It seemed a good idea to her. The
woman refolded the cloth and laid it in the basket.

"There you are," she said. Then, as María picked up her
other bundle, the woman asked, "What is it that you have
there?"

"Corn meal," said María. "Mrs. Gonzales traded it to me for
a cheese."

"That was a good idea," said the woman. She smiled. "You
must be a good trader," she said. "How big a cheese was it?"

"It was one of the little ones," María answered.

"You are a good trader," said the woman. "You must have
fifteen cents' worth of meal there."

"Thank you for telling me," said María. "I have a bigger
piece of cloth than the cheese was wrapped in, too."

"That's just like Mrs. Gonzales," said the woman. "She'd
give away anything she had. She never was a good bargainer."

"Thank you," said María. "Good-bye."

"Good-bye," replied the woman.

After that, selling went better. People were at home in the
next four houses, and María sold a cheese at each one. Everybody was polite and kind. They all asked her in, and they all
said nice things about the cheese and about the way her mother
made it. At the last house, when she had only one small cheese
left, María found the man of the family at home. His wife was
away.

"I don't know," said the man doubtfully, when María told
him why she was there. "That's woman's business. I don't
know whether my wife needs any cheese or not."

María shook her head. She had hoped that the people in this
house would buy her cheese so that she could go home. The
bag of meal was getting heavier and heavier. If all of the cheeses
were out of the basket, she could put the bag in it, and that
would make the carrying easier.

"I'll tell you what," the man said, seeing how unhappy she
looked. "I like cheese, and I believe I could eat that little one
all by myself. I haven't any money with me, because my wife

took it when she went to the store, but I'll trade you something for your cheese. Will you do that?"

"I guess so," María said. "I already made one trade today."

"Well, all right then," said the man. "That's what we'll do. I'll trade you a silver button for the cheese. It's a good Navajo button and it's made out of a ten-cent piece, so I know it's worth as much as the cheese is. I had two on my moccasins, but I lost one, so you can have the other."

"Well, all right," said María. "I guess my mother will like that."

"I think she will," said the man. "You wait here and I'll get it."

He must have had to cut it off his moccasin, for he was gone for some time. When he brought the coin back, there were still sinew threads hanging through the loop on the back of the button.

"Here it is," said the man. "Now you can give me the cheese."

"Have you a plate?" asked María. All of the ladies had known that cheese had to go on a plate, but the man seemed to think she could put it right into his hand.

"A plate?" asked the man. "Yes. I'll get it."

He made a lot of noise moving the dishes around before he came back with the plate. María unwrapped the cheese, and put it on the plate that the man held out to her. Then she tied the silver button in the wrapping, and put the cloth in the basket. Last of all, she put the meal sack in on top of the cloths. She picked the whole pile up in both arms.

"Good-bye," she said to the man, and started home.

María walked slowly, because the basket with the meal was so heavy that it seemed to press her bare feet down into the gravel. She set the basket down twice on the ground, and sat down beside it to rest before she went on. Once she tried to put the basket on her head, but her arms were too short to lift and hold it. It was a wide, flaring basket that her mother had got from a Jicarilla Apache woman, and it was just too big for María to handle easily.

Little by little, though, María went towards home. Once

some of the Spanish children who lived just outside the wall of the village called to her to come and play, but she shook her head.

"I have to take this home to my mother," she said.

A little girl of about María's own age stuck out her tongue and called María by her middle name, which she hated. "Toñita, Toñita, you're red-headed mad!" the Spanish girl yelled.

María wanted to stick her own tongue out in return. She could think of worse things to say. But she was doing something to help her mother now, and she did not want to spoil it. Still holding the basket before her in both arms, she walked solidly up the hill to home.

She knew her mother was in the kitchen, for the front door was closed. María went to the back door and kicked at it with her toe. Mother came to open the door.

"Well," Reyes said, "you got back soon. Did you sell all the cheese?"

"All but two," María said. She was beginning to worry about telling her mother what had happened.

"Two didn't sell?" asked her mother. "What was the matter?"

"I traded for them," said María. "You didn't tell me to do it, but the people said they hadn't any money, and they wanted the cheese."

"What did you trade?" her mother inquired.

"Well," said María, slowly, "for one I got a Navajo button, and for the other I got this corn meal. Mrs. Gonzales traded me the meal, and that's her cloth it's wrapped in."

"Was it for a big cheese or a little one?" her mother wanted to know.

"A little one."

The mother smiled. "You're a good trader," she said. "Wasn't it heavy to carry?"

"Yes," María answered. "Sometimes I almost dropped it."

"Well," said her mother, looking at the silver button, "this was a good trade, too. When people trade you little things like this you can carry them home. But when someone trades you something big, like the meal, leave it. Then your father or Ana can go in the evening and get the things and bring them home. You can't carry all these bundles, not if you're going into the trading business."

She smiled again, and María knew her mother was pleased.

"Do you like to trade?" her mother asked.

"Yes," said María solemnly, "I like it. When I grow up, I'm going to have a trading post of my own and sell things all the time."

But this time her mother shook her head. "That's a lot of work for a woman. You'd better wait till you have a man to help you with it, before you start."

The Butcher

By Wilma Shore

Wilma Shore (1913–) was born in New York City. She moved to Hollywood when her mother, Viola Brothers Shore, a well-known short-story writer, was offered a job writing for silent films. She left high school without finishing and spent two years in Paris studying painting. After an early marriage and the birth of her first daughter, she learned secretarial skills and worked for some years as a legal stenographer and secretary. Since that time, she has published about fifty stories, some of which have appeared in Best Short Stories *and in* Prize Short Stories: The O. Henry Awards. *She has also taught short-story writing workshops for adults and written lyrics and television plays for children. Her books include* Women Should Be Allowed *(1964), a collection of stories each of which is prefaced by an essay on female stereotypes, and* Who in the Zoo *(1976), a children's book. She lives in New York City with her husband and is working on a young adult biography of Beatrix Potter.*

"The Butcher," Wilma Shore's second published story, and, according to her, her "first serious one," appeared first in

the prestigious Story Magazine *in 1940. It was then selected by Edmund O'Brien for the* Best Short Stories of 1940.

I n the Bronx, where Millie Patron grew up, a girl who wanted to work knew she would be either a school teacher or a stenographer. One or the other. And long before Millie finished high school she had made up her mind. For one thing, she knew she wasn't smart enough to be a school teacher without a lot of work; and for another thing she knew it would only be a few years anyhow till she got married.

It was funny that she knew for sure, that way, because she wasn't any beauty. Her skin was nice and white and she had beautiful hair, they called her Red in grammar school, but when she ordered a chocolate malted in the afternoon her friends would always kid about her weight. She didn't care, though. Millie never minded kidding. And besides, she liked chocolate malteds. She figured a couple of extra pounds wouldn't make much difference when somebody wanted to marry her.

When she finished business school she got her mother to give her money for a new hat, and went to sit in the agencies; she got a job the first week. Her boss was a nice middle-aged man who didn't want to pay very much but didn't resent her because she was underpaid. She worked out a good-looking shorthand abbreviation for Paramount Linoleum, Inc., made friends with the rest of the staff, and bought herself a crochet needle and enough twine to make a bedspread for a double bed.

When she had been working two years the other girl in the office left to get married; Millie became the boss's secretary and they got a new girl to take her place. She finished the bedspread and went to work on a set of doilies for the table.

In the evenings she had dates with the different boys she knew from high school. But as time passed there were fewer and fewer extra boys and sometimes her married friends had to scout around for a boy for Millie. Millie knew what was going on, she was nobody's fool, but she didn't mind. She liked to go out and have a good time, but as far as flirting or being popular was concerned, it just never meant anything to her. Like the job, the dates were only to kill time for a couple of years till she met the right man, the way you have a soda until the feature you want to see goes on, and the soda is good enough but not important.

Because even when she was still a little kid she knew that the only important thing was getting married, having her own house, and maybe a couple of kids, loving her husband, and getting to have the warmth and assurance she saw in her own mother. Marriage was all that, and it was something more, something she couldn't put into words, even to herself, but that she could feel all the way through, starting in the small of her back and out to her fingers, sweet and rich, like a chocolate malted with ice cream.

She met Lou in the country, the summer she was twenty-two. He was slightly built and shorter than she was, and he spoke in a quiet husky voice, almost a whisper. He looked older than he was, which was twenty-seven. The way she knew she was in love with him was because he gave her that same feeling, kind of warm and full. She mentioned him in a letter to her mother when she had only known him four days. "He's a very nice boy," she wrote, "with a steady job in the printing business."

He proposed two months later. "We could get married," he whispered, "if you'd like. . . . I'm crazy about you, Millie. . . ."

He had money saved up and so did she, and she had the bedspread and doilies and a half dozen cross-stitched hand towels. She gave her boss a month's notice and he was sorry to see her go and sent them linoleum for their kitchen.

They took an apartment, two rooms and kitchenette, halfway between his mother's house and hers, and she began fixing it up. She ran down to Fourteenth Street for material for curtains, she compared mattresses in half a dozen stores, she tacked chintz edging on the closet shelves. In the evening they sat with pencil and paper figuring how much money should go for a rug, or whether they should wait till next year and in the meantime get a better armchair. Sometimes she ran over to her mother's in the afternoon. "Should I put oilcoth on the kitchen shelves? They say it draws bugs."

In the morning she got up to make breakfast for Lou and it made her happy to do it because she knew she could have slept. After lunch she would stretch out on the couch with a magazine and remember how a month ago she had been running back to the office. That was the thing about being at home; you could do what you wanted, if you had a headache you could lie down all day. But usually when she was halfway through a story she would forget about it and lie looking at the wall, wondering whether she should change the glasses from the second shelf to the first or leave them the way they were.

The last stitch on the curtains went in about a month after they were married. She ran right out and got the curtain rods and hung them herself. That night when Lou came home he did just the right thing; he stopped in the door and stood there shaking his head. "Well, well," he whispered, fondly, "don't they look beautiful? Some girl I married!"

The curtains were the finishing touch. The next morning after she cleaned house she lit a cigarette ceremoniously and sat down to look at them. Now everything was just the way it had always looked in her mind. I'm a lucky girl, she thought solemnly. When the cigarette was burned down she put it out and her mind went on to the next thing to do. But it was all finished, there was nothing else to do. She opened the door of the kitchenette and looked at the neat rows of dishes and then she went into the bedroom and patted the crocheted bedspread, and after a while she put on her hat and coat and went to visit her mother. "Listen, Mama," she said, "I want you to tell me how to make honey cake."

She learned to make all the things her mother had always made, the cakes and the puddings and the twist-bread. She got so she made them as well as her mother. Lou had to laugh. "And to think when I married you I didn't even know you could cook. Honest to God," he would say, "I didn't even care. Honest to God."

But even though she baked nearly every day there were still whole hours when she didn't know what to do with herself. You couldn't take the bed apart and make it over again; you couldn't polish the furniture more than a couple of times a week. Before she was married she had always imagined herself in a spotless house dress taking care of a couple of kids, arranging flowers, surprising Lou with good things to eat, *busy*; not finished at half-past twelve and nothing to do till five. Six months after they were married Lou's wages had been cut; they had enough to get along on, but nothing to put aside for a baby. It didn't matter very much, she was willing to wait another year or two; having kids was only part of marriage. But a baby would have filled her day, at least while it was little. Well, it's nice I have so much time to myself, she thought, and she went and got her crochet needle from her mother's, but she really had enough doilies and the bedspread would last a lifetime.

She knew something was wrong and yet she didn't. Because how could anything be wrong when she was married, with her own house, and a good kind husband? Lou was a wonderful man.

But the funny thing was that although she knew he was wonderful and she loved him, sometimes she was cross with him, sometimes she hurt his feelings. Every so often, in the evening, he would put down his paper and come to sit on the couch and put his arm around her, and after a while she would move a little as if she were uncomfortable, and he would get up and go back to the armchair and put up his paper so she couldn't see his face.

She thought it must be gaining so much weight that made her unhappy; with her own cooking and being in the house all day she had put on nearly fifteen pounds. So she went on a diet. "I like you the way you are," said Lou, "but if it makes you happy, go ahead—starve. Just so you don't make yourself sick."

She took off the fifteen pounds in a few months. Her face was a little thin, but otherwise she looked swell; she stood and turned around in front of the glass every day, holding up the hand mirror to see herself from the back.

While she was reducing it kept her busy just finding ways not to go off her diet, but when she got thin she started to feel awfully restless. She got so she wanted to go out every evening or have some friends in. "Now you have a new figure so you have to go out and show off," said Lou, but he was glad she liked the way she looked. Only most evenings he was tired, and they couldn't afford the movies more than a couple of times a week. Of course she didn't make a fuss about it, like some girls she knew. But she began going out during the day, taking walks, visiting her married friends, window shopping.

One day she went out at half-past two. It was a nice day, clear and fresh, and she took the subway downtown. When she came up the stairs she discovered she had gotten out at the old station without thinking, so she dropped in at the office.

It felt pretty good, walking in like that at three in the afternoon. They all made a fuss over her, the boss even came out to shake hands. There was something homey about it, the way it smelled, and the noise of the typewriters, and Dora and she laughed together because there was still the same hole in the linoleum just inside the door. "I miss you like anything," said Dora. "Why don't you come back?"

"No, sir!" said Millie. "Not on your life. I'm a woman of leisure, now. Besides, I've got my house to take care of."

"The other girl is leaving the end of the month," said Dora. "Her folks are going out West. Gee, it'd be fun to have you back."

"Thanks, kid," said Millie, "but when I left, I left for good. . . . Why don't you come up for dinner sometime, Dora? I'm a good cook." Then she saw Dora's fingers resting on her typewriter keys and she put on her gloves to go, thinking how nice it was to be able to leave at half-past three and do whatever she wanted. But when she got outside she found it was turning cold, and she buttoned up her coat and got back into the subway.

That night she told Lou about her visit to the office, and how Dora wanted her to come back.

"Yeah?" said Lou. With her eyes on her cigarette she knew he was watching her. "What did you say?"

She inhaled the smoke fiercely. "I said no. What else should I say? Why should I have to grab a cup of coffee and run out every morning? And sit over a machine all day. I told her I'm finished punching a time clock. What do I want to work for, so

long as we don't need the money? I said, I'm finished with all
that, I have the house and all. Why should I go back?"

"Sure," said Lou. "That's right. Sure. . . ."

He looked at her one morning at breakfast and said, "My,
you're smoking a lot, Millie."

"Yeah, I guess so," she said. She got up to take the dishes
into the kitchenette.

He brought in the coffee cups. "Why don't you try and cut
down a little?" he asked. "I think maybe it's making you nervous."

"Yeah, I guess so," she said, and after a while he went inside
and put on his hat and coat.

"Well, so long," he called from the door.

"So long." She laid the dripping dishes on the drainboard and
picked up a towel. One of the plates still had egg stain on it, but
instead of washing it over she scraped off the egg with her
fingernail and dried it. She knew Lou was unhappy when she
acted that way, he would be worried all day at the shop, but
there wasn't anything she could do about it. It was just the way
she felt.

She finished the dishes and then it just seemed as though she
had to get out of the house right away, and she put on her hat
and coat over her house dress and went out to market. It was a
gray day and windy, and the damp got inside the coat and inside
her skin, right to the middle of her. Her hands were terribly
cold and she knew they would get chapped, but she didn't take
the trouble to put on her gloves.

She went to the grocer and to the vegetable man and then to
the butcher. She gave her order to the old man who usually
waited on her, an old man with a smooth pink face like a baby's
and a gray felt hat, and then she looked around. In all the
months she had been trading there she had never seen the store
so empty; she was surprised until she realized that it wasn't
nine o'clock yet. The butcher was even eating his breakfast; he
was drinking coffee from a white enameled tin, and there was
a big piece of coffee cake lying on some wax paper on the
butcher's table.

When he saw her looking at him he gave her a smile. "Have

some, Mrs. Berk?" he asked. He was a foreigner of some kind, and he had a long head with black kinky hair just beginning to get gray.

She was surprised and then she saw it was only a joke, so she smiled. "I had mine already."

"Ah, you see?" said the butcher to the girl at the cashier's desk. "I knew I could get Mrs. Berk to smile."

Kind of fresh, she thought to herself, but she didn't really mind. "Why, you saw me smile before!" she said.

Another woman came into the store. "No, you always look so serious," kidded the butcher, and then he nodded to the other woman. "Morning, Mrs. Halloran, you want some nice broilers?"

She took her veal chops and paid the girl; there was a retort in her mind, Sure I'm serious, look at what you charge me, but he was talking to the other woman. She pulled her coat around her and went out.

For several days after that she did her shopping at the usual time, and the old man waited on her. Then she woke up one morning feeling good. She kidded with Lou across the breakfast table and flew into her work with more energy than she had had for weeks. Outside the sun was shining and the wash hanging between the buildings flapped briskly in the wind. She suddenly thought that she would open all the windows and give the place a good airing while she did her marketing.

So when she got to the butcher's it was early again and again he offered her some coffee. "I take mine black," she said, making a little face at the light coffee in the enameled pail.

"What's the matter?" he asked. "Scared to get fat?"

She tossed her head, a little. "What do you think?"

"Say," he said. "You don't have to worry!" He turned to the old man. "Does she?"

She dropped her eyes to the steaks laid out in a neat row in the showcase. She was afraid she was blushing. "I'll take one of those," she said. "Give me a nice one."

"Why, sure, Mrs. Berk," he said. "I'm going to pick you the very best," and the way his fingers hovered over the steaks it was like a boy buying a valentine. "There, how's that?" he said, pulling out a piece of sirloin and holding it up proudly by the tail.

"It looks good enough to take a bite out of," said the old man.

"Who?" said the butcher. "Mrs. Berk?"

Everyone smiled but she couldn't, although she knew she ought to. "I thought you meant Mrs. Berk looked good enough to take a bite out of," said the butcher, looking at her over his shoulder.

The old man leaned across the counter. "This is no place for a minister's son," he said, smiling slyly.

"What's the matter with this place?" said the butcher, loud. "Mrs. Berk likes it all right, don't you, Mrs. Berk?" He caught her eye and winked.

"Why—why sure," she said. And then she picked up her package and the check and paid for it and went out quickly, not meeting his eyes as she turned.

That afternoon she decided that her hair needed washing, and she gave it a lemon rinse and spent a long time setting it. Lou noticed how nice she looked when he came in at the door. And later, when they were eating dinner, he said so again. "You look so nice. And you seem . . . you seem so high."

"High? Well," she said, realizing it, "I feel kind of good today."

"You look good," he said. "You look all lit up. I bet something nice happened today to make you look like that."

"Something nice?" she said. "No, nothing happened. You ready for some more meat?"

It was when she was cutting the steak that it occurred to her. She sat looking at the blood running out under her knife and letting the thought hit her. "I only went to the butcher's," she said, as if she were talking to herself.

"He gave you a nice piece of meat," said Lou, but she didn't hear him. She was thinking, I only went to the butcher's.

But it shouldn't matter, she thought, it shouldn't make any difference what a butcher says to me, how could it change the way I feel? And she looked around at the couch, the rug, the lamp, the curtains, Lou. "Lou," she said, leaning toward him, desperately almost, "Lou, maybe I ought to get out of the house. Don't you think so? Get a job, something—" And she knew she was saying that because she couldn't say, Lou, what's the matter with my marriage? She couldn't say that to him.

"What do you mean?" he whispered. "I thought you—" There was a puzzled look on his face. He didn't understand.

She didn't either. That was the awful part.

I Stand Here Ironing

By Tillie Olsen

Born in Omaha, Nebraska, Tillie Olsen (1913–) was the daughter of Russian Jewish immigrants. Her father was the State Secretary of the Nebraska Socialist party during her childhood. Though she read avidly and wrote for the high school paper, she did not finish high school. By the time she was seventeen, she was in jail for labor organizing in Kansas City. For the next twenty years of her life, she worked at an enormous variety of jobs: in slaughterhouses, laundries, factories, warehouses, restaurants, and offices. Since 1933, she has lived in California, where, in addition to working for pay and in movements for social change, she married Jack Olsen and with him reared four daughters.

In the early thirties, as a young writer then named Tillie Lerner, Olsen published several poems, stories, and essays in Partisan Review. *The necessity to work for pay forced her to set writing aside for two decades. In the midfifties, she began again, first by taking a creative writing course at San Francisco State University, then by writing her first new story, the one we print here, "I Stand Here Ironing." Since the late fifties, Olsen has published a volume of four stories,* Tell Me a Riddle *(1961); half of a novella still to be completed,* Requa I *(1971; and included in* The Best Short Stories of 1971); *an edition of Rebecca Harding Davis's* Life in the Iron Mills *(1972); and a novel reclaimed from her youth,* Yonnandio *(1974). A collection of her critical prose appeared in 1978, and she has been at work for some time on the second half of* Requa *and on a major novel.*

Olsen has received a number of honors and awards, including the O. Henry Award for the best American short story in 1961 and a Guggenheim Fellowship. She has taught at Amherst College, the University of Massachusetts/Boston, and the Massachusetts Institute of Technology.

The subjects and themes of Olsen's fiction—family life, poverty, working-class life—are all present in "I Stand Here Ironing," a story as fresh today as it was when written nearly twenty-five years ago. The working-class mother, now twice the age of her nineteen-year-old daughter, recalls the early years of that first child's life—in the thirites. "Dredging the past," the mother's authentic voice records, in simple language chosen with the care of a poet, the work of mother-hood—its joys and failures, its guilt, and most of all its awesome responsibility for "all that compounds a human being."

I stand here ironing, and what you asked me moves tormented back and forth with the iron.

"I wish you would manage the time to come in and talk with me about your daughter. I'm sure you can help me understand her. She's a youngster who needs help and whom I'm deeply interested in helping."

"Who needs help." Even if I came, what good would it do? You think because I am her mother I have a key, or that in some way you could use me as a key? She has lived for nineteen years. There is all that life that has happened outside of me, beyond me.

And when is there time to remember, to sift, to weigh, to estimate, to total? I will start and there will be an interruption and I will have to gather it all together again. Or I will become engulfed with all I did or did not do, with what should have been and what cannot be helped.

She was a beautiful baby. The first and only one of our five that was beautiful at birth. You do not guess how new and uneasy her tenancy in her now-loveliness. You did not know

(text continued on page 168)

Portraits
of the Authors

Carmen Tafolla: 1978

Rosellen Brown: 1976

Wilma Shore: 1977

Sheila Ballantyne: 1977

Ellen Bryant Voigt: 1976

Patricia Cumming: 1976

August Strindberg: circa 1900

Tillie Olsen: 1977

Alice Lee Marriott: 1960

her all those years she was thought homely, or see her poring over her baby pictures, making me tell her over and over how beautiful she had been—and would be, I would tell her—and was now, to the seeing eye. But the seeing eyes were few or non-existent. Including mine.

I nursed her. They feel that's important nowadays. I nursed all the children, but with her, with all the fierce rigidity of first motherhood, I did like the books then said. Though her cries battered me to trembling and my breasts ached with swollenness, I waited till the clock decreed.

Why do I put that first? I do not even know if it matters, or if it explains anything.

She was a beautiful baby. She blew shining bubbles of sound. She loved motion, loved light, loved colour and music and textures. She would lie on the floor in her blue overalls patting the surface so hard in ecstasy her hands and feet would blur. She was a miracle to me, but when she was eight months old I had to leave her daytimes with the woman downstairs to whom she was no miracle at all, for I worked or looked for work and for Emily's father, who "could no longer endure" (he wrote in his good-bye note) "sharing want with us."

I was nineteen. It was the pre-relief, pre-WPA world of the depression. I would start running as soon as I got off the streetcar, running up the stairs, the place smelling sour, and awake or asleep to startle awake, when she saw me she would break into a clogged weeping that could not be comforted, a weeping I can yet hear.

After a while I found a job hashing at night so I could be with her days, and it was better. But it came to where I had to bring her to his family and leave her.

It took a long time to raise the money for her fare back. Then she got chicken pox and I had to wait longer. When she finally came, I hardly knew her, walking quick and nervous like her father, looking like her father, thin, and dressed in a shoddy red that yellowed her skin and glared at the pock marks. All the baby loveliness gone.

She was two. Old enough for nursery school they said, and I did not know then what I know now—the fatigue of the long day, and the lacerations of group life in nurseries that are only parking places for children.

Except that it would have made no difference if I had known. It was the only place there was. It was the only way we could be together, the only way I could hold a job.

And even without knowing, I knew. I knew the teacher that was evil because all these years it has curdled into my memory, the little boy hunched in the corner, her rasp, "why aren't you outside, because Alvin hits you? that's no reason, go out, scaredy." I knew Emily hated it even if she did not clutch and implore "don't go Mommy" like the other children, mornings.

She always had a reason why we should stay home. Momma, you look sick, Momma. I feel sick. Momma, the teachers aren't there today, they're sick. Momma, we can't go, there was a fire there last night. Momma, it's a holiday today, no school, they told me.

But never a direct protest, never rebellion. I think of our others in their three-, four-year-oldness—the explosions, the tempers, the denunciations, the demands—and I feel suddenly ill. I put the iron down. What in me demanded that goodness in her? And what was the cost, the cost to her of such goodness?

The old man living in the back once said in his gentle way: "You should smile at Emily more when you look at her." What *was* in my face when I looked at her? I loved her. There were all the acts of love.

It was only with the others I remembered what he said, and it was the face of joy, and not of care or tightness or worry I turned to them—too late for Emily. She does not smile easily, let alone almost always as her brothers and sisters do. Her face is closed and sombre, but when she wants, how fluid. You must have seen it in her pantomimes, you spoke of her rare gift for comedy on the stage that rouses a laughter out of the audience so dear they applaud and applaud and do not want to let her go.

Where does it come from, that comedy? There was none of it in her when she came back to me that second time, after I had had to send her away again. She had a new daddy now to learn to love, and I think perhaps it was a better time. Except when we left her alone nights, telling ourselves she was old enough.

"Can't you go some other time, Mommy, like tomorrow?" she would ask. "Will it be just a little while you'll be gone? Do you promise?"

The time we came back, the front door open, the clock on the floor in the hall. She rigid awake. "It wasn't just a little while. I didn't cry. Three times I called you, just three times, and then I ran downstairs to open the door so you could come faster. The clock talked loud. I threw it away, it scared me what it talked."

She said the clock talked loud again that night I went to the hospital to have Susan. She was delirious with the fever that comes before red measles, but she was fully conscious all the week I was gone and the week after we were home when she could not come near the new baby or me.

She did not get well. She stayed skeleton thin, not wanting to eat, and night after night she had nightmares. She would call for me, and I would rouse from exhaustion to sleepily call back: "You're all right, darling, go to sleep, it's just a dream," and if she still called, in a sterner voice, "now go to sleep, Emily, there's nothing to hurt you." Twice, only twice, when I had to get up for Susan anyhow, I went in to sit with her.

Now when it is too late (as if she would let me hold and comfort her like I do the others) I get up and go to her at once at her moan or restless stirring. "Are you awake, Emily? Can I get you something, dear?" And the answer is always the same: "No, I'm all right, go back to sleep, Mother."

They persuaded me at the clinic to send her away to a convalescent home in the country where "she can have the kind of food and care you can't manage for her, and you'll be free to concentrate on the new baby." They still send children to that place. I see pictures on the society page of sleek young women planning affairs to raise money for it, or dancing at the affairs, or decorating Easter eggs or filling Christmas stockings for the children.

They never have a picture of the children so I do not know if the girls still wear those gigantic red bows and the ravaged looks on the every other Sunday when parents can come to visit "unless otherwise notified"—as we were notified the first six weeks.

Oh it is a handsome place, green lawns and tall trees and fluted flower beds. High up on the balconies of each cottage the children stand, the girls in their red bows and white dresses, the boys in white suits and giant red ties. The parents stand below shrieking up to be heard and the children shriek down to be heard, and between them the invisible wall "Not To Be Contaminated by Parental Germs or Physical Affection."

There was a tiny girl who always stood hand in hand with Emily. Her parents never came. One visit she was gone. "They moved her to Rose Cottage," Emily shouted in explanation. "They don't like you to love anybody here."

She wrote once a wcck, the laboured writing of a seven-year-old. "I am fine. How is the baby. If I write my leter nicly I will have a star. Love." There never was a star. We wrote every other day, letters she could never hold or keep but only hear read—once. "We simply do not have room for children to keep any personal possessions," they patiently explained when we pieced one Sunday's shrieking together to plead how much it would mean to Emily, who loved so to keep things, to be allowed to keep her letters and cards.

Each visit she looked frailer. "She isn't eating," they told us.

(They had runny eggs for breakfast or mush with lumps, Emily said later, I'd hold it in my mouth and not swallow. Nothing ever tasted good, just when they had chicken.)

It took us eight months to get her released home, and only the fact that she gained back so little of her seven lost pounds convinced the social worker.

I used to try to hold and love her after she came back, but her body would stay stiff, and after a while she'd push away. She ate little. Food sickened her, and I think much of life too. Oh she had physical lightness and brightness, twinkling by on skates, bouncing like a ball up and down up and down over the jump rope, skimming over the hill; but these were momentary.

She fretted about her appearance, thin and dark and foreign-looking at a time when every little girl was supposed to look or thought she should look a chubby blonde replica of Shirley

Temple. The door-bell sometimes rang for her, but no one seemed to come and play in the house or be a best friend. Maybe because we moved so much.

There was a boy she loved painfully through two school semesters. Months later she told me how she had taken pennies from my purse to buy him candy. "Liquorice was his favourite and I brought him some every day, but he still liked Jennifer better'n me. Why, Mommy?" The kind of question for which there is no answer.

School was a worry to her. She was not glib or quick in a world where glibness and quickness were easily confused with ability to learn. To her overworked and exasperated teachers she was an overconscientious "slow learner" who kept trying to catch up and was absent entirely too often.

I let her be absent, though sometimes the illness was imaginary. How different from my now-strictness about attendance with the others. I wasn't working. We had a new baby, I was home anyhow. Sometimes, after Susan grew old enough, I would keep her home from school, too, to have them all together.

Mostly Emily had asthma, and her breathing, harsh and laboured, would fill the house with a curiously tranquil sound. I would bring the two old dresser mirrors and her boxes of collections to her bed. She would select beads and single ear-rings, bottle tops and shells, dried flowers and pebbles, old postcards and scraps, all sorts of oddments; then she and Susan would play Kingdom, setting up landscapes and furniture, peopling them with action.

Those were the only times of peaceful companionship between her and Susan. I have edged away from it, that poisonous feeling between them, that terrible balancing of hurts and needs I had to do between the two, and did so badly, those earlier years.

Oh there are conflicts between the others too, each one human, needing, demanding, hurting, taking—but only between Emily and Susan, no Emily toward Susan that corroding resentment. It seems so obvious on the surface, yet it is not obvious. Susan, the second child, Susan, golden- and curly-haired and chubby, quick and articulate and assured, everything in appearance and manner Emily was not; Susan, not able to resist Emily's precious things, losing or sometimes clumsily breaking them; Susan telling jokes and riddles to company for applause while Emily sat silent (to say to me later: that was *my* riddle, Mother, I told it to Susan); Susan, who for all the five years' difference in age was just a year behind Emily in developing physically.

I am glad for that slow physical development that widened the difference between her and her contemporaries, though she suffered over it. She was too vulnerable for that terrible world of youthful competition, of preening and parading, of constant measuring of yourself against every other, of envy, "If I had that copper hair," or "If I had that skin. . . ." She tormented herself enough about not looking like the others, there was enough of the unsureness, the having to be conscious of words before you speak, the constant caring—what are they thinking of me? What kind of an impression am I making?—there was enough without having it all magnified by the merciless physical drives.

Ronnie is calling. He is wet and I change him. It is rare there is such a cry now. That time of motherhood is almost behind me when the ear is not one's own but must always be racked and listening for the child cry, the child call. We sit for a while and I hold him, looking out over the city spread in charcoal with its soft aisles of light. *"Shoogily,"* he breathes and curls closer. I carry him back to bed, asleep. *Shoogily.* A funny word, a family word, inherited from Emily, invented by her to say: *comfort.*

In this and other ways she leaves her seal, I say aloud. And startle at my saying it. What do I mean? What did I start to gather together, to try and make coherent? I was at the terrible, growing years. War years. I do not remember them well. I was working, there were four smaller ones now, there was not time for her. She had to help be a mother, and housekeeper, and shopper. She had to set her seal. Mornings of crisis and near hysteria trying to get lunches packed, hair combed, coats and shoes found, everyone to school or Child Care on time, the baby ready for transportation. And always the paper scribbled on by a smaller one, the book looked at by Susan then mislaid, the homework not done. Running out to that huge school where she was one, she was lost, she was a drop; suffering over the unpreparedness, stammering and unsure in her classes.

There was so little time left at night after the kids were bedded down. She would struggle over books, always eating (it was in those years she developed her enormous appetite that is legendary in our family) and I would be ironing, or preparing food for the next day, or writing V-mail to Bill, or tending the baby. Sometimes, to make me laugh, or out of her despair, she would imitate happenings or types at school.

I think I said once: "Why don't you do something like this in the school amateur show?" One morning she phoned me at work, hardly understandable through the weeping: "Mother, I did it. I won, I won; they gave me first prize; they clapped and clapped and wouldn't let me go."

Now suddenly she was Somebody, and as imprisoned in her difference as she had been in anonymity.

She began to be asked to perform at other high schools, even in colleges, then at city and state-wide affairs. The first one we went to, I only recognized her that first moment when thin, shy, she almost drowned herself into the curtains. Then: Was this Emily? The control, the command, the convulsing and deadly clowning, the spell, then the roaring, stamping audience, unwilling to let this rare and precious laughter out of their lives.

Afterwards: You ought to do something about her with a gift like that—but without money or knowing how, what does one do? We have left it all to her, and the gift has as often eddied inside, clogged and clotted, as been used and growing.

She is coming. She runs up the stairs two at a time with her light graceful step, and I know she is happy tonight. Whatever it was that occasioned your call did not happen today.

"Aren't you ever going to finish the ironing, Mother? Whistler painted his mother in a rocker. I'd have to paint mine standing over an ironing-board." This is one of her communicative nights and she tells me everything and nothing as she fixes herself a plate of food out of the icebox.

She is so lovely. Why did you want me to come in at all? Why were you concerned? She will find her way.

She starts up the stairs to bed. "Don't get me up with the rest in the morning." "But I thought you were having mid-terms." "Oh, those," she comes back in, kisses me, and says quite lightly, "in a couple of years when we'll all be atom-dead they won't matter a bit."

She has said it before. She *believes* it. But because I have been dredging the past, and all that compounds a human being is so heavy and meaningful in me, I cannot endure it tonight.

I will never total it all. I will never come in to say: She was a child seldom smiled at. Her father left me before she was a year old. I had to work her first six years when there was work, or I sent her home and to his relatives. There were years she had care she hated. She was dark and thin and foreign-looking in a world where the prestige went to blondness and curly hair and dimples, she was slow where glibness was prized. She was a child of anxious, not proud, love. We were poor and could not afford for her the soil of easy growth. I was a young mother, I was a distracted mother. There were the other children push-ing up, demanding. Her younger sister seemed all that she was not. There were years she did not want me to touch her. She kept too much in herself, her life was such she had to keep too much in herself. My wisdom came too late. She has much to her and probably nothing will come of it. She is a child of her age, of depression, of war, of fear.

Let her be. So all that is in her will not bloom—but in how many does it? There is still enough left to live by. Only help her to know—help make it so there is cause for her to know that she is more than this dress on the ironing-board, helpless before the iron.

They Call Me Mummy

By Sheila Ballantyne

Sheila Ballantyne (1936–) was born and raised in Seattle, Washington. She graduated from Mills College in 1958 and has worked as a researcher, medical secretary, switchboard operator, and book reviewer for The New York Times Book Review. *Her novel,* Norma Jean the Termite Queen, *was published in 1975 by Doubleday & Company. Her short stories have appeared in* Aphra, Ms., American Review, The New Yorker, Prize Stories of 1977: The O. Henry Awards, *and* Short Story International. *She now lives in Berkeley, California, with her husband and two children.* "They Call Me Mummy" *was first published in* Aphra *in 1972.*

Monday: This morning's paper carries the news that there have been two more mystery killings during the night. That brings the total of mystery killings in our area to five since April. Someone's really getting a lot of use out of his little .38. I light a cigarette and my attention wanders out the window where the wind is shaking an old apple tree. I see myself running through orchards. The details are unclear, but I do know they are far away.

"I have to make a pee pee, Mummy. Mummy! My pee pee is coming out!" screams Johnny.

Into the bathroom we go, to sit again on haunches. Eternal Mother, waiting for the pee pee to begin. But wait. There in the bowl floats a little pair of pants—fetid, dead, languishing in a sea of golden excrement. "Wait a minute, dear. Mummy has to take care of your poopie."

"I can't wait. My pee pee is coming OUT!" he wails. Slosh, slosh. Up and down, around and around. Loving hands at home, as the decorators are fond of saying. "There now, up you go, make your pee pee, that's a good boy."

Ah, child, hurry and eat your peanut butter sandwich. Mummy has important business to attend to. Come on, eat it up, and take your nap. While you sleep I must get a letter off to Dow Chemical. They left that little sample of Touch of Sweden hand lotion in the mailbox this morning. Touch of Sweden. What tempting images the little tube evoked: Green, cool, icily smooth. Smelled the way one would imagine Sweden to smell too. Subtle. Fir-tree green. How nice of Dow to know it was just what I needed for my raw chapped loving hands.

Dow Chemical Company
Midland, Michigan 48640

Dear Dow Chemical:

It was very thoughtful of you to send me the little tube of Touch of Sweden lotion for my hands. It arrived this morning, just in time for my 10 A.M. shake-out. You know, someone in your ad department is very clever to have thought of that Sweden approach; and the design is good too. We mothers are always a touch for a product that suggests far-away places and cool glacial calm. Not just a treat for our hands, you might say, but a little vicarious vacation for our minds.

"Use generously on hands, elbows, face, knees, anywhere your skin is dry and needs nourishment.
NOURISHES
A special skin nourishing formula, Touch of Sweden is a blend of rich emollients and skin moisturizers."

Then I noticed the words "Dow Chemical Company" at the bottom of the tube. It pains me to tell you this, but that spoiled my day. "Dow Chemical" does something to me. It brings on little mind pictures of delicate yellow children, far away, trying to hold their blistering skin on. You might tell your ad man that if he really knew his word-association business, he would have sent the lotion out anonymously. Because I couldn't stop thinking of the napalm you make for those other mothers far away. I thought how peculiar it was: here you are sending out little tubes of smooth silky Touch of Sweden to *us* mothers, and great big tubes of smooth jelly-like napalm to *those* mothers. My mind really went kind of wild. It's true we mothers are understimulated, and most anything is likely to set off a little mental static. But I couldn't read your description of what *I* was supposed to do with your lotion (use generously on my hands, elbows, face, knees, anywhere) without getting these little pictures of what *they* were supposed to do with the napalm you send them (generously burning their hands, elbows, faces, knees, anywhere . . .).

Now the suggestion I have is this: It would be so nice of you if you would take my little tube of Touch of Sweden, which I herewith return to you, and send it instead to a Vietnamese mother. She really needs it much more than I do. (I notice also on the tube it specifically says ". . . to prevent skin discomforts." You people have sort of a thing for skin, don't you?) Well, you get the point: she must be feeling a lot more skin discomfort than I am.

If I'm not being too presumptuous, you could even recall *all* the little samples of Touch of Sweden which you have for us American mothers, and send them to the Vietnamese mothers *instead* of the napalm. It would cost you less to send Touch of Sweden lotion to

Vietnam than it does to send napalm. Once all those mothers see how good it feels on their skin they will want more of it. It is so soothing, you create an instant market for it. As I'm sure you have noticed, there is a limited market for napalm, since you can't burn up the same skin twice.

Sincerely yours,
Mrs. J.P. Jones, Occupant
23 Pleasant Way
Berkeley, Calif.

It is 2:30. The door slams, shaking the house. Sally is back from school. Here is a brown paper bag, full of the things she has made. A collage, made of gum wrappers; a bas-relief, very nice, of sea shells and beer tabs. And an 8 by 10 charcoal, on yellow butcher paper, entitled "Mouse With Diarrhea." Pinned to her dress is the school lunch menu for the following month. Like any good mother, I light up a cigarette and take the time to sit down and read it, to see that she's getting the proper nourishment. The menu reads like the Palace Hotel. Someone in the public school system has been paid a salary to come up with a list of adjectives with which to describe the monthly lunch menu for Kindergarten through 3rd Grade. For a moment I consider that they might have hired an advertising agency to do it, but dismiss this thought as unduly paranoid. Still, it seems inconceivable that they couldn't just say, for instance: Monday: French fries; Tuesday: carrots. Well, see for yourself:

Oven French fries;	*Whipped* potatoes;
Tossed green salad;	*Sunshine* salad;
Rosy applesauce;	*Chilled* peaches;
Buttered green beans;	*Delicious* peas;
Hot buttered French bread;	*Butterfly* ravioli;
Crusty fish sticks;	*Confetti* salad;
Crisp celery sticks;	and *Fluffy* rice.

Well, that's nice. What difference does it make if they try to make institutional food sound more glamorous than it really is? I am just about to let it go at that when my eyes fall on the lunch for the last Friday of the month: "Vegetables *Delicieux*" and "Fruit *Medley*." I start to fall apart; well I don't know what you would call it, but I am experiencing mild convulsions and the children are staring at me. At first I pass it off as laughter, but gradually become aware that I am feeling outraged to think that someone really thinks she can pass off plain rotten over-cooked vegetables on me as something other than plain rotten overcooked vegetables by affixing the term *"Delicieux"* after them. And, although I know on some level that it is highly illogical and unreasonable of me, I do see myself going for the throat of whomever it was who could conceive of the term "Fruit Medley."

"Now you and John go play upstairs. Mummy has to pick up the downstairs." I have decided against a tranquilizer. I will work things off cleaning house. Where do all those toys come from? This house eats essentials such as bottle openers and pens, regurgitates nonessentials such as Deely Bobbers and Tinker Toys.

Tuesday: Only Tuesday, and already I feel consumed by nursery-school schedules, car pools, and play-group activities. Leaning against my dark brown G.E. side-by-side refrigerator-freezer, I stare at the scraps of peanut butter crusts turning slimy in the sun. It is only 3 o'clock. It is too early for the vodka. Or is it? By whose schedule must I wait the extra two hours that would make it civilized, acceptable, commonplace? By whose sacred proclamation must I wait for the magic cocktail time to begin, when all the other mothers on the block reach for the potion that dulls the memory of their days?

I am an individual, I think. I am, I am. I will have my vodka at 3 o'clock. I reach. I pour. It sparkles there, among the crusts. As it slides down my throat, I am my own person, engaging in ritual by choice. My son sleeps on no-iron crib sheets. There is a mess in his pants. I will clean it up when he awakens. I will put it to soak in the toilet. I will shake it up and down in the toilet this evening, and my husband will complain that all the toilets in the house have diapers in them.

Wednesday: Just as I am drawing in my first mouthful of coffee I see in the paper that a man was shot in the head by a sniper while driving on the freeway. "His wife and baby riding beside him were unhurt. He remains in critical condition with a .38 caliber bullet in his head." Now how does one interpret these things to one's children? Margaret Mead says I have to. It's my role as a mother, to interpret reality to my children. God knows, I try.

Dear, you see, the reason you can't *swim* in this water is because it's polluted.

What's polluted?

It means the water is full of beer cans, garbage, dixie cups, B.M.'s, and toxic chemicals.

Can we play in the sand?

Yes, but keep your shoes on and watch for broken glass and twist-off tabs.

Mr. Harold Burnside, President
Consolidated Can Company
111 Market Street
San Francisco, Calif.

Dear Mr. Burnside:

I am in receipt of your response to my letter of October 5, in which I chided you for telling the ecology demonstrators in your office that it was no concern of yours what people did with your cans, once they had sucked the beer out.

Thank you very much for the little pamphlet about your support of the Boy Scouts of America, and the little colored children at the Y, and all you are doing for them. Thanks also for your plastic Beautify America bag, which you suggest I put in my car, for immediate use whenever I chance to see one of your beer cans on the highway. I notice you've got your company name stenciled on it; that's a clever promotional stunt.

Yours truly,
Mrs. J.P. Jones
23 Pleasant Way
Berkeley, Calif.

Thursday: AMPUTEE SLAIN IN STREET SHOOTING. It's going to be that kind of a day. Well, maybe not. Here's an article about the mackerel that have been called back in L.A. due to their high level of mercury. The president of the fish-packing firm wants the government to raise its acceptable levels of mercury so he won't go broke. It's going to be that kind of a day.

"The effects of mercury poisoning include listlessness, headache, nausea, stiffness of the joints, and in its extreme form it is capable of causing brain damage," the official was quoted as saying.

I begin to wonder about the fish we had for dinner last night. Was it stream or ocean? It makes a difference. The home economist at Co-op says so. Fresh water, or stream, fish are the most suspect, while ocean fish are less so: the deeper into the ocean they are, the less suspect. Or so they think at this time. I find myself having profound thoughts about red snappers. They sound fierce—like ocean fish. I decide we are safe, at least for the time being, but later discover myself surreptitiously watching the children for signs of subtle brain damage.

There is a terrible noise upstairs. The terrible noise continues, only it is coming downstairs. It is John, I think, in a panic. (My mind slowly begins to move in the direction of the noise, to focus on the noise.) It *is* John and he is falling down the stairs. I move from the kitchen to the stairs in a terrible silence. As I reach the stairs, John is screaming. John's head is covered with blood. This is serious, I think. This isn't like the time he almost bit off his tongue. Or even the time he broke his foot jumping off Sally's dresser ("Sally *said* we could fly"). No, this is a mess. And the mess is slowly seeping into the Persian rug. There is a hole in his head, I see as I sponge it off. Yes, a definite hole, in the middle of his forehead. And the car is in the garage today, having its muffler fixed.

I phone the doctor, who says bring him in right away. "In" is on the other side of town. John is writhing on my lap and won't keep the ice cube on his hole. He throws it across the kitchen. I phone Yellow, but they say it will be fifteen or twenty minutes. That means a half-hour. I phone the hippie cab, and they say "Wow. We're splitting right now; stay cool." We go and sit on the curb, trying to stay cool. The blood just won't stop. I rummage around in my purse to see if I have any extra Kleenex, and discover I have locked myself out of the house. I also notice I have no shoes on. Then they're here, rounding the corner on two wheels. The cab has a dragon painted on one side and Power To The People on the other. The driver is very stoned. And very concerned. It only takes him seven minutes to get the door closed. He takes the long way, but turns the meter off and goes through all the stop signs. I am so grateful I write out a check for the Peoples' Park Defense Fund, and drop it in the little basket they have hanging on the back seat for that purpose, bloody thumb prints and all.

Back home, stitched and looking like a miniature, lobotomized Frankenstein, John is banging on the table for some lunch. "What kind of yogurt do you want, John?"

"What kind do we have?"

"We have Strawberry, Blueberry, Boysenberry, Mandarin Orange, Spiced Apple, Red Raspberry, Cherry, and Pineapple." There is a pause. I know just what it portends.

"I'll have Daffodil yogurt."

Control yourself. In fifteen minutes, twenty at the most, he will be in bed napping.

"There is no such thing as Daffodil yogurt. How about some nice Blueberry instead?"

"I want Daffodil! I want it right now!"

Dear Golden Rich Dairy:

I am writing you on behalf of my son, John. Your failure to include Daffodil among the flavors currently in your repertoire of yogurts seems a gross oversight.

In this competitive world it is essential to keep abreast of the rapidly changing tastes of your young consumers.

Friday: I am sitting here in the parking lot, waiting for the bank to open. The cars are all nosed in at the bank, sucking. You have to see it to believe it: this big mother bank, nursing all these little cars. Detroit steel feeding off Wall Street concrete.

I feel, sitting here, as though I've finally become that species,

Berkeley Mother, that I always looked upon with mixed awe and amusement in the past. Here we sit, the kids fighting in the back seat, and me up front, watching the local obsessive maneuvering his car into the slot next to ours, waiting for the bank to open. I wear an eight-year-old car coat and a Boycott Grapes button and a Defend the Park button. If I also wore Free Huey, Save the Bay, Legalize Abortion, and Make Love Not War buttons, I'd look ridiculous. You have to make choices when you live in Berkeley.

After the bank we go to the Co-op to get the week's groceries. It's been bothering me lately that I always come out of the Co-op crying. I would like to blame it on the Co-op, but whispers in my head say it's me. After all, they point out, how many other mothers do you see coming out the door crying? I've tried to convince them that the others are merely skilled in holding back their tears. See that one there, for instance. See how she's biting her lip? Holding back tears, I say. And that one over there, whose child just dropped the jar of mayonnaise from the basket—there, where the bagger is working away at all that mayonnaise and glass on the floor. Now to the casual observer she seems unruffled; but I know she is pretending to look for her checkbook in her purse. Deep inside, she is weighing whether to buy another jar of mayonnaise; whether to do without mayonnaise this week; and whether to hit the kid in the parking lot, or in the privacy of her car after the groceries are paid for. And holding back tears.

Furthermore, anyone can see that the checkers are not doing the job they are paid for. It's true they are pleasant. But they spend all their time flirting with the baggers and chewing gum. I have been standing in this line twenty minutes, waiting to get through the check stand. And my frozen foods are melting. I have heard that they can't be re-frozen, but I will do it anyway. You go crazy if you believe everything you hear. No, my voices say, you're all washed up. Do you know anyone else who spends half an hour each week trying to find organic peanut butter? Not just unhydrogenated peanut butter, but peanut butter made from organically grown peanuts. Do you know anyone else who cares that DDT has a special affinity for peanuts? No, I have to tell them, I do not. Maybe you're right. Now that I think about it, everyone else I know thinks only of the convenience of peanut butter, and the fact that it is high in protein.

Leaving Co-op is always a draw: from time to time I let my voices convince me that I'm the only one in this special category—Co-op Criers—but I know what I know, and if there's one thing I pride myself on being able to detect in others, it's held-back tears.

Back home, I hurry the children through lunch. My mind wanders back, through spilled organic apple juice and acres of dead sandwiches, to my breakthrough of five months ago, after the Cambodian invasion, when I hired a sitter and spent three days taking petitions around town. I felt futile, but not hopeless, because the headlines still aroused anger in me. I spent half the night before drawing up the petitions, just as the senator on TV suggested. "You can do something tonight, my fellow Americans" is what he said. That fired me up again.

The petitions themselves had something about them which said, "I will end the war; all you do is sign." You had to believe that in order to drag them around, but you knew they lied, were impotent, that the war would eventually wear itself out, but not because of anything you did. Still, it is necessary from time to time, just to keep from losing one's sanity, to keep alive the illusion that individual commitment matters and that grassroots democracy is effective.

"Come on, Sally, *finish* that stuff; it's nap time."

"I won't finish this until you promise to get me a Suzy Homemaker Popcorn Popper."

"Suzy what?"

"You know! On television. Everyone has one, and I don't, and you're hurting my feelings and making me very sad."

"Now Sally, you *know* I won't get you a Suzy Homemaker Popcorn Popper—we have a pan, and we make our own popcorn that way. We don't *need* another one."

"Yes we *do!* We *do!* Oh, I can't stand it. I knew this would happen. Why can't I have one? Why? Tell me why!" She's crying now; the tears are coming and soon—there is no question,

absolutely none—there will be full-blown hysteria, any minute, right here in my Betty Crocker kitchen.

"I told you why. I will tell you again: Mummy thinks those
toys are dangerous. They are also unnecessary. And the people
on television who tell you to tell your mom to get them are
evil, stupid people. You can't have it because you can't have
everything you want. Just like the time you wanted the Barbie
Doll. Remember?"

". . . You're a terrible mummy. You won't let me have anything. Everyone has a Barbie Doll. Why can't I have a Barbie
Doll and a Suzy Homemaker Popcorn Popper? You're not a
kind lady. I hate you."

I take her hands in mine. My little flower, my angel. Her face
is full of storms, unforgiving. It sets out to annihilate me. Just
in time, I remember I am bigger than she is.

"You can't have it because Mummy thinks it's icky."

Dear President Nixon:

I've been meaning to write you about my experiences of five
months ago, when I walked the streets, rang doorbells, and canvassed
supermarkets and laundromats to enlist the signatures of your fellow
Americans on a petition to end the war. I see that the war is still on
however, and I thought I should get a letter off to you right away, to
light a fire under you, so to speak, just in case you had forgotten
about it.

It is tempting to think of them as "my" people, because I saw them,
handed them the pen, and talked with them. Some of them were
tough, and pressed down hard; their wish to end the war was a powerful one and it showed, along with their frustration, in this small direct
action. Some were wistful, fragile, their hands moved like feathers
over the paper. They weren't sure that a thing as small as their signature was enough to stop a bomb. Others were so alienated they merely
said "why not," and scribbled their names listlessly before moving on.

Let me tell you about Mrs. Harris. She had just come out of her
room in the Shattuck Hotel to take the air. She was in her seventies
and not too strong. She lingered over the petition, drawing out the
contact between us. Her face was covered with rouge; she had dressed
carefully for her walk around the block. She signed slowly, and smiled
at the others who had gathered around us to sign, like an actress at the

stage door after a successful performance. I was the first person who
had spoken to her, although it was three in the afternoon. She handed
it back reluctantly, and moved down the street. It is a fair guess that
Mrs. Harris was a member of your Silent Majority, until that day.

In Oakland there was a man in a green business suit and very short
hair. I approached him because I had decided at the beginning that I
would not prejudge anyone on the basis of his appearance. I asked him
if he would like to sign a petition against the war. "Yes, I would," he
said. He was very collected, and signed it as he would have a bank
statement. He asked me if I represented some organization. I told him
no, that I was an individual, and was sending these petitions to my
senator. He said he thought there should be more people like me, and
I said there were; they were all over town with their own petitions.

And Travis and Obie. You should get to know them. They's black.
They's in high school. They's going to be called to fight this war, any
day now. They say, yeah, they sign. Nothin else to do on a hot day, and
they don't hold much respect for this war anyhow. Travis, he start to
sign, but Obie, he smart, he cynic. He say "Travis, just put down
'mother' ain't goin' to do no good anyhow." But Travis, he believe, he
not been asked for his signature before. He know he too young to
vote, but old enough to die for his country. He go ahead, he do the one
small thing that might save his life some day soon: he put down
"Travis." Obie, he get the idea, he think maybe it can't hurt, he put
down "Obie" for all to see, in thick black ink. Can you doubt that his
blue-eyed congressman will be grateful?

Now I want you to listen to Mr. Smith. He's black, too, but old.
He's pushing a huge vacuum around the Co-op, getting the floors oh,
so clean. He wears Big Mack overalls, and I think you could say he's
not too political. But he says, "Yeah, I'll sign! I'm right sick of this
war, no question about that. You want me to sign twice? I'll sign as
many times as I can." What could I tell him, but that once would be
enough. One voice, one vote; we wouldn't want the senator from
California to think Berkeley was cheating again.

I will admit, the retired colonel on my block thinks you're a peachy
prez. He turned his hose on me. And there was a woman on the street
who thought I should go to Hanoi if I didn't like the way you were
running things. But there were 250 others who wanted you to know
they are tired of the war.

Now my purpose for writing you at this time is that I notice that
not only is the war still on, but that you are thinking of escalating it
again. When I was a little girl my mother would always tell me that
whenever something seemed impossible, all one had to do was write
to the President; and according to her he always came through. Why
just the other day I read in the paper about that poor little boy in
Nebraska, who had some incurable disease and wasn't expected to be

around at Christmas, and his mother wrote to you about it, and sure enough, you sent him a great big Christmas card, even though it was July.

Now it doesn't seem too unreasonable to think that if you could make one little boy so happy, you could make thousands more just as happy, and their mothers too, if you would just get together with those men in the Pentagon and find a way to end the war. I know that if you will think about it, and maybe even consult your religious advisor, you will agree.

Sincerely yours,
Mrs. J.P. Jones
23 Pleasant Way
Berkeley, Calif.

I put a stamp on the letter, and place it by the door. I will take the children for a walk and they will fight over who gets to put it in the mailbox. Johnny is up from his nap, and has taken an old piece of bread with peanut butter on it, and dropped it on the floor, smearing it over a two-foot-square area.

"Come and see my mess, quickly," he says.

As I clean it up, he gets the garden shovel and starts to turn the earth over, right where I planted my English poppy seeds last week. I throw the shovel into the hedge, and call for Sally to come and get her sweater on, we're going for a walk, and the one who gets his sweater on first can mail Mummy's letter. She is watching "Sesame Street," however, and insists we wait until it is over. I insist we mail the letter now because it will be dark when "Sesame Street" is over; and since the old man was beaten up on our block last month, I haven't felt too keen about walking around after dark. Of course I feel I can't give her the real reason, so she says I am unfair and do not understand her.

I decide that Nixon has made it so far without hearing from me; he can wait another day. I mix myself a drink and sit down on the big chair to watch "Sesame Street" with my children. One of the cartoon figures (I think it's Ernie) is singing "Gone With the Wind." (Not a bad voice, either, for a puppet.) The song is so poignant and simple, the way things seemed in the forties. They will grow up feasting on acid rock. I sit, sipping vodka, letting myself be carried back to adolescent dreams,

Gone with the wind,
My romance has gone away . . .

wondering whether to cry now or wait until they are in bed. But with each sip it seems a little less disturbing to wonder what their future will be like. I begin to feel a sensation of timelessness; it settles in there next to some vague thoughts about historical migrations and impermanence. I have survived, and each generation before me survived. My children will adapt. The last thought sets up a little malfunctioning in my mental circuitry, however. I begin receiving the words "future shock" over and over.

But Ernie sings on, and the drink is moving through my veins now. How peaceful the house is, how still we three, sitting here at day's end (my golden creatures and I): a tableau of domestic tranquility, frozen in TV light, waiting for Daddy, and being moved by a clown singing "Gone With the Wind." They're exquisite children, I am thinking, they really are. But every time they call me Mummy, I get these funny little pictures of ancient Egyptian sarcophagi. I do admit I feel all tied up and unable to move at times.

An Attempt at Reform

By August Strindberg

August Strindberg (1848–1912) was born in Stockholm, Sweden. The son of a former waitress and servant mother and a grocer father, his early life was beset by poverty. He managed, however, to study at Uppsala University and to earn his living as a journalist before his first novel,
The Red Room *(1879), established him as a writer at the age*

of 30. For the next fifteen years, he traveled restlessly through
Europe, joining bohemian circles in Berlin, Paris, and
London. At various times in his life, he embraced socialism,
pietism, naturalism, and mysticism.

Strindberg is best known as a dramatist, and in the
United States, his most frequently performed plays are
"Miss Julie" (1888), "The Dance of Death" (1900), and
"A Dream Play" (1901). He also wrote numerous short stories,
poems, and essays, and his collected works fill fifty-five
volumes. Strindberg's work often both exalts women and
debases them, and in several plays, his antagonist is an
emancipated woman who victimizes a man by her masculine
strength. "An Attempt at Reform" is from Married, *a*
volume of stories about relationships between men and
women, published in the United States in 1913.

S he had noticed with indignation that girls were solely
brought up to be housekeepers for their future husbands.
Therefore she had learnt a trade which would enable her to
keep herself in all circumstances of life. She made artificial
flowers.

He had noticed with regret that girls simply waited for a
husband who should keep them; he resolved to marry a free
and independent woman who could earn her own living; such a
woman would be his equal and a companion for life, not a
housekeeper.

Fate ordained that they should meet. He was an artist and
she made, as I already mentioned, flowers; they were both living in Paris at the time when they conceived these ideas.

There was style in their marriage. They took three rooms at
Passy. In the centre was the studio, to the right of it his room,
to the left hers. This did away with the common bed-room and
double bed, that abomination which has no counterpart in
nature and is responsible for a great deal of dissipation and
immorality. It moreover did away with the inconvenience of
having to dress and undress in the same room. It was far better
that each of them should have a separate room and that the
studio should be a neutral, common meeting-place.

They required no servant; they were going to do the cooking themselves and employ an old charwoman in the mornings and evenings. It was all very well thought out and excellent in theory.

"But supposing you had children?" asked the sceptics.

"Nonsense, there won't be any!"

It worked splendidly. He went to the market in the morning and did the catering. Then he made the coffee. She made the beds and put the rooms in order. And then they sat down and worked.

When they were tired of working they gossiped, gave one another good advice, laughed and were very jolly.

At twelve o'clock he lit the kitchen fire and she prepared the vegetables. He cooked the beef while she ran across the street to the grocer's; then she laid the table and he dished up the dinner.

Of course, they loved one another as husbands and wives do. They said good-night to each other and went into their own rooms, but there was no lock to keep him out when he knocked at her door; but the accommodation was small and the morning found them in their own quarters. Then he knocked at the wall:

"Good morning, little girlie, how are you to-day?"

"Very well, darling, and you?"

Their meeting at breakfast was always like a new experience which never grew stale.

They often went out together in the evening and frequently met their countrymen. She had no objection to the smell of tobacco, and was never in the way. Everybody said that it was an ideal marriage; no one had ever known a happier couple.

But the young wife's parents, who lived a long way off, were always writing and asking all sorts of indelicate questions; they were longing to have a grandchild. Louisa ought to remember that the institution of marriage existed for the benefit of the children, not the parents. Louisa held that this view was an old-fashioned one. Mama asked her whether she did not think that the result of the new ideas would be the complete extirpation of mankind? Louisa had never looked at it in that light, and moreover the question did not interest her. Both she and her husband were happy; at last the spectacle of a happy married couple was presented to the world, and the world was envious.

Life was very pleasant. Neither of them was master and they shared expenses. Now he earned more, now she did, but in the end their contributions to the common fund amounted to the same figure.

Then she had a birthday! She was awakened in the morning by the entrance of the charwoman with a bunch of flowers and a letter painted all over with flowers, and containing the following words:

"To the lady flower-bud from her dauber, who wishes her many happy returns of the day and begs her to honour him with her company at an excellent little breakfast—at once."

She knocked at his door—come in!

And they breakfasted, sitting on the bed—his bed; and the charwoman was kept the whole day to do all the work. It was a lovely birthday!

Their happiness never palled. It lasted two years. All the prophets had prophesied falsely.

It was a model marriage!

But when two years had passed, the young wife fell ill. She put it down to some poison contained in the wall-paper; he suggested germs of some sort. Yes, certainly, germs. But something was wrong. Something was not as it should be. She must have caught cold. Then she grew stout. Was she suffering from tumour? Yes, they were afraid she was.

She consulted a doctor—and came home crying. It was indeed a growth, but one which would one day see daylight, grow into a flower and bear fruit.

The husband did anything but cry. He found style in it, and then the wretch went to his club and boasted about it to his friends. But the wife still wept. What would her position be now? She would soon not be able to earn money with her work and then she would have to live on him. And they would have to have a servant! Ugh! those servants!

All their care, their caution, their wariness had been wrecked on the rock of the inevitable.

But the mother-in-law wrote enthusiastic letters and repeated over and over again that marriage was instituted by God
for the protection of the children; the parents' pleasure counted
for very little.

Hugo implored her to forget the fact that she would not be
able to earn anything in future. Didn't she do her full share of
the work by mothering the baby? Wasn't that as good as
money? Money was, rightly understood, nothing but work.
Therefore she paid her share in full.

It took her a long time to get over the fact that he had to
keep her. But when the baby came, she forgot all about it. She
remained his wife and companion as before in addition to being
the mother of his child, and he found that this was worth more
than anything else.

The Famous Writers School
Opens Its Arms in the
Next Best Thing to Welcome

By Rosellen Brown

*Rosellen Brown (1939–) has been writing since she was nine.
Her first published poem, written in a Barnard College English
class, appeared in the* New York Times. *In 1965, she
and her husband, Marvin Hoffman, went to Mississippi to
work in the civil rights movement; she as a teacher at
Tougaloo College, he with a Headstart Program. Although
she had a B.A. from Barnard College and an M.A. from
Brandeis University, she says that she learned most about
writing from her experience in Mississippi and from teaching
elsewhere—in Brooklyn's ghettos and in rural towns. In
order to write down the stories of people "who don't write
themselves," she listens and records the "human voices*

of common people" around her. As a member of the Teachers
and Writers Collaborative, an organization aimed at
bringing poets into schools, she has taught children in
New York City as well as in Vermont and New Hampshire.
She lives in Peterborough, New Hampshire, with her
husband and two daughters.

   Brown's poems and reviews have appeared in Ms., The
New Republic, The Nation, Parnassus, *and elsewhere.*
She has published two volumes of poems, Some Deaths in
the Delta *(1970) and* Cora Fry *(1977); a volume of stories,*
Street Games; *and a novel,* The Autobiography of My
Mother. *"The Famous Writers School Opens Its Arms in the*
Next Best Thing to Welcome" is from her first volume
of poems.

(for A.B.)

Good writing, the book tells you,
begins at home.
If it's anything like charity.
Hope for the best, try to relax,
and ignore the spelling.

You are obedient. You write about your kitchen.
"Everything I hate.
It is the place where all the accidents happen."
You are standing at the stove
shaking the saucepan
the way you'd shake a child,
to hurry along the coffee-water.
Oh it is green in here,
the green that punishes public walls,
never the color of leaves or moss
spreading, soft, on the shady side.
The pennies in the linoleum cracks
you're leaving there for luck.
The walls, the floors, the chairs have their flesh scrubbed off,

flayed no-color. All of it shatter-lines,
but holding.

"I think I have something to say,"
you say, separating some of your children,
always tangled up like hair.
Once a year you can expect to disappear
so far down your own throat and belly
a doctor with a miner's lamp
comes looking, calling out names,
some of them yours.
He tells you
you mustn't want to be destroyed
ever again,
admires your youth, your height, your hair,
whatever catches his nearest eye.
But you are the place
where all the accidents happen.
You have a cache of reasons
he isn't going to see.

This morning, though,
with a branch of sunlight
moving against the kitchen window,
words are—cheap? free?
No. Possible.
In the air.
They blow around
in the wind of your dreams.
"I was dreaming about the word 'surprise'
with a 'z' in it.
Nothing else happened, there was only this word
coming out of my typewriter.
A tickertapeworm, surprizesurprize."
You laugh, slouch a little,
and wait for something surprising to begin.

To saddle the word "surprize"
and ride out the kitchen window forever

over the limp roofs of Brownsville,
across the stone badlands,
Red Hook, Gowanus,
right through the twin castles,
empty purple castles of the Brooklyn Bridge.
Or out to sea past the softening
Staten Island meadows,
dotted with old trees and genuine, pale lakes.

You pour the water
into the Maxwell House,
and turn to the paragraph you've made
with your own limber hands.
You are turning soil,
looking for the place to plant fresh syllables.
The only garden on your block.

FOUR:
Transforming Work
Moment of Assertion

IN THIS FINAL SECTION are stories and poems that might have been placed in earlier sections. What distinguishes the literature included here is the effort of the central characters—women alone or in groups—to do work that is either more difficult or different in form or substance from what they or others

have done before. A quiltmaker attempts a supremely complex design. Factory workers participate in slowdowns. A housewife organizes a peace walk. A climbing team attempts a difficult mountain peak. Such efforts often transform the lives of workers dramatically. In some instances, the actions are also part of a conscious or unconscious effort to transform the conditions under which people work.

In Edward Field's poem, "Notes from a Slave Ship," the effort to transform work takes the form of a "moment of assertion": typing a poem on company time when "the boss's eyes are on you." Although this deliberate rebellion appears as an attempt to modify working conditions, it is also personally

transforming, "the moment when you say I exist." Varieties of
rebellion also occur in "The Triangle Fire," the excerpt from
Sholem Asch's early twentieth-century novel. When the sweat-
shop owner stands over the women at their sewing machines,
they work so fast they "make the foot pedals fly." But as soon
as he steps away, the workers, acting in unison, slow down the
speeded pace set for them. In this excerpt also, Asch recreates
the Triangle shirtwaist fire of 1911 in which 146 workers died.
Although these victims had no chance to change their own
working conditions, unknowingly, they helped transform factory work. Fifty years later, in 1961, the International Ladies
Garment Workers Union installed a plaque at the site of the
fire:

On this site, 146 workers lost their lives in the Triangle Shirtwaist
Company fire on March 25, 1911. Out of their martyrdom came new
concepts of social responsibility and labor legislation that have helped
make American working conditions the finest in the world.

A different kind of change takes place in Dorothy Canfield
Fisher's "The Bedquilt." Sixty-eight-year-old Aunt Mehetabel
carries the idea of an extraordinary design in her head through
months of her customary domestic drudgery. "For a long
time," the author tells us, "she did not once think of putting an
actual quilt together following that pattern, even though she
herself had invented it." From Aunt Mehetabel's perspective,
it takes great strength and daring to begin the first square.
Creating the square transforms her drab and narrow existence.
Once palpable, her artistry gains her the respect and admiration from the household in which she has been little more than
a servant. Her work as an artist changes the conditions under
which she continues to perform the necessary household tasks.
"Now," for the first time in Aunt Mehetabel's long life, "things
had a meaning."

Still different work and unusual circumstances are portrayed in Meridel Le Sueur's "I Was Marching." A middle-class
woman's consciousness is transformed through her involve-
ment in a larger movement to change working conditions.

Accustomed to the pleasures of individual recognition, to the habit of competition, she finds herself an uncomfortable observer at the headquarters of a large, city-wide strike in Minneapolis in 1934. Soon she joins other women preparing coffee and serving meals as an anonymous part of a cooperative effort. Later, out of doors with thousands, building a barricade, attending a rally, then marching, she feels the "strange, powerful trance of movement together." Though working anonymously, without individual recognition, at first felt "strange" to her, at the end she says, "I feel good."

Like Meridel Le Sueur's heroine, Lila Horton in Sue Davidson's "The Peace Walk" also feels good at the end of that story —and energized by the work she has done. Lila's ability to assert herself, to transform her beliefs into organizing work although she has little support from others, transforms her view of herself.

Even when workers have the will and capacity to assert themselves, change is difficult and slow—as the stories and poems in this section indicate. Lila's story illuminates how difficult it is to organize social action. Aunt Mehetabel works five years on her quilt: she is seventy-three when it wins first prize. While the Triangle Fire of 1911 was followed by decades of strikes and other tactics to improve conditions in factories and mines, on railroads, in mills and shipyards, American workers still lose their lives because of hazardous working conditions.

If change is difficult and slow, it is also not customarily associated with women's actions. Partly, we have forgotten women's history in such efforts as the movement for the abolition of slavery, for women's suffrage, for improved working conditions. Partly, we do not have available enough literature that portrays rebellious women. Also, women's "moments of assertion" may take unexpected forms: quiltmaking or writing a poem on company time. Several characters in earlier sections of this volume mourn decisions not to rebel. By contrast, the women in this final section have "battered down doors," as Alice Walker says in "Women." They survive the consequences of rebellion and affirm their will to change.

Notes from a Slave Ship

By Edward Field

*Born in Brooklyn, New York, Edward Field (1924–) went to
college, dropped out, then joined the army. When he got
out, he never expected to support himself by writing. After
stints as a machinist and warehouseman, he found typing
"wonderful work—wonderful people you met—and you
could work irregularly." For ten years, Field earned his living
as a temporary typist in New York City. "Notes from a
Slave Ship" appears in his first book of poems,* Stand Up
Friend with Me *(1963), published during his typing decade.*

Field's poems have been published in such magazines as
Prairie Schooner, Poetry, The New Yorker, Evergreen Review,
and Floating Bear. *Besides* Stand Up Friend with Me, *his
books include* Variety Photo Plays *(1967),* Eskimo Songs and
Stories *(1974),* A Full Heart *(1977), and a novel,* The
Potency Clinic, *written with a friend under the pseudonym
Bruce Elliot.*

It is necessary to wait until the boss's eyes are on you
Then simply put your work aside,
Slip a fresh piece of paper in the typewriter,
And start to write a poem.

Let their eyes boggle at your impudence;
The time for a poem is the moment of assertion,
The moment when you say I exist—
Nobody can buy my time absolutely.

Nobody can buy me even if I say, Yes I sell.
There I am sailing down the river,
Quite happy about the view of the passing towns,
When I find that I have jumped overboard.

There is always a long swim to freedom.
The worst of it is the terrible exhaustion
Alone in the water in the darkness,
The shore a fading memory and the direction lost.

Girl Held Without Bail

By Margaret Walker

*See page 49 for biographical information on Margaret Walker.
This poem comes from Walker's second volume of poems,
Prophets for a New Day, published in 1970. The opening
quotation is from Henry David Thoreau, who went to jail
to protest the condition of slavery.*

*"In an unjust state the only place
for a just man is in jail."*

I like it here just fine
And I don't want no bail
My sister's here
My mother's here
And all my girl friends too.
I want my rights
I'm fighting for my rights
I want to be treated
Just like *anybody* else
I want to be treated
Just like *everybody* else

*I like it fine in Jail
And I don't want no Bail.*

Women

By Alice Walker

*Born in Eatonton, Georgia, like her "mama's generation,"
Alice Walker (1944–) first worked in her family's corn and
cotton fields. Summers during her high school and college
years, she says, "You worked where you could get work—as
a waitress, as a secretary-typist." Alice Walker attended*

Spelman College and graduated from Sarah Lawrence College.
During two summers in the sixties, she returned to the South
as a civil rights worker in Georgia and Mississippi. She
has also worked in the New York City Department of Welfare.
In the past decade, she has published two novels, The Third
Life of Grange Copeland *(1970) and* Meridian *(1976); two*
volumes of poems, Once *(1969) and* Revolutionary Petunias
and Other Poems *(1973); and a volume called* In Love and
Trouble: Stories of Black Women *(1973). She has collected*
and edited an anthology of Zora Neale Hurston's work to be
published by The Feminist Press. As a contributing editor of
Ms., *Walker's writing appears there frequently. Her work has*
also been published in The Best Short Stories by Negro
Writers, Harpers Magazine, Black World, Freedomways, *and*
elsewhere. She earns her living by writing and, on occasion,
teaches, lectures, or reads her work on college campuses.
In 1977, she was awarded a Guggenheim Fellowship. She
lives in Brooklyn, New York, with her daughter Rebecca.

As a novelist, poet, and theorist of black feminism, Alice
Walker often writes about the strong black southern women
among whom she was raised. "Women," a celebration of
earlier generations, comes from her second volume of poems.

They were women then
 My mama's generation
Husky of voice—Stout of
Step
With fists as well as
Hands
How they battered down
Doors
And ironed
Starched white
Shirts
How they led
Armies
Headragged Generals
Across mined
Fields

Booby-trapped
Ditches
To discover books
Desks
A place for us
How they knew what we
Must know
Without knowing a page
Of it
Themselves.

The Bedquilt

By Dorothy Canfield Fisher

Dorothy Canfield (1879–1958) was born in Lawrence, Kansas, and grew up there and in Nebraska. Her mother was a painter and sculptor and her father, a university administrator and librarian. Dorothy Canfield earned a B.A. at Ohio State University, and then, in 1904, a Ph.D. in Old French at Columbia University. She spent more than a year abroad with her mother, living in Paris, studying at the Sorbonne, and visiting museums in other parts of Europe. After her marriage to John Fisher, they moved to Arlington, Vermont in 1907—her home for the rest of her life and the scene of much of her writing.

Dorothy Canfield Fisher's work included rearing two children, running a home for sick children in France during World War I, and organizing a Braille printing shop in Paris during the same period. She was one of the five original editorial board members of the Book-of-the-Month Club and served in that capacity for twenty-five years. She was the first woman elected to Vermont's state board of education. After a visit to Italy, where she became acquainted with Montessori education, she wrote A Montessori Manual for Teachers and Parents *(1913; 1964);* Mothers and Children *(1914); and* A Montessori Mother *(1916). In and around all this work, she wrote ten novels, nine volumes of short*

stories, seven children's books, seven other volumes of
prose, and two volumes of translation. Her novels include
The Squirrel Cage (*1912*), The Bent Twig (*1915*), The Brimming
Cup (*1921*), *and* The Deepening Stream (*1930*); *her stories,*
Hillsboro People (*1915*), Fables for Parents (*1937*), *and*
Four-Square (*1949*). *Her first book, published in 1904, was*
Corneille and Racine in England. *She wrote the introduction*
to the first American edition of Isak Dinesen's Seven Gothic
Tales (*1934*).

Though Dorothy Canfield Fisher has received some
recognition as a champion of books and libraries, and as an
educational reformer, she has not yet been noticed as a
significant woman writer. Her stories are not usually
anthologized, and her other works are all but unknown. As
in "The Bedquilt," she writes often about the work of
women, including mothering and art, and often also about
the very old and the very young. "The Bedquilt" appeared
in her first volume of stories, Hillsboro People.

O f all the Elwell family Aunt Mehetabel was certainly the
most unimportant member. It was in the old-time New
England days, when an unmarried woman was an old maid at
twenty, at forty was everyone's servant, and at sixty had gone
through so much discipline that she could need no more in the
next world. Aunt Mehetabel was sixty-eight.

She had never for a moment known the pleasure of being
important to anyone. Not that she was useless in her brother's
family; she was expected, as a matter of course, to take upon
herself the most tedious and uninteresting part of the household labors. On Mondays she accepted as her share the washing
of the men's shirts, heavy with sweat and stiff with dirt from
the fields and from their own hardworking bodies. Tuesdays
she never dreamed of being allowed to iron anything pretty or
even interesting, like the baby's white dresses or the fancy
aprons of her young lady nieces. She stood all day pressing out
a monotonous succession of dish cloths and towels and sheets.

In preserving-time she was allowed to have none of the
pleasant responsibility of deciding when the fruit had cooked
long enough, nor did she share in the little excitement of pour-

ing the sweet-smelling stuff into stone jars. She sat in a corner
with the children and stoned cherries incessantly, or hulled
strawberries until her fingers were dyed red.

The Elwells were not consciously unkind to their aunt, they
were even in a vague way fond of her; but she was so insignifi-
cant a figure in their lives that she was almost invisible to
them. Aunt Mehetabel did not resent this treatment; she took
it quite as unconsciously as they gave it. It was to be expected
when one was an old maid dependent in a busy family. She
gathered what crumbs of comfort she could from their occasional careless kindnesses and tried to hide the hurt which
even yet pierced her at her brother's rough joking. In the winter
when they all sat before the big hearth, roasted apples, drank
mulled cider, and teased the girls about their beaux and the
boys about their sweethearts, she shrank into a dusky corner
with her knitting, happy if the evening passed without her
brother saying, with a crude sarcasm, "Ask your Aunt Mehetabel about the beaux that used to come a-sparkin' her!" or,
"Mehetabel, how was't when you was in love with Abel Cum-
mings?" As a matter of fact, she had been the same at twenty
as at sixty, a mouselike little creature, too shy for anyone to
notice, or to raise her eyes for a moment and wish for a life of
her own.

Her sister-in-law, a big hearty housewife, who ruled indoors
with as autocratic a sway as did her husband on the farm, was
rather kind in an absent, offhand way to the shrunken little old
woman, and it was through her that Mehetabel was able to
enjoy the one pleasure of her life. Even as a girl she had been
clever with her needle in the way of patching bedquilts. More
than that she could never learn to do. The garments which she
made for herself were lamentable affairs, and she was humbly
grateful for any help in the bewildering business of putting
them together. But in patchwork she enjoyed a tepid importance. She could really do that as well as anyone else. During
years of devotion to this one art she had accumulated a con-
siderable store of quilting patterns. Sometimes the neighbors
would send over and ask "Miss Mehetabel" for the loan of her
sheaf-of-wheat design, or the double-star pattern. It was with
an agreeable flutter at being able to help someone that she

went to the dresser, in her bare little room under the eaves, and drew out from her crowded portfolio the pattern desired.

She never knew how her great idea came to her. Sometimes she thought she must have dreamed it, sometimes she even wondered reverently, in the phraseology of the weekly prayer-meeting, if it had not been "sent" to her. She never admitted to herself that she could have thought of it without other help. It was too great, too ambitious, too lofty a project for her humble mind to have conceived. Even when she finished drawing the design with her own fingers, she gazed at it incredulously, not daring to believe that it could indeed be her handiwork. At first it seemed to her only like a lovely but unreal dream. For a long time she did not once think of putting an actual quilt together following that pattern, even though she herself had invented it. It was not that she feared the prodigious effort that would be needed to get those tiny, oddly shaped pieces of bright-colored material sewed together with the perfection of fine workmanship needed. No, she thought zestfully and eagerly of such endless effort, her heart uplifted by her vision of the mosaic-beauty of the whole creation as she saw it, when she shut her eyes to dream of it—that complicated, splendidly difficult pattern—good enough for the angels in heaven to quilt.

But as she dreamed, her nimble old fingers reached out longingly to turn her dream into reality. She began to think adventurously of trying it out—it would perhaps not be too selfish to make one square—just one unit of her design to see how it would look. She dared do nothing in the household where she was a dependent, without asking permission. With a heart full of hope and fear thumping furiously against her old ribs, she approached the mistress of the house on churning-day, knowing with the innocent guile of a child that the country woman was apt to be in a good temper while working over the fragrant butter in the cool cellar.

Sophia listened absently to her sister-in-law's halting petition. "Why, yes, Mehetabel," she said, leaning far down into the huge churn for the last golden morsels—"why, yes, start another quilt if you want to. I've got a lot of pieces from the spring sewing that will work in real good." Mehetabel tried honestly to make her see that this would be no common quilt, but her limited vocabulary and her emotion stood between her and expression. At last Sophia said, with a kindly impatience: "Oh, there! Don't bother me. I never could keep track of your quiltin' patterns, anyhow. I don't care what pattern you go by."

Mehetabel rushed back up the steep attic stairs to her room, and in a joyful agitation began preparations for the work of her life. Her very first stitches showed her that it was even better than she hoped. By some heaven-sent inspiration she had invented a pattern beyond which no patchwork quilt could go.

She had but little time during the daylight hours filled with the incessant household drudgery. After dark she did not dare to sit up late at night lest she burn too much candle. It was weeks before the little square began to show the pattern. Then Mehetabel was in a fever to finish it. She was too conscientious to shirk even the smallest part of her share of the housework, but she rushed through it now so fast that she was panting as she climbed the stairs to her little room.

Every time she opened the door, no matter what weather hung outside the small window, she always saw the little room flooded with sunshine. She smiled to herself as she bent over the innumerable scraps of cotton cloth on her work table. Already—to her—they were arranged in orderly, complex, mosaic-beauty.

Finally she could wait no longer, and one evening ventured to bring her work down beside the fire where the family sat, hoping that good fortune would give her a place near the tallow candles on the mantelpiece. She had reached the last corner of that first square and her needle flew in and out, in and out, with nervous speed. To her relief no one noticed her. By bedtime she had only a few more stitches to add.

As she stood up with the others, the square fell from her trembling old hands and fluttered to the table. Sophia glanced at it carelessly. "Is that the new quilt you said you wanted to start?" she asked, yawning. "Looks like a real pretty pattern. Let's see it."

Up to that moment Mehetabel had labored in the purest spirit of selfless adoration of an ideal. The emotional shock given her by Sophia's cry of admiration as she held the work towards the candle to examine it, was as much astonishment as joy to Mehetabel.

"Land's sakes!" cried her sister-in-law. "Why, Mehetabel Elwell, where did you git that pattern?"

"I made it up," said Mehetabel. She spoke quietly but she was trembling.

"No!" exclaimed Sophia. "Did you! Why, I never see such a pattern in my life. Girls, come here and see what your Aunt Mehetabel is doing."

The three tall daughters turned back reluctantly from the stairs. "I never could seem to take much interest in patchwork quilts," said one. Already the old-time skill born of early pioneer privation and the craving for beauty, had gone out of style.

"No, nor I neither!" answered Sophia. "But a stone image would take an interest in this pattern. Honest, Mehetabel, did you really think of it yourself?" She held it up closer to her eyes and went on, "And how under the sun and stars did you ever git your courage up to start in a-making it? Land! Look at all those tiny squinchy little seams! Why, the wrong side ain't a thing *but* seams! Yet the good side's just like a picture, so smooth you'd think 'twas woven that way. Only nobody could."

The girls looked at it right side, wrong side, and echoed their mother's exclamations. Mr. Elwell himself came over to see what they were discussing. "Well, I declare!" he said, looking at his sister with eyes more approving than she could ever remember. "I don't know a thing about patchwork quilts, but to my eye that beats old Mis' Andrew's quilt that got the blue ribbon so many times at the County Fair."

As she lay that night in her narrow hard bed, too proud, too excited to sleep, Mehetabel's heart swelled and tears of joy ran down from her old eyes.

The next day her sister-in-law astonished her by taking the huge pan of potatoes out of her lap and setting one of the younger children to peeling them. "Don't you want to go on with that quiltin' pattern?" she said. "I'd kind o' like to see how you're goin' to make the grapevine design come out on the corner."

For the first time in her life the dependent old maid contradicted her powerful sister-in-law. Quickly and jealously she
said, "It's not a grapevine. It's a sort of curlicue I made up."

"Well, it's nice-looking anyhow," said Sophia pacifyingly.
"I never could have made it up."

By the end of the summer the family interest had risen so
high that Mehetabel was given for herself a little round table in
the sitting room, for *her*, where she could keep her pieces and
use odd minutes for her work. She almost wept over such kind-
ness and resolved firmly not to take advantage of it. She went
on faithfully with her monotonous housework, not neglecting
a corner. But the atmosphere of her world was changed. Now
things had a meaning. Through the longest task of washing
milk-pans, there rose a rainbow of promise. She took her place
by the little table and put the thimble on her knotted, hard
finger with the solemnity of a priestess performing a rite.

She was even able to bear with some degree of dignity the
honor of having the minister and the minister's wife comment
admiringly on her great project. The family felt quite proud of
Aunt Mehetabel as Minister Bowman had said it was work as
fine as any he had ever seen, "and he didn't know but finer!"
The remark was repeated verbatim to the neighbors in the following weeks when they dropped in and examined in a per-
verse Vermontish silence some astonishingly difficult tour de
force which Mehetabel had just finished.

The Elwells especially plumed themselves on the slow progress of the quilt. "Mehetabel has been to work on that corner
for six weeks, come Tuesday, and she ain't half done yet," they
explained to visitors. They fell out of the way of always expecting her to be the one to run on errands, even for the children.
"Don't bother your Aunt Mehetabel," Sophia would call.
"Can't you see she's got to a ticklish place on the quilt?" The
old woman sat straighter in her chair, held up her head. She
was a part of the world at last. She joined in the conversation
and her remarks were listened to. The children were even told
to mind her when she asked them to do some service for her,
although this she ventured to do but seldom.

One day some people from the next town, total strangers,
drove up to the Elwell house and asked if they could inspect

the wonderful quilt which they had heard about even down in their end of the valley. After that Mehetabel's quilt came little by little to be one of the local sights. No visitor to town, whether he knew the Elwells or not, went away without having been to look at it. To make her presentable to strangers, the Elwells saw to it that their aunt was better dressed than she had ever been before. One of the girls made her a pretty little cap to wear on her thin white hair.

A year went by and a quarter of the quilt was finished. A second year passed and half was done. The third year Mehetabel had pneumonia and lay ill for weeks and weeks, horrified by the idea that she might die before her work was completed. A fourth year and one could really see the grandeur of the whole design. In September of the fifth year, the entire family gathered around her to watch eagerly, as Mehetabel quilted the last stitches. The girls held it up by the four corners and they all looked at it in hushed silence.

Then Mr. Elwell cried as one speaking with authority, "By ginger! That's goin' to the County Fair!"

Mehetabel blushed a deep red. She had thought of this herself, but never would have spoken aloud of it.

"Yes indeed!" cried the family. One of the boys was dispatched to the house of a neighbor who was Chairman of the Fair Committee for their village. He came back beaming, "Of course he'll take it. Like's not it may git a prize, he says. But he's got to have it right off because all the things from our town are going tomorrow morning."

Even in her pride Mehetabel felt a pang as the bulky package was carried out of the house. As the days went on she felt lost. For years it had been her one thought. The little round stand had been heaped with a litter of bright-colored scraps. Now it was desolately bare. One of the neighbors who took the long journey to the Fair reported when he came back that the quilt was hung in a good place in a glass case in "Agricultural Hall." But that meant little to Mehetabel's ignorance of everything outside her brother's home. She drooped. The family noticed it. One day Sophia said kindly, "You feel sort o' lost without the quilt, don't you Mehetabel?"

"They took it away so quick!" she said wistfully. "I hadn't hardly had one good look at it myself."

The Fair was to last a fortnight. At the beginning of the second week Mr. Elwell asked his sister how early she could get up in the morning.

"I dunno. Why?" she asked.

"Well, Thomas Ralston has got to drive to West Oldton to see a lawyer. That's four miles beyond the Fair. He says if you can git up so's to leave here at four in the morning he'll drive you to the Fair, leave you there for the day, and bring you back again at night." Mehetabel's face turned very white. Her eyes filled with tears. It was as though someone had offered her a ride in a golden chariot up to the gates of heaven. "Why, you can't *mean* it!" she cried wildly. Her brother laughed. He could not meet her eyes. Even to his easy-going unimaginative indifference to his sister this was a revelation of the narrowness of her life in his home. "Oh, 'tain't so much—just to go to the Fair," he told her in some confusion, and then "Yes, sure I mean it. Go git your things ready, for it's tomorrow morning he wants to start."

A trembling, excited old woman stared all that night at the rafters. She who had never been more than six miles from home—it was to her like going into another world. She who had never seen anything more exciting than a church supper was to see the County Fair. She had never dreamed of doing it. She could not at all imagine what it would be like.

The next morning all the family rose early to see her off. Perhaps her brother had not been the only one to be shocked by her happiness. As she tried to eat her breakfast they called out conflicting advice to her about what to see. Her brother said not to miss inspecting the stock, her nieces said the fancy-work was the only thing worth looking at, Sophia told her to be sure to look at the display of preserves. Her nephews asked her to bring home an account of the trotting races.

The buggy drove up to the door, and she was helped in. The family ran to and fro with blankets, woolen tippet, a hot soapstone from the kitchen range. Her wraps were tucked about

her. They all stood together and waved goodby as she drove out
of the yard. She waved back, but she scarcely saw them. On her
return home that evening she was ashy pale, and so still that
her brother had to lift her out bodily. But her lips were set in a
blissful smile. They crowded around her with questions until
Sophia pushed them all aside. She told them Aunt Mehetabel
was too tired to speak until she had had her supper. The young
people held their tongues while she drank her tea, and absent-
mindedly ate a scrap of toast with an egg. Then the old woman
was helped into an easy chair before the fire. They gathered
around her, eager for news of the great world, and Sophia said,
"Now, come, Mehetabel, tell us all about it!"

Mehetabel drew a long breath. "It was just perfect!" she said.
"Finer even than I thought. They've got it hanging up in the
very middle of a sort o' closet made of glass, and one of the
lower corners is ripped and turned back so's to show the seams
on the wrong side."

"What?" asked Sophia, a little blankly.

"Why, the quilt!" said Mehetabel in surprise. "There are a
whole lot of other ones in that room, but not one that can hold
a candle to it, if I do say it who shouldn't. I heard lots of people
say the same thing. You ought to have heard what the women
said about that corner, Sophia. They said—well, I'd be ashamed
to *tell* you what they said. I declare if I wouldn't!"

Mr. Elwell asked, "What did you think of that big ox we've
heard so much about?"

"I didn't look at the stock," returned his sister indifferently.
She turned to one of her nieces. "That set of pieces you gave
me, Maria, from your red waist, come out just lovely! I heard
one woman say you could 'most smell the red roses."

"How did Jed Burgess' bay horse place in the mile trot?"
asked Thomas.

"I didn't see the races."

"How about the preserves?" asked Sophia.

"I didn't see the preserves," said Mehetabel calmly.

Seeing that they were gazing at her with astonished faces
she went on, to give them a reasonable explanation, "You see
I went right to the room where the quilt was, and then I didn't
want to leave it. It had been so long since I'd seen it. I had to

look at it first real good myself, and then I looked at the others to see if there was any that could come up to it. Then the people begun comin' in and I got so interested in hearin' what they had to say I couldn't think of goin' anywheres else. I ate my lunch right there too, and I'm glad as can be I did, too; for what do you think?"—she gazed about her with kindling eyes. "While I stood there with a sandwich in one hand, didn't the head of the hull concern come in and open the glass door and pin a big bow of blue ribbon right in the middle of the quilt with a label on it, 'First Prize.' "

There was a stir of proud congratulation. Then Sophia returned to questioning, "Didn't you go to see anything else?"

"Why, no," said Mehetabel. "Only the quilt. Why should I?"

She fell into a reverie. As if it hung again before her eyes she saw the glory that shone around the creation of her hand and brain. She longed to make her listeners share the golden vision with her. She struggled for words. She fumbled blindly for unknown superlatives. "I tell you it looked like—" she began, and paused.

Vague recollections of hymnbook phrases came into her mind. They were the only kind of poetic expression she knew. But they were dismissed as being sacrilegious to use for something in real life. Also as not being nearly striking enough.

Finally, "I tell you it looked real *good*," she assured them and sat staring into the fire, on her tired old face the supreme content of an artist who has realized his ideal.

The Triangle Fire

By Sholem Asch

Sholem Asch (1880–1957) was born in a Polish shtetl *(small town) to a poor Jewish family. Until he went to Warsaw to earn his living at age sixteen, his only education was in the village religious school. Within a year after his move, he had absorbed much of European culture and had pub-*

lished a collection of short stories in Hebrew. Almost all his
work, however, was written in Yiddish, a Hebrew-German
dialect spoken by Eastern European Jews the world over. It
was among Jews in Europe and America that Asch established
his reputation for realistically portraying conditions in
the impoverished shtetl and the urban ghetto.

Until the outbreak of the first World War, Asch and his
family lived in Switzerland; then he, his wife, and their
four children came to the United States and became American
citizens. From 1908 on, Asch wrote regularly for the
Forward, a New York Yiddish paper where several of his best-
loved novels—including Mottke the Thief (1917) and
Uncle Moses (1920)—first appeared in serial form. Many
of Asch's plays had long runs at the Yiddish Theatre in New
York. Asch, however, continued to live periodically
in Europe and spent months in the newly established Jewish
colonies of Palestine—the present Israel.

"The Triangle Fire" is a chapter from East River (1964),
a chronicle of immigrant Jewish and Catholic families who
live near each other on New York's Lower East Side
during the early part of this century. Mary, like many of her
neighbors in "The Triangle Fire," works in the garment
industry. Later in the book, Mary becomes a designer.

The shop where Mary found work was in a long, large cellar
in the neighborhood of 34th Street and Second Avenue. The
cellar opened on a large yard full of grain stores and warehouses
for merchandise, with a cheap restaurant for the truckmen who
worked in the vicinity. The cellar, formerly used as a laundry,
was under the restaurant, and the stench of decayed food and
greasy cooking permeated the cellar workroom. There was no
ventilation; only a single window, always closed, which faced
a blank wall, grimy with cobwebs. There was no daylight,
except for the light that came in through the open door to the
cellar together with the waves of heat of the summer and the
cold blasts of the winter. The cellar was illuminated by electric
bulbs which hung naked from the low ceiling, without cover-
ing of any kind. In the summer, when the heat scorched the
walls of the warehouses, the fetid smell of meat, cheese, fish,

and other foods kept in them would be borne into the workroom. Piles of garbage were strewn about the yard. Stray cats and bedraggled beggars dug into the garbage cans outside the restaurant kitchen and the warehouses.

Wagons laden with merchandise rattled in and out of the yard all day. The heavy creaking of truck wheels, the noise and shouts of the truckmen and porters poured in through the workroom door. Overhead, through the ceiling, came the noise of footsteps and the clatter of dishes from the restaurant above.

In this cellar Mendel Greenspan, the owner of the workroom, had placed a row of sewing machines purchased on time payments. The machines were so constructed that they could be operated by foot pedals or by electric power. For the present, until Greenspan had enough money to equip a real shop and get enough orders, they were operated by foot pedals.

Before the twelve machines, each of them set below a naked electric bulb hanging from the low ceiling, sat twelve girls—Irish, Jewish, Italian—of whom Mary was now one. In addition to the machines there were long tables at which sat seven or eight finishers, hand workers. These were all middle-aged Jews, with grizzled beards and orthodox ear curls. Two sad-faced youths stood at ironing boards, in the midst of clouds of vapor raised by the hot irons on damp cloth.

Greenspan was a man in his thirties, with a carefully trimmed beard, artfully cropped so as to avoid the impression that he was one of the modern "pagan" Jews addicted to the use of the razor; in the trim of his sidelocks there was even the slight suggestion of the ear curls. He wore a skullcap. He stood at the long table and from paper patterns cut piles of cheap printed fabrics to be made into dresses. His meek-eyed wife, about the same age as himself and wearing a smock, worked on a bundle of garments at the head of the row of sewing machines and kept an eye on the girls to see that they labored with proper diligence.

The Greenspans, with their two children and Mrs. Greenspan's mother, lived in the two rooms that shut off the front end of the factory, thus blocking off the only windows leading onto the street below the restaurant.

Greenspan and his wife hardly slept or ate. He worked at the bench himself, and even found jobs to do for his old mother-in-law, and his two children, for all their tender years. He was acquainted with some pious Jews who frequented the same synagogue on the East Side. He talked it into them that at his shop they would be able to gather for the afternoon prayers without interruption—and on his time, too; that they would be able to wear their cherished skullcaps, and even be able to chant from the sacred Psalms as they worked—something they certainly wouldn't be able to do in a union shop. In this way, he exploited their piety by working them long hours and paying them starvation wages. He hired young, inexperienced girls forced by the desperate poverty in their homes to help contribute to the family larder. He convinced the girls that the union shops wouldn't take them in, and that, to get into the union, they'd have to pay enormous initiation fees.

He worked side by side with them, his wife, too, at one of the machines, and speeded up their work by putting before them the example of his own industry. He got up at dawn to prepare the work for the hands, and he sat at the bench until late at night—he, his wife, and often his mother-in-law—to finish the work the hands hadn't completed during the long day. He begrudged himself a single minute's rest, hastily gulping food his mother-in-law would set beside him at the cutting table. It was as though he were saying to his employees: "How can you have the heart to take off to eat your lunch in peace when I, the boss, work until I'm ready to drop!"

When Mary came to the factory early on Monday morning, Greenspan welcomed her with a broad smile.

"You're a good girl," he said, "to help out your family. I know your mother; she worked for us. Homework. Come, sit down here. They'll show you how it goes."

He had his own system for breaking in green hands. He sat Mary between two experienced operators, old employees in the shop, who knew how to make the foot pedals fly. One of them sewed one edge of a dress and handed it over to Mary to complete the other side. The operations had to dovetail so that the dress could be handed over to the finishers to complete.

"You'll catch on! You'll learn! In the beginning it's a little bit hard. You'll get used to it," Greenspan said to the embarrassed girl who in her inexperience was not able to drive the pedal as fast as the other two.

Mary was swimming in perspiration; her cheeks flushed with embarrassment, and although she had been used to operating a sewing machine at home at a fair speed, now her limbs seemed to be made of lead. She began to make clumsy blunders; the thread came out of the needle time after time. But Greenspan was patient.

"Don't worry! You'll do it! You'll be all right!"

And she did do it. She managed to catch up with the fast tempo and keep abreast of the others.

"You see!" Greenspan said. "I told you you could do it! You're a smart girl."

Greenspan left her side and went back to the cutting table.

But no sooner had Greenspan left them than the two girls at either side of Mary began to slow down. Now it was Mary who was finished with her part of the garment first. She caught a wink from the bright black eyes of the girl who sat at her right, and heard the quiet whisper: "Take it easy!"

Mary caught on and answered with a smile from her own dark eyes.

Now she found the tempo of the machine much easier and as natural as her handling of it at home.

Her feet were getting tired and her hands weary. The heavy footsteps and clatter from the restaurant above the shop hammered into her head. Her throat was suffocating from the smell of the fumes of frying lard which came down from the restaurant kitchen. But she stuck to the work. Gradually she got used to the constant thump of footsteps and the kitchen smells. Then at last it was time for lunch.

The old Jews in the shop had their lunch indoors. The girls went out into the courtyard, where some of them found seats on the tailboard of a truck, and opened up the packages of sandwiches they had brought along with them.

For Mary's first day at the factory, Grandma McCarthy had prepared a corned beef sandwich, of meat she had managed to save from the Sunday meal, with a bit of lettuce and spread

with mayonnaise, the way Mary liked it. She had also given her
a nickel for a cup of coffee, but Mary preferred to invest it in
some ice cream.

On the way out of the shop, the girl who had advised Mary
to take it easy came over.

"This is your first day here, isn't it?" she said. "Where do
you come from?"

"I live on 48th Street. We know the boss. He used to give
my mother work to take home."

"You know that this isn't a union shop."

"I couldn't help myself. This is the first place I ever
worked. My family needs my wages."

"My parents, too. My father's in the hospital for two months
already. They say that he needs an operation. Something to do
with his stomach. I looked for work in a union shop, but I
couldn't find a job. Besides, you have to work on Saturday in a
union shop, and my parents are orthodox; they wouldn't let me
work on Saturday. They said it's better to work even for less
wages as long as you don't have to work on the Sabbath. That's
why I'm working here. I had no choice. It's only for a while,
anyway. I know the boss is taking advantage of us. He uses
green hands—old orthodox Jews and inexperienced girls. We
ought to get the union to organize the place. What's your
name?"

Mary told her.

"My name is Sarah Lifschitz. Look, Mary, we ought to stick
together. I already talked to the other girls. Some are willing,
but the others are afraid. Will you stick with us?"

"Sure."

"Fine, Mary! Gee, I'd like to have you for a friend."

"Why not?" Mary said. Their eyes met in a warm glance.
They broke into spontaneous laughter.

Mary had been working at Greenspan's shop for about two
months. She and Sarah Lifschitz had become close friends. One
day, as the two girls sat together eating lunch, Sarah said:

"Listen to this, Mary. The Triangle Waist Company on
Washington Place is looking for girls to work on blouses. It's
easy work, one of the girls who works there told me, because

this season's styles are simple, not much fancy stuff. It's not a union shop, but even if you're a union member you can get in—you just don't have to tell them. The pay's wonderful, ten or twelve dollars a week, if you work from half-past seven in the morning to six. With overtime some of the girls make fourteen dollars a week, even though they don't pay extra rates for overtime. It's a big shop, and the working conditions are pretty good. I'm going to try to get a job there; I wouldn't mind earning more money; they need it at home. What do you say? Do you want to come with me?"

"Twelve dollars a week!" Mary could hardly believe it. "And fourteen with overtime! Sure I'll go with you. I'm sick of this place, with all the smells of that darned restaurant. And I can't stand working with all those old men. I'd like to work among a lot of girls in a real shop for a change, even though it would take longer to get all the way down there. I get up early, anyway. I have to make breakfast for my father—my grandma hasn't been feeling well lately and my mother's supposed to stay in bed as much as she can. I could use a few extra dollars. The kids at home are in rags; my mother can't patch Jimmy's pants any more. I'd like to earn some extra money and get some new clothes for the kids as a surprise for Easter."

A few days later both girls went over to the Triangle firm on Washington Place to ask about jobs. When they satisfied the foreman that they were experienced hands and didn't belong to the union, he took them on.

That evening Mary came home radiant. At last she would be working in a real shop. Besides she would be earning at least six dollars a week more than she was getting at Greenspan's; with some overtime she might even make as much as fourteen dollars a week.

The Triangle firm was housed in a modern building, practically a skyscraper, situated on the edge of the enormous open square in the heart of the city. The factory took up several floors of the building. The offices, showrooms, and cutting rooms were on the lower floors. On the ninth floor about two hundred and thirty girls and a few men worked at sewing machines. Other hands worked on the eighth floor. The tenth floor housed the finishers, cleaners, and examiners. Besides a large number of men, cutters and pressers, Triangle employed more than seven hundred girls.

Entrance and exit to the ninth floor were furnished by two doors, one opposite the other. One of them, the one giving on the stairway on the Washington Square side, was always kept locked. The other door opened on the corridor and elevator leading to Greene Street. This door was constantly guarded by a watchman who looked the girls over each time they left the shop. His beady eyes were like exploring, impudent fingers, making sure that a girl didn't have a blouse or a stray piece of material concealed under her dress or coat. Nor did he hesitate to paw them for a more thorough inspection. There was no other way for the girls to enter or leave the shop except through the door guarded by the watchman.

March twenty-fifth fell on a Saturday. Through the wide windows overlooking Washington Place the afternoon sky was snowladen and gloomy. The ninth floor bustled with activity. Rows of girls sat at the sewing machines, the electric bulbs gleaming over their bowed heads. The work was going on at full speed; all the girls were hurrying to get through with the day's work so as to get home as early as possible. Although Saturday was a full working day, the girls were permitted to leave an hour earlier if the day's quota was disposed of. Saturday was payday, another inducement to hurry; everyone had plans for the evening, to go visiting, to go shopping, to go to the movies or to a dance.

Mary and Sarah sat at adjoining machines. As they worked they chatted of their evening plans. The electricity-driven leather belts of the machines clattered so noisily they were barely able to hear one another.

Sarah was in an elated mood. This week she had managed to earn, with overtime, all of fourteen dollars, an enormous sum. Besides, she was going to a dance in the evening; Jack Klein, who worked in the factory, had invited her. Her problem was what to wear, the new evening dress she had bought with her increased earnings at Triangle, or her black skirt and waist; the waist was a Triangle number; she might even have worked on it herself.

"Gee, Sarah," Mary commented, "I love those new waists with the ribbon at the collar that we're making now. But I guess it's really a question of how interested you are in Jack. Do you want to look gorgeous—or just attractive?"

"Well, naturally, a girl wants to look gorgeous when a fellow takes her out to a dance for the first time," Sarah replied.

"In that case you better wear your evening dress. A girl looks more—more important in an evening dress. That's what the fellows like."

As they talked above the whirr of the machines a sudden quiet fell on the shop; even the machines sounded subdued. Something seemed to be happening at the far end of the room. Sarah stood up to see what was going on. Mary scrambled up beside her. They could see nothing.

"What is it?" Mary asked in sudden alarm.

"I don't know," Sarah answered.

All at once they saw puffs of thick smoke coming up between the cracks of the floor boards near the door leading to the elevator. Forked flames of fire followed the smoke. All the fright in the world broke out in a chorus of hysterical screams.

"Fire! Fire! Fire!"

Panic swept through the room. There was the noise of running feet, the clatter of chairs and stools being thrown over. The two girls began to run with the rest.

The running mob pushed them toward the exit door on the Greene Street side. It was near the door leading to the elevator that the flames were licking through the planks of the floor. They remembered that no stairway descended from the corridor. The elevator was the only exit. They would be trapped in the corridor by the flames. The smoke and fire coming through the floor near the door terrified them. The crowd veered and dashed to the other side of the loft, where the door led to the stairway that went down to Washington Place. Mary and Sarah, holding each other by the hand, ran with the rest.

They stumbled over chairs and upended stools. They were blocked by hysterical girls who were too terrified to move. Sarah and Mary tried to drag some of them along with them. Here and there tongues of fire were coming up through the floor. Around the sewing machines the heaps of remnants of material and trimmings, silks, linings, padded cotton, the oil-soaked rags which the girls used to clean the machines after oiling them, blazed into flame. The oil-soaked rags were the first to catch fire, setting alight the piles of cuttings and feeding the flames from one machine to the next. The grease-covered machines themselves began to blaze together with the piles of material on them. The fire grew in volume by the minute. It spread like a stream overflowing its banks. The waves of living flame licked at the skirts of the fleeing, screaming, trapped girls.

Barely had they escaped through the corridor of flame between the rows of machines when they were blocked by a wall of smoke which rose up from the large stacks of finished blouses. With the smoke came a suffocating odor. The smoke arose to the ceiling, where it hung like a cloud. They began to suffocate, gagging and choking. Her eyes blinded and her throat gasping, Sarah dragged Mary along. The door, when they reached it, was blocked with a mass of bodies. Hair loosed, clothing torn, the mob pulled and tore at each other in panicked attempts to get to the door. From the packed mass of bodies came a high-pitched keening, a hysterical yammering.

Those nearest the door were jammed against it, beating at it with their fists, tearing at it with their fingers, clawing at it with their nails. Some, in an ecstasy of terror, beat against it with their heads. The door did not budge.

The press around the door grew thicker. Sarah and Mary, midway in the mob, were held immovable and helpless in the tightly pressed crush of girls' bodies.

Some of the cooler heads among them tried to shout out advice to those nearest the door. Their shouts were lost in the hysterical shrieks of the terrified girls. Someone, more resourceful, managed to pass the metal head of a sewing machine over the struggling mob to the girls at the door. One of them began to beat the door frantically with the heavy metal head. The door did not yield.

The press of bodies was now an immovable mass. Sarah and Mary saw themselves hopelessly hemmed in. Sarah kept her senses. Unless they got out of the packed crowd around the door they were lost. She could see the tongues of flame coming closer and closer. With an energy born of desperation she grabbed Mary by the arm and began to drag her after her. With heads, shoulders, feet, and arms they managed to force their way through the mass of bodies and away from the door. Biting, scratching, tearing and clawing at arms, bodies, and legs, Sarah, half crawling, pulled Mary along after her, until they reached the outer edge of the crush.

Desperately Sarah looked around. Half of the floor was in flames, and the flames were coming toward them. The space near the windows which overlooked Washington Place was still untouched. In front of the windows frantic girls were weaving, clutching at the window sills, desperately trying to find some way of escape.

Near one of the windows the flames were coming closer. Here only a few girls were gathered. If there was any escape it would have to be through this window, the thought flashed through Sarah's mind. They would have to get through it before the flames reached it. She began to drag Mary toward the window. Mary showed no resistance. She was only half conscious. She let the other do what she willed.

The window was nailed down. It resisted all Sarah's efforts to open it. There was a small, jagged break in the pane, stained with blood about the edges; others had tried to shatter the glass. Sarah banged her clenched fist against the glass again and again and made the opening larger.

When the opening was big enough she put her head through. On the street below she could see crowds of people. She could see firemen holding safety nets to catch the girls who dropped from the openings in other windows. From the crowd came frantic shouts. The wails of the girls answered them. The firemen made unavailing attempts to raise their too-short ladders to the upper floors. One girl after another dropped from the windows. Sarah looked to see if there was a ledge below the window which she might be able to reach with her toes. Outside the eighth floor window there was a small iron balcony. It might be possible to reach that, and from there to the balcony outside the seventh floor window, and so on down to safety.

She turned to Mary. "Quick, crawl through to the window ledge!"

"I'm afraid. . . ."

"Quick! Come on! Here, through the broken glass."

"I can't! I can't! What will I hold on to?"

"I'll hold your arms. Try to get your toes on the iron balcony down there. Look, the other girls are doing it."

"You go first, Sarah."

"No, I'm stronger than you. I'll be able to hold on to you. You're too weak to hold on to me. I'll come after you. Go ahead!"

The flames came closer. Urged on by Sarah and driven by the terrifying spectacle of the approaching tongues of flame, Mary scrambled onto the sill, and, with her back to the street, managed to get her legs through the hole in the window, holding on frantically to Sarah's shoulders. She gashed her knee on the jagged edges of the glass but never felt the pain. Holding tightly to Sarah, she groped for some projecting ledge to support her. Except for the balconies outside the line of windows below her, the wall fell sheer. But the balcony was too far down; she couldn't reach it. Sarah, holding Mary firmly by the arms, reached out of the window as far as she dared, trying to lower her as close as possible to the balcony. It was still too far to be reached.

Yells came up to Mary's ears from the street, but she could not understand what they were shouting. Only one thought possessed her, how to get a toehold on the iron balcony below. She still gripped Sarah's arms in an iron clutch. Sarah managed to shift her hold so as to grab Mary by both hands, thus lowering her body farther down. Mary strained to reach the balcony; still it was no use. Sarah strained even farther out of the window; she was now halfway out of the jagged opening. The sharp edges of the broken glass cut into her arms and chest. As Mary strained with her feet to find a hold, the jagged edges cut deeper and deeper into Sarah's flesh. She felt the raw edges going into her, but she felt no pain. There was only the one overwhelming urge—to lower Mary closer to the balcony. She strained farther out. Suddenly she felt a fierce wave of heat licking at her legs.

The anguish was so intense, the instinct for self-preservation so compelling, that all thoughts of Mary disappeared from her mind. She couldn't withdraw her body into the room to face the enemy that was attacking her. But she knew what the enemy was. The flames were licking at her stockings. In another moment her dress would be on fire.

"Mama!" she screamed hysterically. Her body went farther out through the window. The broken edges of the jagged glass tore at her flesh.

With the tips of her toes Mary could feel the balcony under her feet. The faint hint of safety only served to heighten her terror. Through the mist of consciousness left to her Sarah saw that Mary could now find a footing. "Just a little more. Just a little more," she thought. She could feel herself moving farther forward. She could feel the flames licking up from her shoes, climbing her legs. Then she could feel nothing. If only she could lean out a little more, Mary would reach the balcony. She dare not let go of Mary's hands. She was no longer herself. She no longer existed. She had become a part of Mary. She was only an instrument to help her reach the balcony. . . . Now she could reach it. Sarah threw the upper half of her body violently forward. Mary felt below her feet the firm surface of the balcony. Her hands, suddenly released, clutched at the bare sides of the building. Above her, out of the shattered window, a flaming body fell, like a living torch down to the street below.

Mary knew that flaming torch. She opened her mouth to shriek Sarah's name. In her pain and terror no sound came from her lips. Now the single thought of escape obsessed her. From the window outside of which she stood, a wave of blasting heat came to her from the roaring flames inside.

She threw a terrified glance to the street below. It was so far away that it seemed to her that it must be a distant, unattainable world. The area immediately below her was an empty expanse. The crowds had been herded away by lines of police; there were only the firemen and fire-fighting apparatus. She could see safety nets held out spread by groups of firemen. She could see bodies falling from the walls of the building with hair and clothing aflame. She could hear voices calling to her; she did not know what they were shouting. She looked around her at the other windows of the building. She could see girls crawling through the windows on hands and knees, trying frantically to hold on to the bare walls. Others seemed to be hanging in mid-air, their falling bodies caught by projecting cornices.

The second that she remained crouched on the balcony seemed like an eternity. Angry flames were shooting out through the window, licking at her. She was alone now; there was no Sarah holding on to her hands. Her consciousness and resourcefulness began to function; she would have to depend on her own initiative now. Driven more by fear of the flames that licked at her from the window than by any considered design, she held on to the iron rail of the balcony and let her body down. Her feet swung in the air; she hadn't looked first to see whether she could reach the landing below. She was afraid to let go of the rail. Her feet sought for a foothold; they found none; the wall was smooth and unbroken. Again and again her toes sought out a niche in the wall, but they found only a sheer surface. Her hands were getting weak, she would have to let go the iron rail; it was hot from the flames which were shooting farther and farther through the window. The palms of her hands burned. She could feel her fingers relaxing. She would let herself go, like the others, to fall into the safety net—or to crash onto the sidewalk.

She couldn't summon up the courage to let go. But she knew if she didn't let go herself, her fingers would slip from the rail and she would fall onto the sidewalk. She must jump. She must try to jump to the nets spread below. Her lips kept murmuring "Jesus, Christ, Jesus, Mary." She closed her eyes for a second. She saw before her the carved wooden figure of Jesus to which she prayed in the Italian church. She knelt before it and prayed her familiar prayer. "Sweet Jesus, save me." As her lips murmured the words her fingers let go their clutch on the iron balcony rail and her body fell.

She did not fall to the ground. Her dress caught on the iron bar of a sign extending outside the third floor window. In the second that she remained suspended, strong arms reached out of the window and pulled her in.

For three weeks Mary was kept at the hospital. By the end of that time her gashed knee had healed. Also her shattered nerves.

More than one hundred and fifty girls had lost their lives in the fire. They were buried at mass funerals; the Jewish girls in the Jewish cemeteries, the Christian girls in Christian cemeteries. The survivors soon began to search for work in other factories. The wave of excitement and anger that swept through the city and all through the country didn't last very long. A commission was appointed to investigate fire hazards in the state's garment factories. Some bills were introduced into the Assembly. There were heated debates; some measures were adopted, others were defeated. When it was all over, everything in the needle industries remained the same.

The McCarthy family had become accustomed to Mary's contributions to the household; now they found it impossible to manage on the reduced scale. Patrick McCarthy renewed his old, endless arguments. Although most of the victims were Jewish girls, only a few Gentile girls having been killed, McCarthy blamed the fire and everything about it on the Jews. He swore he would not allow Mary to go back to work, but he soon began to drown his troubles in drink—with the help of the rent money to which Mary had so substantially contributed in the weeks past. After she had been out of the hospital for about two weeks, the McCarthy larder was so empty that Mary had to go out looking for a job.

She found work in a factory whose owner assured her it was fireproof. McCarthy made a show of protesting, but, like the rest of the family, he knew well enough what Mary's earnings meant. Since she had been working he had been able to go more often to the rent money in the bowl in the cupboard with less pangs of conscience.

"Fire or no fire," Grandma McCarthy said, "the world has to go on about its business. Coal miners go back to the pit after a mine disaster."

They all had to agree with her.

One vivid vision remained in Mary's memory: Sarah's terrified eyes staring from below her flaming hair.

I Was Marching

By Meridel Le Sueur

*Meridel Le Sueur (1900–) was born in Iowa and grew up
mainly in Minnesota under the influence of three independent women—her mother, her homesteading grand-
mother, and a Native American woman named Zona.
(Her great-grandmother had been an Iroquois.) Her mother
Marian and her mother's second husband, Arthur Le Sueur, were
political activists: he was the first Socialist mayor of
Minot, Minnesota; she, a lifetime feminist, ran for the
senate when she was seventy-five. Meridel Le Sueur's
irregular schooling included a year at the Academy of
Dramatic Arts in New York City. In Hollywood, looking
for acting parts, she worked as a stunt artist for several
years. In 1928, Le Sueur returned to Minnesota to work as
a journalist and to devote herself to populist causes and the
labor movement. In the thirties, she reared two daughters
on her meager earnings as a writer. She now lives with
one of her daughters and her daughter's family in St. Paul,
Minnesota, where she continues to write. She is pleased
that she has seven grandchildren and seven great-
grandchildren.*

*The stories Le Sueur published in the early thirties gained
her a national reputation. Like her later work similarly honored, her earliest published story, "Persephone," appeared
in Edmund O'Brien's* Best Short Stories of 1927. *Her
poems and journalism, as well as her stories, appeared in
a great variety of publications, including* Poetry, Dial,
American Mercury, The Daily Worker, Partisan Review,
The Nation, Scribner's Magazine, Prairie Schooner,
New Masses, *and the* Yale Review. *She published volumes
of stories at regular intervals until the fifties:* Annuncia-
tion *(1935),* Salute to Spring *(1940), and* North Star
Country *(1945). Blacklisted in the fifties during the
McCarthy period, she found most channels of publication
closed to her. Nevertheless, she continued to write, filling*

one hundred and fifty volumes of journals, as well as
producing stories and poems and experimenting with new
forms.

    Recently, Le Sueur's work has been rediscovered, and
some of it is now available again. In 1977 and 1978, West
End Press issued two volumes of previously published
stories, Song for My Time *and* Harvest, *and an unpub-*
lished novel, The Girl; *and International Publishers re-*
printed Salute to Spring. *A feminist collective in Minneap-*
olis has written and produced a film of Le Sueur's life
called My People Are My Home. *Le Sueur cooperated with*
the group and opened her journals to them. An anthology
of Le Sueur, that shows the range of her prose and poetry,
will be published by The Feminist Press.

    "I Was Marching" was written after a 1934 strike in
Minneapolis. As in much contemporary journalism, Le
Sueur herself is a participant in as well as an observer of
the events she records and describes.

I have never been in a strike before. It is like looking at
something that is happening for the first time and there are
no thoughts and no words yet accrued to it. If you come from
the middle class, words are likely to mean more than an event.
You are likely to think about a thing, and the happening will
be the size of a pin point and the words around the happening
very large, distorting it queerly. It's a case of "Remembrance of
things past." When you are in the event, you are likely to have
a distinctly individualistic attitude, to be only partly there, and
to care more for the happening afterward than when it is
happening. That is why it is hard for a person like myself and
others to be in a strike.

    Besides, in American life, you hear things happening in a
far and muffled way. One thing is said and another happens.
Our merchant society has been built upon a huge hypocrisy, a
cut-throat competition which sets one man against another
and at the same time an ideology mouthing such words as
"Humanity," "Truth," the "Golden Rule," and such. Now in a
crisis the word falls away and the skeleton of that action shows
in terrific movement.

For two days I heard of the strike. I went by their head-quarters. I walked by on the opposite side of the street and saw the dark old building that had been a garage and lean, dark young faces leaning from the upstairs windows. I had to go down there often. I looked in. I saw the huge black interior and live coals of living men moving restlessly and orderly, their eyes gleaming from their sweaty faces.

I saw cars leaving filled with grimy men, pickets going to the line, engines roaring out. I stayed close to the door, watching. I didn't go in. I was afraid they would put me out. After all, I could remain a spectator. A man wearing a polo hat kept going around with a large camera taking pictures.

I am putting down exactly how I felt, because I believe others of my class feel the same as I did. I believe it stands for an important psychic change that must take place in all. I saw many artists, writers, professionals, even business men and women standing across the street, too, and I saw in their faces the same longings, the same fears.

The truth is I was afraid. Not of the physical danger at all, but an awful fright of mixing, of losing myself, of being un-known and lost. I felt inferior. I felt no one would know me there, that all I had been trained to excel in would go un-noticed. I can't describe what I felt, but perhaps it will come near it to say that I felt I excelled in competing with others and I knew instantly that these people were *NOT* competing at all, that they were acting in a strange, powerful trance of move-ment *together*. And I was filled with longing to act with them and with fear that I could not. I felt I was born out of every kind of life, thrown up alone, looking at other lonely people, a con-dition I had been in the habit of defending with various atti-tudes of cynicism, preciosity, defiance, and hatred.

Looking at that dark and lively building, massed with men, I knew my feelings to be those belonging to disruption, chaos, and disintegration and I felt their direct and awful movement, mute and powerful, drawing them into a close and glowing cohesion like a powerful conflagration in the midst of the city. And it filled me with fear and awe and at the same time hope. I knew this action to be prophetic and indicative of future actions and I wanted to be part of it.

Our life seems to be marked with a curious and muffled violence over America, but this action has always been in the dark, men and women dying obscurely, poor and poverty marked lives, but now from city to city runs this violence, into the open, and colossal happenings stand bare before our eyes, the street churning suddenly upon the pivot of mad violence, whole men suddenly spouting blood and running like living sieves, another holding a dangling arm shot squarely off, a tall youngster, running, tripping over his intestines, and one block away, in the burning sun, gay women shopping and a window dresser trying to decide whether to put green or red voile on a mannikin.

In these terrible happenings you cannot be neutral now. No one can be neutral in the face of bullets.

The next day, with sweat breaking out on my body, I walked past the three guards at the door. They said, "Let the women in. We need women." And I knew it was no joke.

At first I could not see into the dark building. I felt many men coming and going, cars driving through. I had an awful impulse to go into the office which I passed, and offer to do some special work. I saw a sign which said "Get your button." I saw they all had buttons with the date and the number of the union local. I didn't get a button. I wanted to be anonymous.

There seemed to be a current, running down the wooden stairs, towards the front of the building, into the street, that was massed with people, and back again. I followed the current up the old stairs packed closely with hot men and women. As I was going up I could look down and see the lower floor, the cars drawing up to await picket call, the hospital roped off on one side.

Upstairs men sat bolt upright in chairs asleep, their bodies flung in attitudes of peculiar violence of fatigue. A woman nursed her baby. Two young girls slept together on a cot, dressed in overalls. The voice of the loudspeaker filled the room. The immense heat pressed down from the flat ceiling. I stood up against the wall for an hour. No one paid any attention to me. The commissary was in back and the women came

(text continued on page 234)

Portraits
of the Authors

Meridel Le Sueur: 1937

Dorothy
Canfield
Fisher:
circa 1905

Sholem Asch: circa 1950

Marge Piercy: 1976

Alice Walker: 1974

Adrienne Rich: 1972

Sue Davidson: 1962

Margaret Walker: 1973

Edward Field: 1977

out sometimes and sat down, fanning themselves with their aprons and listening to the news over the loudspeaker. A huge man seemed hung on a tiny folding chair. Occasionally some one tiptoed over and brushed the flies off his face. His great head fell over and the sweat poured regularly from his forehead like a spring. I wondered why they took such care of him. They all looked at him tenderly as he slept. I learned that he was a leader on the picket line and had the scalps of more cops to his name than any other.

Three windows flanked the front. I walked over to the windows. A red-headed woman with a button saying, "Unemployed Council," was looking out. I looked out with her. A thick crowd stood in the heat below listening to the strike bulletin. We could look right into the windows of the smart club across the street. We could see people peering out of the windows half hidden.

I kept feeling they would put me out. No one paid any attention. The woman said without looking at me, nodding to the palatial house, "It sure is good to see the enemy plain like that." "Yes," I said. I saw that the club was surrounded by a steel picket fence higher than a man. "They know what they put that there fence there for," she said. "Yes," I said. "Well," she said, "I've got to get back to the kitchen. Is it ever hot?" The thermometer said ninety-nine. The sweat ran off us, burning our skins. "The boys'll be coming in," she said, "for their noon feed." She had a scarred face. "Boy, will it be a mad house?" "Do you need any help?" I said eagerly. "Boy," she said, "some of us have been pouring coffee since two o'clock this morning, steady, without no let-up." She started to go. She didn't pay any special attention to me as an individual. She didn't seem to be thinking of me, she didn't seem to see me. I watched her go. I felt rebuffed, hurt. Then I saw instantly she didn't see me because she saw only what she was doing. I ran after her.

I found the kitchen organized like a factory. Nobody asks my name. I am given a large butcher's apron. I realize I have never before worked anonymously. At first I feel strange and then I feel good. The forewoman sets me to washing tin cups. There are not enough cups. We have to wash fast and rinse them and set them up quickly for buttermilk and coffee as the line thickens and the men wait. A little shortish man who is a professional dishwasher is supervising. I feel I won't be able to wash tin cups, but when no one pays any attention except to see that there are enough cups I feel better.

The line grows heavy. The men are coming in from the picket line. Each woman has one thing to do. There is no confusion. I soon learn I am not supposed to help pour the buttermilk. I am not supposed to serve sandwiches. I am supposed to wash tin cups. I suddenly look around and realize all these women are from factories. I know they have learned this organization and specialization in the factory. I look at the round shoulders of the woman cutting bread next to me and I feel I know her. The cups are brought back, washed and put on the counter again. The sweat pours down our faces, but you forget about it.

Then I am changed and put to pouring coffee. At first I look at the men's faces and then I don't look anymore. It seems I am pouring coffee for the same tense, dirty sweating face, the same body, the same blue shirt and overalls. Hours go by, the heat is terrific. I am not tired. I am not hot. I am pouring coffee. I am swung into the most intense and natural organization I have ever felt. I know everything that is going on. These things become of great matter to me.

Eyes looking, hands raising a thousand cups, throats burning, eyes bloodshot from lack of sleep, the body dilated to catch every sound over the whole city. Buttermilk? Coffee?

"Is your man here?" the woman cutting sandwiches asks me.

"No," I say, then I lie for some reason, peering around as if looking eagerly for someone, "I don't see him now."

But I was pouring coffee for living men.

For a long time, about one o'clock, it seemed like something was about to happen. Women seemed to be pouring into headquarters to be near their men. You could hear only lies over the radio. And lies in the paper. Nobody knew precisely what was happening, but everyone thought something would happen in a few hours. You could feel the men being poured out of the hall onto the picket line. Every few minutes cars left and more drew up and were filled. The voice at the loudspeaker was accelerated, calling for men, calling for picket cars.

I could hear the men talking about the arbitration board, the truce that was supposed to be maintained while the board sat with the Governor. They listened to every word over the loudspeaker. A terrible communal excitement ran through the hall like a fire through a forest. I could hardly breathe. I seemed to have no body at all except the body of this excitement. I felt that what had happened before had not been a real movement, these false words and actions had taken place on the periphery. The real action was about to show, the real intention.

We kept on pouring thousands of cups of coffee, feeding thousands of men.

The chef with a woman tattooed on his arm was just dishing the last of the stew. It was about two o'clock. The commissary was about empty. We went into the front hall. It was drained of men. "The men are massed at the market," he said. "Something is going to happen." I sat down beside a woman who was holding her hands tightly together, leaning forward listening, her eyes bright and dilated. I had never seen her before. She took my hands. She pulled me towards her. She was crying. "It's awful," she said. "Something awful is going to happen. They've taken both my children away from me and now something is going to happen to all those men." I held her hands. She had a green ribbon around her hair.

The action seemed reversed. The cars were coming back. The announcer cried, "This is murder." Cars were coming in. I don't know how we got to the stairs. Everyone seemed to be converging at a menaced point. I saw below the crowd stirring, uncoiling. I saw them taking men out of cars and putting them on the hospital cots, on the floor. At first I felt frightened, the close black area of the barn, the blood, the heavy movement, the sense of myself lost, gone. But I couldn't have turned away now. A woman clung to my hand. I was pressed against the body of another. If you are to understand anything you must understand it in the muscular event, in actions we have not been trained for. Something broke all my surfaces in something that was beyond horror and I was dabbing alcohol on the gaping wounds that buckshot makes, hanging open like crying mouths. Buckshot wounds splay in the body and then swell like a blow. Ness, who died, had thirty-eight slugs in his body, in the chest and in the back.

The picket cars keep coming in. Some men have walked back from the market, holding their own blood in. They move in a great explosion, and the newness of the movement makes it seem like something under ether, moving terrifically towards a culmination.

From all over the city workers are coming. They gather outside in two great half-circles, cut in two to let the ambulances in. A traffic cop is still directing traffic at the corner and the crowd cannot stand to see him. "We'll give you just two seconds to beat it," they tell him. He goes away quickly. A striker takes over the street.

Men, women, and children are massing outside, a living circle close packed for protection. From the tall office building business men are looking down on the black swarm thickening, coagulating into what action they cannot tell.

We have living blood on our skirts.

That night at eight o'clock a mass-meeting was called of all labor. It was to be in a parking lot two blocks from headquarters. All the women gather at the front of the building with collection cans, ready to march to the meeting. I have not been home. It never occurs to me to leave. The twilight is eerie and the men are saying that the chief of police is going to attack the meeting and raid headquarters. The smell of blood hangs in the hot, still air. Rumors strike at the taut nerves. The dusk looks ghastly with what might be in the next half hour.

"If you have any children," a woman said to me, "you better not go." I looked at the desperate women's faces, the broken feet, the torn and hanging pelvis, the worn and lovely bodies of women who persist under such desperate labors. I shivered, though it was 96 and the sun had been down a good hour.

The parking lot was already full of people when we got there and men swarmed the adjoining roofs. An elegant cafe stood across the street with water sprinkling from its roof and splendidly dressed men and women stood on the steps as if looking at a show.

The platform was the bullet riddled truck of the afternoon's fray. We had been told to stand close to this platform, so we did, making the center of a wide massed circle that stretched as far as we could see. We seemed buried like minerals in a mass, packed body to body. I felt again that peculiar heavy silence in which there is the real form of the happening. My eyes burn. I can hardly see. I seem to be standing like an animal in ambush. I have the brightest, most physical feeling with every sense sharpened peculiarly. The movements, the masses that I see and feel I have never known before. I only partly know what I am seeing, feeling, but I feel it is the real body and gesture of a future vitality. I see that there is a bright clot of women drawn close to a bullet riddled truck. I am one of them, yet I don't feel myself at all. It is curious, I feel most alive and yet for the first time in my life I do not feel myself as separate. I realize then that all my previous feelings have been based on feeling myself separate and distinct from others and now I sense sharply faces, bodies, closeness, and my own fear is not my own alone, nor my hope.

The strikers keep moving up cars. We keep moving back together to let cars pass and form between us and a brick building that flanks the parking lot. They are connecting the loudspeaker, testing it. Yes, they are moving up lots of cars, through the crowd and lining them closely side by side. There must be ten thousand people now, heat rising from them. They are standing silent, watching the platform, watching the cars being brought up. The silence seems terrific like a great form moving of itself. This is real movement issuing from the close reality of mass feeling. This is the first real rhythmic movement I have ever seen. My heart hammers terrifically. My hands are swollen and hot. No one is producing this movement. It is a movement upon which all are moving softly, rhythmically, terribly.

No matter how many times I looked at what was happening I hardly knew what I saw. I looked and I saw time and time again that there were men standing close to us, around us, and then suddenly I knew that there was a living chain of men standing shoulder to shoulder, forming a circle around the group of women. They stood shoulder to shoulder slightly moving like a thick vine from the pressure behind, but standing tightly woven like a living wall, moving gently.

I saw that the cars were now lined one close fitted to the other with strikers sitting on the roofs and closely packed on the running boards. They could see far over the crowd. "What are they doing that for?" I said. No one answered. The wide dilated eyes of the women were like my own. No one seemed to be answering questions now. They simply spoke, cried out, moved together now.

The last car drove in slowly, the crowd letting them through without command or instruction. "A little closer," someone said. "Be sure they are close." Men sprang up to direct whatever action was needed and then subsided again and no one had noticed who it was. They stepped forward to direct a needed action and then fell anonymously back again.

We all watched carefully the placing of the cars. Sometimes we looked at each other. I didn't understand that look. I felt uneasy. It was as if something escaped me. And then suddenly, on my very body, I knew what they were doing, as if it had been communicated to me from a thousand eyes, a thousand silent throats, as if it had been shouted in the loudest voice.

THEY WERE BUILDING A BARRICADE.

Two men died from that day's shooting. Men lined up to give one of them a blood transfusion, but he died. Black Friday men called the murderous day. Night and day workers held their children up to see the body of Ness who died. Tuesday, the day of the funeral, one thousand more militia were massed downtown.

It was still over ninety in the shade. I went to the funeral parlors and thousands of men and women were massed there waiting in the terrific sun. One block of women and children were standing two hours waiting. I went over and stood near them. I didn't know whether I could march. I didn't like marching in parades. Besides, I felt they might not want me.

I stood aside not knowing if I would march. I couldn't see how they would ever organize it anyway. No one seemed to be doing much.

At three-forty some command went down the ranks. I said foolishly at the last minute, "I don't belong to the auxiliary— could I march?" Three women drew me in. "We want all to march," they said gently. "Come with us."

The giant mass uncoiled like a serpent and straightened out ahead and to my amazement on a lift of road I could see six blocks of massed men, four abreast, with bare heads, moving straight on and as they moved, uncoiled the mass behind and pulled it after them. I felt myself walking, accelerating my speed with the others as the line stretched, pulled taut, then held its rhythm.

Not a cop was in sight. The cortege moved through the stop-and-go signs, it seemed to lift of its own dramatic rhythm, coming from the intention of every person there. We were moving spontaneously in a movement, natural, hardy, and miraculous.

We passed through six blocks of tenements, through a sea of grim faces, and there was not a sound. There was the curious shuffle of thousands of feet, without drum or bugle, in ominous silence, a march not heavy as the military, but very light, exactly with the heart beat.

I was marching with a million hands, movements, faces, and my own movement was repeating again and again, making a new movement from these many gestures, the walking, falling back, the open mouth crying, the nostrils stretched apart, the raised hand, the blow falling, and the outstretched hand drawing me in.

I felt my legs straighten. I felt my feet join in that strange shuffle of thousands of bodies moving with direction, of thousands of feet, and my own breath with the gigantic breath. As if an electric charge had passed through me, my hair stood on end. I was marching.

The Peace Walk

By Sue Davidson

Sue Davidson (1925–) was born and raised in Texas and worked there on the Galveston Daily News. *She attended several universities, earning an M.A. in English from the University of Chicago. Her articles and short stories have appeared in* The Progressive, The Nation, Commonweal, Antioch Review, Western Political Quarterly, WIN, *and other periodicals. She is the author of a book on alternatives to war,* What Do You Mean Non-Violence? *and has held a Saxton Memorial Fellowship and a Stanford Fellowship in Creative Writing. Her work was included in* Twenty Years of Stanford Short Stories *(1966).*

Throughout her adult life, Davidson has been an out-spoken activist—for peace, civil rights, and women's rights. She has worked as a journalist, editor, researcher, teacher, citizens' planner, and educational evaluator, and currently is an editor for The Feminist Press. *She and her husband, Alex Gottfried, live in Seattle. They have one daughter, Erika. "The Peace Walk," first published in the* Northwest Review *in 1959, reflects some of Davidson's political concerns.*

Lying awake that night, after she and Jim had watched the late T.V. news, the idea of organizing the Peace Walk first came to Lila. The news had included an item about an anti-H-bomb demonstration moving toward Washington, D.C., a still photograph of men and women carrying placards in the hot sun. She recalled reports of similar demonstrations in recent months.

She tossed and turned most of the night, planning. In the morning, the idea still seemed feasible. She spoke to Jim about it over breakfast, before he left for the plant lab. He shrugged. "Could be. We don't know anything about this town."

"I assume the people in this town are like people any-where," Lila said. "If that's the case, there must be a few of them, anyway, who don't want the human race destroyed."

Jim said, "Yes. It's a long jump from that assumption, even if it's correct, to being able to get up the kind of public protest you have in mind." He kissed her. "See you at six."

Lila admitted that she didn't know the town. They had been in Fainville only three months, and probably would not remain over a year. Jim's company found it convenient to move him about a good deal—four towns in three years of marriage. Lila didn't mind moving about; she regarded it as an adventure, after having lived all her life in the same house in the same city, even going to the local university. She was not very social; she liked to read and dream, and this could be done anywhere.

In the present case there were, of course, disadvantages. Lila knew no one personally who might be interested in the Peace Walk, and the yellow pages of the telephone book yielded the names of no organizations which might be interested, not even a local United Nations association or a Quaker congregation. But perhaps, she thought, that had to be expected in the South. She got off letters to the national offices of the Sane Nuclear Policy Committee and the American Friends Service Committee, asking for local contacts and advice. Then she made a list of Fainville's churches and women's organizations, using the telephone book as a source. She did not telephone anyone that day; she wanted time to work out the verbal approach.

After dinner she reported to Jim on what she had done. He was pouring out their coffee in the living room. He brought her cup over to the sofa and sat down.

"I didn't realize you were serious."

"Well, I am. I've got to do something. I can't bear reading the newspapers and just sitting around and doing nothing about it."

"About what?"

"About what?" Lila stared. "About everything! About H-bombs and the arms race and preparations for a war that will end the world—the whole business."

"Oh," Jim said. "Do you think this will do something?"

"It's a start," Lila said. "If enough people show that they

simply won't have it. . . . This is a democracy, isn't it? Don't you believe that public opinion means anything?"

"I believe it means something."

"Well?"

"I just wanted to make sure of what you had in mind," Jim said. "Is there any more cake?"

"On the kitchen table. Put it away, will you, Jim? The ants. . . ."

Jim reseated himself on the couch. Lila was smoking a cigarette and drumming her fingers upon the end table. She watched the smoke spiraling from her cigarette, her blue eyes narrowed.

"It ought to be inter-racial," she said.

"What?"

"The Peace Walk. It's important that it be inter-racial. I have no lines to the colored community here. I wish there were a branch of the N.A.A.C.P. There isn't, can you imagine? In times like these?"

"You might work on that," Jim said.

"On what?"

"Local organization of the N.A.A.C.P. You'd probably be able to interest more colored people in the N.A.A.C.P. than in your peace march."

"Walk," Lila said. "Not march. I don't see why. Colored people are capable of seeing that if we're all going to be blown to bits, segregation becomes a side issue. They can see that. Anyone can see it. Everything's a side issue, compared to this. Yet everybody just sits around twiddling their thumbs, waiting to get slaughtered, like a lot of dumb cattle. To say nothing of cooperating, by supporting a huge military. . . ."

"Yes. All right. Please don't get so worked up, darling."

"It's appropriate to be worked up, under the circumstances!" Lila jumped up from her chair. She went to the windows and stood looking down into the street. She said, more quietly, "Can't you see that?"

Jim did not reply. After a moment, he said: "Lila?"

"Yes?"

"This is a little off the subject, but I've been thinking. . . .

Since we made this last move, I think we've racketed around long enough, don't you? I think I ought to ask for a permanent assignment, maybe back East. We can settle down, get a house of our own, begin to raise a family. . . ."

Lila's shoulders stiffened. "Family?" She turned around. "Family?"

Jim went on quickly, "We can easily afford to, now. There's no question of security, of my job, nor of promotion. . . ."

"I don't intend to have a family."

"Oh?" Jim set his plate carefully on the coffee table. He gave a short laugh. "Well, thanks for telling me."

"I have told you. I've said it repeatedly, especially in the past year. I won't bring children into a world like this. I'd consider it a crime—against you and myself, to say nothing of the child. Won't our sufferings be great enough in the event of an atom war, without adding the anguish of having children? Besides, we're polluted. All the radiation we've been subjected to, there's an excellent chance our children would be defective. I've told you, I won't take that chance."

Jim shook his head. "I didn't think you were serious."

"That's the second time you've said that tonight. I'm amazed at you, Jim. When have I ever not been serious?" He made no response, and she went on, "I'm afraid what you mean isn't that I am not serious, but that you don't *take* me seriously." She turned back to the window.

"No, darling, that's not true. I only meant—well, you're pretty emotional, and sometimes you say things in the heat of the moment that you don't really mean. . . ."

"I mean this," Lila said, without turning around.

"All right. Family or no, I think we should begin to think in terms of settling down somewhere. We've been strangers among strangers long enough. I think it's . . . not good for you. There's never time to get acquainted, we're always just getting acquainted by the time we move on. You're alone too much. You read too much and brood too much. You should be seeing people more frequently, be involved in community affairs. . . ."

"Wouldn't you say that the probable extinction of the community is a community affair?"

Jim shook his head. "I doubt that the community would see it that way. Most people would take a statement like that as pretty wild and extremist, Lila. If you're going to go around talking like that. . . ."

Lila interrupted him thoughtfully. "It's funny, when anybody is serious about a really serious matter, when you face reality, people think you're crazy. Whereas the people who ignore reality are regarded as sane." She turned around to him. "I'm sorry you're opposed, Jim."

"Darling, I'm not opposed." He stood up and went to her. Putting his arms about her, he said, "I just don't want you to be hurt. I honestly don't think you'll be able to get any cooperation in this thing."

"You needn't worry about my getting hurt, Jim. I'm not made of papier-mache."

"You always seem to me so . . . delicate." He buried his face in her hair. "Darling, I love you so much. Let's not quarrel."

"No," Lila said. "We won't talk about it any more now. . . ." She gazed past him abstractedly.

In the next few days Lila called on a dozen Fainville ministers. They received her politely, without exception. Only one tried to argue her out of the Peace Walk on the ground that military preparedness was necessary because of the threat of atheistic Red communism. Two of them agreed to announce the Peace Walk, when the date was scheduled. These, however, as well as the others, said that they could give Lila no help in organizing it, as they were short-handed during the summer, and already snowed under their work. They were unable to suggest the names of any among their congregations who would be interested. Only the Congregationalist minister—a shy, pleasant, very young man—could suggest any name at all. He said there was an old pensioner who did odd jobs around the church, who might want to help Lila. The man, a Mr. Jorgenson, had no telephone; but the minister wrote out his address.

Mr. Jorgenson lived in a poor section of the town. Lila felt guilty and self-conscious as she pulled the convertible to the curb in front of his cottage. She wished she hadn't let the top down—a new convertible was even more conspicuous with the top down.

Lila had been discouraged by her failure with the spiritual leadership of Fainville. When Mr. Jorgenson opened his door, she felt more discouraged still. Mr. Jorgenson did not look especially intelligent, and he was not very clean. There were tufts of coarse gray hair growing out of his ears, a thing that always made Lila slightly ill.

But she smiled and forced herself to enter his dark little house, which smelled of fuel oil and bacon fat. As she talked to Mr. Jorgenson, she had the disconcerting impression that he was not listening to anything she said; his eyes never met hers, his expression was remote. Yet as soon as she had finished speaking, he said that he would be glad to participate in the Peace Walk. He added:

"Not just me. I can get you lotsa people. Old people. They ain't got nothing to do."

Lila's heart sank. The minister had played a cruel joke on her. Undoubtedly he believed her insane, but harmless, and thought that Mr. Jorgenson would make a suitable companion to her madness. Mr. Jorgenson was not a man of pacifist convictions. He merely had nothing to do with his time.

But a moment later, she saw that she had been mistaken in her evaluation of Mr. Jorgenson. He said suddenly and loudly:

"Socialist Party always been opposed to war. Capitalist conspiracy to keep the working people down."

She perked up. "You're a Socialist?"

He nodded. "Sure. Forty-two years."

"And these friends of yours—they're Socialists, too?"

He shook his head. "Oh, no, lady. Ain't another Socialist in the county, nor the next county, nor the one after that. They're just old working people I know. Dumb, but nice. Too old to change. I talk to them plenty, and they listen, but they never change."

"Well—I wouldn't want anybody to participate who didn't feel strongly about the H-bomb."

"Don't worry. Old people dumb, but not dumb enough to like H-bombs."

"Oh," Lila said. "That's fine. Mr. Jorgenson, another thing—
I think Negroes should be asked to participate in the Peace
Walk, don't you?"

"Sure," Mr. Jorgenson said. "Why not? They're working
people."

Lila warmed to him. "You know, Mr. Jorgenson, there isn't
even a local branch of the National Association for the Ad-
vancement of Colored People here. Has anybody tried to do
anything about that?"

Mr. Jorgenson shook his head. "No use," he said, "no
use. No use trying to do anything about the colored, not with
things like they are."

"Well, yes, it's a minor issue compared to . . ."

"Got to change the system first. It's the capitalist dictators.
Can't change anything in the capitalist system."

"Oh—yes." It occurred to her to wonder why, in that case,
Mr. Jorgenson should see any use in the Peace Walk. But she
reminded herself that human beings are never completely con-
sistent. Mr. Jorgenson's heart, she felt sure, was in the right
place—that was the important thing.

She rose and shook him by the hand. "You've been so encouraging, Mr. Jorgenson. You're the first person I've talked
with who's responded at all. I'm really very grateful."

"Sure. Anything I can do."

"I was wondering, Mr. Jorgenson, about a name, a handle.
We haven't the sponsorship of any organization, and we have
to call ourselves something—I mean, for the newspaper publicity and so on."

"Nothing to it," Mr. Jorgenson said. "It's an ad hoc committee. Ad Hoc Committee for the March for Freedom Peace
and Equality."

" 'Walk,' I think, don't you? 'March' is awfully—military."

"You're right, Mrs. Horton. Walk is lots better."

Before she went out of the door, he shoved a handful of
Socialist literature at her. She took it home and dutifully read
it. She had been exposed to all of the basic ideas before, and
acquiesced generally in those which concerned her. Nevertheless, the reading was useful to her, for the Socialist tracts were
written in a shrill, hysteric tone, which she warned herself

must be guarded against at all costs in presenting the Peace
Walk.

Her voice was carefully controlled, even a trifle dry, the next
morning as she telephoned the chairwoman of the Fainville
Milk Fund, whose name she had picked up from the daily
newspaper. The chairwoman of the Fainville Milk Fund cut her
off as soon as she understood what was wanted, however; and
Lila fared no better with the next five women she contacted,
although they were inclined to be more chatty. Lila found that
her palms were sweating. Her neck had become stiff with
tension as she sat with the receiver glued against her ear. She
pushed the telephone away and went out into the hall to look
for the mail.

May Brooks, who lived in the opposite apartment, was
standing in the hallway with a paper sack of groceries. A
divorcee living with an eleven-year-old son, May was de-
pressive and alcoholic, and Lila felt sorry for her. She had
helped May to bed on a couple of occasions, and last week had
given the little boy lunch when his mother became incapaci-
tated before noon.

The bottom of the paper sack split open; oranges and apples
rained upon the hall carpet. Mrs. Brooks said, "Oh, my God."

Lila helped May retrieve the fruit and carry the groceries
into the kitchen. May took off her gloves and passed a trembling hand over her forehead. "My God," she repeated. "Thank
you, Lila. I'd ask you to stay for a cup of coffee, but if I get
to talking I won't be ready in time. How did I get into this?"

She scooped up the apples and dumped them into the
vegetable-bin. "It's something to do with the Sea Scouts. The
mothers of Timmy's pack or crew or something. They called
one day last week when I was . . . I said they could meet here,
Timmy tells me."

"Is there anything I can do?"

"Oh, my God, I don't know. I've got to get the place straight
and have coffee and cake ready by one-thirty for twenty
women."

Lila had a sudden inspiration. "May, will you do something
for me?"

"Oh, honey, yes, but not now!"

"I'll get everything ready for you, and you can lie down and rest. But I wish you'd do something for me, too."

She told May about the Peace Walk. Although she was brief, she tried to make herself very clear about its objectives; she did not wish to victimize May Brooks, or her guests, for that matter.

"If you'll just introduce me to them when their meeting is over. I'll explain that I'm not going to speak about Sea Scouts, and that they don't have to stay if they don't want to listen."

"So long as you don't want me to march, too, honey, it's O.K. You're a pal, Lila. I got an awful head."

"Walk," Lila said, "not march. . . ." But May Brooks was on her way.

Lila sighed and went into the living room. As she carried ashtrays from the living room to the kitchen sink, she squared her shoulders. Her eyes grew thoughtful, then bright. . . .

She began to rehearse her words for the Scout mothers.

Everything took an upward swing beginning with that afternoon. Lila did not at first anticipate good results. When she had finished speaking—to a stony silence—the women coughed, gathered up their bags, and began an exodus to the hallway. One of them stopped beside Lila. Her mouth was tight with fury. "You'll be sorry," she said, "when the Russians start dropping bombs on you!"

"Why, yes," Lila said. "Of course, I'd be sorry if we dropped bombs on them, too. That's just what we want to prevent. . . ."

Behind the angry woman's shoulder, a blonde girl in a low-cut peasant blouse asked: "Wheahbouts you from, anyways?"

"Massachusetts," Lila said. She added, smiling a little, "It's in the United States."

"Uh huh," the blonde girl said. "That's what Ah thought. Come on, Betty Jane."

When a pale, thin, forty-fivish woman in a dark cotton dress laid a hand on her arm, Lila jumped. The pale woman said, "My name is Mrs. Bunje. I'd like very much to help with the Peace Walk, Mrs. Horton." Glaring after the blonde girl, Lila could not prevent herself from bursting out: "Really? Why?"

The pale woman said, "I'm a Christian."

"Oh—oh, I'm sorry."

The woman laughed, and then Lila saw how beautiful she was. It was not only a beauty of spirit, although it was that, too. Mrs. Bunje's unpainted face looked as though its owner had been scrubbing away at it for years, in an effort to eliminate its purely physical beauty, without success. She said, "Don't be. I'm not!"

"Oh," Lila said, "I didn't mean. . . ."

Still laughing, Mrs. Bunje said, "Of course not. Have you time to talk?"

"You can stay and talk here," May Brooks said. She slammed the door closed and leaned against it. "Thank God that's over! How about a drink?"

Lila shook her head. Her cheeks flamed: she did not want to be associated with Mrs. Brooks in Mrs. Bunje's beautiful presence. But Mrs. Bunje turned to May and said, "Oh that's very kind. I'll just help myself to more coffee, if you don't mind. Are you working with Mrs. Horton on the Peace Walk?"

"Not exactly," May Brooks said. "You all go right on. I'm going to get the ice."

For all her saintly appearance, Mrs. Bunje was a practical woman. In five minutes she had devised a program of action designed to reach more people, more quickly, than Lila's frustrating house-to-house calls—although she approved of this approach, too, and thought it should be continued. She proposed a notice for insertion in the daily newspapers at Fainville and surrounding towns, as well as releases for radio stations and T.V. She sketched out an appeal to be mailed to one hundred church, civic, business and organizational leaders, whose names she could supply—she had lived in Fainville for over fifteen years. She asked Lila if she had looked into the matter of a police permit to hold the Walk; and she criticized Mr. Jorgenson's suggestion of a name for the peace-walk-group, on the grounds that it did not make sense. "Ad hoc committee of *what*?" she said, turning up her slender, unjeweled hands. They settled on "The Citizens Committee for the Fainville Peace Walk."

When Jim came home that night, Lila was bubbling. "I don't

know what would have happened," she told him as she carried the salad bowl into the dining room, "if Mrs. Bunje hadn't turned up. This morning I didn't feel I could go on. She's a tower of moral strength."

"That's fine." Watching Lila, Jim bit his pipe. "Only—nothing's really happened yet, Lila. You mustn't let yourself ride for a fall. The whole thing—in spite of Mrs. Bunje—it may never come to anything."

"I think it will. I suppose I have more confidence in people than you have, Jim. Besides, you're forgetting all the people who turned up for the peace demonstrations in Washington, and in Philadelphia, and New York."

"This isn't Philadelphia or New York. It's a narrow, provincial little Southern city." Jim knocked out his pipe.

"By the way, what does Mr. Bunje do?"

"Mrs. Bunje is a widow." Lila was lighting candles at the buffet. She blew out the match and dropped it slowly into the wastebasket.

"Jim?" She turned to face him. "Are you sure that you . . . that you aren't hoping the Peace Walk will never materialize?"

"What are you talking about?"

Lila grasped the back of a chair. "It's just occurred to me, you might be worried about your job . . . I mean, that my doing this might endanger it. I wouldn't want to . . . I know how much your job means to you."

"To me!" Jim stared at her. "Perhaps I ought to remind you that you were pretty anxious for me to get into the company, three years ago!"

"I was worried about security. I didn't realize there can't be any security, in a world that may destroy itself at any moment. Material security is an illusion, now."

"I have to pretend that it isn't an illusion, Lila. Or there won't be real food on this table."

Lila leaned forward. "All I want to know, is whether you want me to give it up, Jim. You must tell me honestly."

"Have I asked you to?" Jim frowned. "That's your idea, not mine. I've never tried to interfere with anything you want to do."

"I know. You never have."

She slipped into her chair and unfolded her napkin without looking at him.

"But then, you know, it's the first time I've ever tried to do anything."

The problem of Negro participation was to some degree solved the following day, when Lila's charwoman Nancy came to do her weekly chores. Nancy was a pious woman, much given to quoting Scripture and muttering prayers over the dustbin. It was the work of no more than a few minutes to convince her of where her Christian duty lay. She promised to come, and bring friends.

One week after the first news item appeared, the mail brought Mrs. Bunje fifty dollars in cash, from an anonymous donor, with a typed note to the effect that the money was to be used in whatever way might further the Peace Walk. Mrs. Bunje and Lila were jubilant; they went downtown the same afternoon to order a printing of two thousand leaflets for sidewalk distribution. The heading, in bold letters, was to be: "ONE WORLD OR NONE—IT'S UP TO YOU! END BOMB TESTS WITHOUT DELAY!"

The next development was perhaps more surprising. May Brooks, who had listened without a word to the conversation between Lila and Mrs. Bunje in her apartment, the while putting down three bourbon-and-sodas—May Brooks volunteered her services for the Citizens Committee for the Fainville Peace Walk. She offered Lila the explanation that she had been thinking the problem over. "I feel like you do about it," she said. "It's a hell of a note, them poisoning us without so much as a by-your-leave." Her mouth twitched. "Timmy's daddy's family is chock-full of cancer anyway."

May gave earnest of her intentions by accompanying Lila to the first meeting of the Committee at Mrs. Bunje's home. She smelled faintly of bourbon but was steady enough to take minutes. In all, a dozen people were present. They were mainly friends of Mr. Jorgenson and Mrs. Bunje. Lila had telephoned Nancy before the meeting to offer her a ride; and Nancy had said that she could get there in her son's car, but she did not appear. Mrs. Bunje said that Nancy was probably reluctant to meet with whites on anything so like a social basis; they need not give up hope that Nancy would appear for the Peace Walk as promised.

Over a bedtime snack Lila told Jim about the meeting. When she came to the mention of May's participation in it, he said: "Is that good or bad?" He was peeling an apple; he did not look up from his work with the fruit knife. After a little silence, Lila said: "Is that supposed to be funny?"

"No, I mean it. A cracked Negro scrubwoman, a bunch of senile radicals, now an alcoholic. . . ." He put down the knife. "Are you sure you'll be serving the Cause well, parading a crew like that?"

Lila said hotly: "This isn't a style show; it's a demonstration for peace!" Then, recalling Mrs. Bunje's forbearance, she went on gently, "I can't make teetotaling a condition of May's joining us, can I?"

Jim shrugged his shoulders. "I guess not. I was just suggesting that Mrs. Brooks's support may be of doubtful value."

"Perhaps." Lila looked at him. "But if we can't rouse the strong, we must rely upon the weak and helpless. I agree, it's unfortunate when so-called decent people refuse to lift a finger for humanity."

Jim looked back at her, his eyes blank. She went on, after a pause: "However, we have one or two reliable people, it may interest you to know. Mrs. Fienberg, for example."

"Who's she?"

"Mrs. Jack Fienberg? Her husband owns the Bon Marche. He's something in the city government, too—the Council, I think. She knows all the important people. She telephoned the Mayor, right from the meeting, to clear up the matter of the police permit. He said we didn't need a permit—only to let the Police Chief know when and where we want to hold the street meeting, so he can have some extra policemen there. To avoid traffic problems, I suppose. Or," she added, "in case of a riot."

Her face was calm, expressionless. Jim looked startled, then angry. His face had turned a dull red. "Now, look here, Lila. . . ."

Lila regarded him sympathetically. "Yes, dear?"

Jim slowly unclenched his fists. "Nothing," he said. "Never mind." He took a bite of his apple. "What do you plan to do at this street meeting?"

"Well, we'll have speakers, of course. Mrs. Bunje is going to speak on the moral implications of bomb-testing. So far, we've no other qualified speakers. We want at least one man to address the crowd. We can't let Mr. Jorgenson do it. He'd only get up and harangue about Socialism. Sometimes I'm not even sure Mr. Jorgenson belongs with us. . . . Well . . ." she smiled. "I'm not going to worry about it. Someone will turn up."

Jim smiled back at her. "Sure," he said. "Someone will turn up."

As he was turning out the bedroom lamps, Jim said, "This Mrs. Finer—what does her husband do?"

"Mr. Fienberg? I told you. He's the owner of that big department store."

"Oh, yes, sure. You told me." He laughed. "Funny, I forgot."

He switched off the light.

Mrs. Bunje and Lila had put forward a motion that the Peace Walk take place on the anniversary of Tolstoy's birth, falling at a convenient time in late August. Mr. Jorgenson objected that this was a weekday, when working people could not be expected to participate; and Mrs. Fienberg agreed that the Walk should be on a Saturday, because of the greater number of people downtown, shopping.

Mr. Jorgenson suggested the second Saturday in August, the date of the Nagasaki bomb. Spurred on by the Middle East crisis, they unanimously adopted his suggestion.

The choice of this earlier date rushed them. They worked feverishly at last-minute mailings, door-to-door and telephone appeals, the production of placards to be carried by the Peace Walkers. Mrs. Bunje, as delicate as she looked, contracted a bad cold as the result of overexertion; she went on working, carrying everywhere a large box of tissues.

The day of the Peace Walk dawned cloudy, which was all to the good, as the weather was beastly hot. Lila was up at six, scanning the skies. She decided that the clouds did not look like rain clouds.

The Walk was scheduled to form at ten-thirty. By nine o'clock, Lila had finished washing the breakfast dishes and straightening the apartment. She was dressed—all in white—with the exception of her gloves. She sat down in the living room with the newspaper.

Jim came out of the bedroom, wearing shorts and sneakers. In his hand he carried a can of tennis balls. "All set?" he said.

Lila nodded.

"I thought, as long as you're going to be busy this morning, I'd—could you drop me at the municipal courts on your way down?"

"You can take the car. I'm driving down with May Brooks."

"Oh," Jim said. "Fine."

Lila returned to her newspaper. Jim hesitated, hitching at his shorts. "You wouldn't mind if I left right away, would you? The courts are pretty crowded on Saturday. As long as you're going to be leaving pretty soon, anyway."

Lila smiled sweetly. "No, dear. You go right ahead and play tennis."

"O.K." Jim said. He pulled his racket out of the guest closet and took the car keys off the mantle.

"Well—good luck." He went to Lila, bent over and kissed her. "Love me?" He squeezed her arm.

Her blue eyes gazed up into his; she nodded, slowly. Jim patted her shoulder. "See you at lunch, O.K.?" She nodded again.

When the door closed, Lila got up and went into the kitchen to check her wristwatch by the electric clock on the stove. As she was starting back to the living room, the telephone rang.

She jumped nervously and crossed the desk to pick up the receiver. Her eyes were on the windows, where the clouds were darkening.

As she listened to the voice at the other end of the wire, her face drained; she leaned against the wall.

"But, Mrs. Bunje—Oh, I'm so sorry!—But Mrs. Bunje—who will—If we don't have you, I don't see how we can—"

The voice at the other end went on for some time. Lila nodded her head, saying, "Yes. Yes," in a subdued voice. At last, she hung up. She wrung her hands. The doorbell rang.

Lila ran to open the door. May Brooks was standing in the hallway. Lila said dazedly, "You're early. Never mind, we'd better go. Mrs. Bunje's cold is Asian flu, her doctor won't let her get up. I'll just get my bag. . . ."

Lila did not glance at May as she hurried down the steps and got into the car. They were, in fact, nearly downtown when she took a good look at May. It was not until then that she saw that May's dress was on backward.

The rain drove Jim off the tennis courts at about eleven o'clock. He hung around for a while, in a drugstore across the street, thinking the squall might pass; but when the rain began to descend in earnest, he dashed to the car and started home.

As he neared the apartment, driving at a snail's pace in the blinding downpour, he struck his hand against his forehead. The Peace Walk! He had a mental vision of Lila in her white dress and shoes. Jim saw the blue lettering of her placard—NO MORE WAR!—melting into her small white-gloved hands. He moaned.

He ran all the way up the steps and burst into the apartment. It was empty. Crossing the hall to May's apartment, he heard sounds within, and knocked. After a moment, Timmy opened the door.

The room was a sickening jumble of ash trays, bits of clothing, newspapers, a variety of cups and drinking glasses. Timmy put out a hand to turn down the T.V. sound but continued to watch the flickering cartoons out of the corner of his eye. "What is it?"

"Is your mother home?"

"She and Mrs. Horton went downtown." Timmy turned from the screen with an effort, focusing his eyes on Jim. "Mother was drunk." He offered it matter-of-factly.

Jim received the words in shocked silence. After a second he asked, "Are you all right, son?"

"Sure." Timmy's gaze was fixed on the screen again. "Can I do something for you, Mr. Horton?"

"Oh," Jim said. "No. No, thank you."

Jim returned to the apartment and changed into dry clothes. He went into the kitchen and mixed a pitcher of Martinis. As he placed it in the refrigerator, he murmured aloud, "My poor baby. Oh, my poor baby!" He prepared sandwiches, clumsily, and set the table. There did not seem to be anything more to do. He sat down in the living room to wait.

He was on his feet the minute Lila's key turned in the door. When she stepped in, in her sodden dress, her hair dripping, he took her quickly into his arms. "Darling," he said, "Poor darling!"

"Oh, no, Jim. I'll get you all wet!" She pushed gently against his chest. To his surprise, her voice was lively. Her cheeks were flushed with color; she smiled. "I guess I ought to change."

"O.K." He backed away a little. "I made some Martinis to warm you up. I'll bring them into the bedroom."

She said indifferently, "Oh, all right."

When Jim came into the bedroom carrying the pitcher of Martinis, Lila was in her negligee, stripping off her stockings. She hummed a tune under her breath.

Jim set the pitcher on the dresser, carefully.

"How's May?"

"Fine. I had to fix her up a little, at a filling station, before we got downtown. She sobered up in the rain."

"Did you walk very far?"

"Fifteen blocks. As we planned." She looked up. "Why? What did you think?"

"Oh, I—well, I don't know. The rain. I thought you might get—wet."

Lila laughed. "Of course we got wet! It didn't hurt us. Human beings are of pretty solid flesh, you know. Including me. I'm not made of papier-mache."

She leaned against the bed-post, smiling. "I've said that to you before, often. Of course, I've never been utterly sure of it, myself, to tell you the truth—until today. This morning, when Mrs. Bunje took sick, I was terrified." She shrugged. "Then, I found out it didn't matter, I didn't need Mrs. Bunje."

"Well, that was fine."

"Yes. It was a good thing." Lila cupped her chin in her hand, thoughtfully. "Isn't it funny, Jim? I thought I needed you, too. Right up to this morning, I kept hoping you'd understand, and, oh, support me." She shook her head, smiling. "Wasn't that silly?"

"Well, I. . . ."

"I didn't need anybody's support, you see. When I got there, they were terribly worried. Even before it began to rain, they were talking about giving it up, because we were so few. Just eight of us. So I asked them: what had numbers to do with it? So long as we believed in what we were doing? I was perfectly prepared to go alone. I told them so. They came, then. We covered all the streets we planned, and rallied where we'd told the Police Chief we'd stop. Fortunately, it was close to a store-front awning. A crowd of people was already gathered there to shelter from the storm." She paused for a long moment.

"I gave the speech."

"You did?"

Lila nodded, looking at the rain-splashed windows; she seemed to be listening to something in the distance. Then she stopped listening to whatever it was and swung her feet to the floor. "I'm starving! Let's talk in the kitchen while I fix lunch."

"I've fixed lunch. I thought you might be—tired."

"I am, a little. I'll lie down after lunch. The doctor says I'm supposed to rest for fifteen minutes after meals, anyway. I'll begin today."

"What for? What doctor?"

"Well, I hadn't wanted to tell you," Lila said. "I felt so wretched about it. I'm going to have a baby."

"Oh," Jim said. He wet his lips. "That's—that's too bad."

"Oh, no, I don't think so. I think it'll be all right."

"You think . . . ?" Jim's voice was cautious. "What's made you change your mind?"

Lila took his arm. "I'm not afraid any more, Jim. In fact, I'm hopeful. I feel a great deal of confidence in the future, since this morning—since the Peace Walk."

"You do?" He hung back, frowning. "But why? I don't under-stand. What's the Peace Walk got to do with it? It was a coura-geous little demonstration, yes, but, after all, Lila, it hasn't changed anything!"

"Don't you think so?" Lila smiled. "I'd say that remains to

be seen." She dropped his arm and started for the kitchen. "Come along, Jim. Let's have lunch."

He stood looking after her.

Lila dropped off to sleep soon after she lay down. Although it was still raining hard, Jim put on a raincoat and hat and went out. He walked around the block several times.

When he returned to the apartment, he picked up a sheet of paper and began drafting a letter to his employers.

"Dear Sirs," he wrote, "If it's at all possible, I would like a permanent assignment, preferably at the main plant; my wife is not in good health . . ."

But this was untrue. Lila was pregnant, not ill. He tore up the letter and began another one, to Lila's mother. After some polite inquiries, he wrote:

"I think it would be a very good idea if you—you and Don— could come down here for a little visit. I think it would be good for Lila. She has recently been . . ." He thought for a moment, then wrote, "depressed." But this was also untrue, she was not depressed. He flung down the pen and began to pace the living room floor, from the windows to the wall, and back again.

Nothing was wrong with Lila. In some mysterious fashion, Lila had found "hope." Might the trouble be with himself? He could not recall a time when he had felt so uneasy, lost, uncertain of the future.

Phantasia for Elvira Shatayev

By Adrienne Rich

Born into a comfortable Baltimore family, Adrienne Rich (1929–) pleased her father by writing poems. Beneath the conscious craft of her early poems, written while she was an undergraduate at Radcliffe College, one can sense a strong female identity and power. Married in 1953, by the age of thirty Adrienne Rich had mothered three sons and had begun

*to experience what seemed to her later an inevitable conflict—
was she to be "a failed woman" or "a failed poet"? Miracu-
lously, she continued to write "during children's naps . . .
or at 3 A.M."* Snapshots of a Daughter-in-Law *was published
when her youngest child was four. Her most recent books
are* Diving into the Wreck, *which won the National Book
Award in 1974;* Poems: Selected and New *(1975); and a
scholarly, yet personal and speculative, prose work on
motherhood,* Of Woman Born *(1976). She lives in New York
City and teaches at Douglass College, Rutgers University.*

*Since the early seventies, Adrienne Rich has been both a
recorder and prophet of radical feminist culture. In* The Will
to Change *(1971), her seventh book of poetry, she first
explicitly linked personal and political conflict. Two poems
in that book, for example, suggest similar causes for the war
in Vietnam and the inability of a man and a woman to speak
to each other. More recently, her poems have criticized
patriarchal culture and institutions, and have presented
contrasting portraits of female love and energy. Persistent
themes in her poems include women's struggles to cast off
"old ways," the loneliness and exhilaration of changing
oneself, and the strength of women acting together. This last
theme is celebrated in "Phantasia for Elvira Shatayev."
Shatayev was the leader of a women's climbing team, all of
whom died in a storm on Lenin Peak, August 1974.
Later, Shatayev's husband found and buried the bodies.*

T he cold felt cold until our blood
  grew colder   then the wind
died down and we slept

If in this sleep I speak
it's with a voice no longer personal
(I want to say   *with voices*)
When the wind tore   our breath from us at last
we had no need of words
For months   for years   each one of us
had felt her own *yes*   growing in her
slowly forming   as she stood at windows   waited

for trains   mended her rucksack   combed her hair
What we were to learn   was simply   what we had
up here   as out of all words   that *yes*   gathered
its forces   fused itself   and only just in time
to meet a *No* of no degrees
the black hole   sucking the world in

I feel you climbing toward me
your cleated bootsoles leaving   their geometric bite
colossally embossed   on microscopic crystals
as when I trailed you in the Caucasus
Now I am further
ahead   than either of us dreamed   anyone would be
I have become

the white snow packed like asphalt by the wind
the women I love   lightly flung   against the mountain
that blue sky
our frozen eyes unribboned   through the storm
we could have stitched that blueness   together   like a quilt

You come (I know this)   with your love   your loss
strapped to your body   with your tape-recorder   camera
ice-pick   against advisement
to give us burial in the snow   and in your mind
While my body lies out here
flashing like a prism   into your eyes
how could you sleep   You climbed here for yourself
we climbed for ourselves

When you have buried us   told your story
ours does not end   we stream
into the unfinished   the unbegun
the possible
Every cell's core of heat   pulsed out of us
into the thin air   of the universe
the armature of rock beneath these snows
this mountain   which has taken   the imprint of our minds
through changes elemental and minute
as those we underwent
to bring each other here

choosing ourselves   each other   and this life
whose every breath   and grasp   and further foothold
is somewhere   still enacted   and continuing

In the diary I wrote: *Now we are ready*
and each of us knows it   I have never loved
like this   I have never seen
my own forces so taken up and shared
and given back
After the long training   the early sieges
we are moving almost effortlessly in our love

In the diary as the wind   began to tear
at the tents over us   I wrote:
We know now we have always been in danger
down in our separateness
and now up here together   but till now
we had not touched our strength

In the diary torn from my fingers I had written:
What does love mean
what does it mean   "to survive"
A cable of blue fire ropes our bodies
burning together in the snow   We will not live
to settle for less   We have dreamed of this
all of our lives

To Be of Use

By Marge Piercy

A native of Detroit and the first in her family to go to college,
Marge Piercy (1936–) graduated from the University of Michi-
gan. Her poems, reviews, and essays have appeared in a broad
spectrum of periodicals, including The Nation, The Carleton
Miscellany, The Transatlantic Review, Hanging Loose,
and Women: A Journal of Liberation. *She is the most widely*
anthologized feminist poet of her generation. In the past

*ten years, she has published five volumes of poems and five
novels. Her recent novels include* Small Changes *(1973),*
Woman on the Edge of Time *(1976), and* The High Cost of
Living *(1978).* Breaking Camp, *her first volume of poems,
was published in 1968 by Wesleyan University Press. Her
two most recent volumes are* Living in the Open *(1976)
and* The Twelve-Spoked Wheel Flashing *(1978). She now lives
with a group of people on Cape Cod and spends two days
a week in Boston.*

*Since 1967, Piercy has supported herself through her
writing. Before that time, she held "all the part-time jobs
that women do—secretary, door-to-door pollster, artist's
model, department store clerk, switch-board operator, and
waitress." Since the midsixties, she has also been active in
movements for social change, including the women's
movement. Like "To Be of Use" (the title poem of her 1973
volume), many of her poems and some of her novels imagine
future societies in which people enjoy working together
cooperatively, in harmony and peace.*

The people I love the best
jump into work head first
without dallying in the shallows
and swim off with sure strokes almost out of sight.
They seem to become natives of that element,
the black sleek heads of seals
bouncing like half-submerged balls.

I love people who harness themselves, an ox to a heavy cart,
who pull like water buffalo, with massive patience,
who strain in the mud and the muck to move things forward,
who do what has to be done, again and again.

I want to be with people who submerge
in the task, who go into the fields to harvest
and work in a row and pass the bags along,
who stand in the line and haul in their places,
who are not parlor generals and field deserters
but move in a common rhythm
when the food must come in or the fire be put out.

About the Authors

NANCY HOFFMAN is an associate professor of humanities at the College of Public and Community Service, University of Massachusetts / Boston. She received her Ph.D. in comparative literature at the University of California, Berkeley. Hoffman is the author of *Spenser's Pastorals*, and has written articles on education, literature, and women's studies. She chaired the Modern Languages Association Commission on the Status of Women, and helped start a women's studies program at Portland State University in Oregon.

FLORENCE HOWE is a professor of humanities at the State University of New York / College at Old Westbury. She is an authority on women's studies and was one of the founders of The Feminist Press as well as of the National Women's Studies Association. Howe is editor of the *Women's Studies Newsletter*, and a past president of the Modern Languages Association. She co-edited *No More Masks: An Anthology of Poems by Women*, and has published several other books and many essays on literature, politics, education, and women's studies.

A Note on Language

IN EDITING BOOKS, The Feminist Press attempts to eliminate harmful sex and race bias inherent in the language. In order to retain the authenticity of historical and literary documents, however, our policy is to leave their original language unaltered. We recognize that the task of changing language usage is extremely complex and that it will not be easily accomplished. The process is an ongoing one that we share with many others concerned with the relationship between a humane language and a more humane world.

This book was composed on the VIP *in Trump and Olive Antique by Monotype Composition Company, Baltimore, Maryland. It was printed and bound by R. R. Donnelley & Sons Company, Chicago, Illinois. The covers were printed by Algen Press, Queens, New York.*

Index

Authors, Titles, First Lines of Poems

The numbers in boldface type indicate pages on which selections appear. The numbers in italics indicate pages on which the photographs of the authors appear.

(Acknowledgments continued from page vi)

Field, Edward, "Notes From a Slave Ship." From *Stand Up Friend with Me*, copyright © 1965 by Edward Field. Reprinted by permission of Grove Press, Inc.

Giovanni, Nikki, "Poem for Aretha." From *Re: Creation*, copyright © 1970 by Nikki Giovanni. Reprinted by permission of Broadside Press, Detroit, Michigan.

Higgins, Judith, "The Only People." From *The Atlantic Monthly*, 1967. Reprinted by permission of Russell & Volkening, Inc. as agents for the author. Copyright © 1967 by Judith Higgins.

Hurston, Zora Neale, "Mules and Men." From *Mules and Men* by Zora Neale Hurston. Copyright 1935 by Zora Neale Hurston. Copyright © renewed 1963 by John C. Hurston and Joel Hurston. Reprinted by permission of J. B. Lippincott Company.

Le Sueur, Meridel, "I Was Marching." From *Proletarian Literature in the United States*, eds. Granville Hicks, *et al.*, copyright 1935. Reprinted by permission of International Publishers.

Lights, Rikki, "Medicine Man." © 1978 by Vernether Lights. All rights reserved. Originally published in *Aphra*.

Marriott, Alice Lee, "The Indian Trader." From *Maria: The Potter of San Ildefonso* by Alice Marriott. Copyright 1948 by the University of Oklahoma Press.

Marriott, Alice Lee, "The Whole Pot." From *Maria: The Potter of San Ildefonso* by Alice Marriott. Copyright 1948 by the University of Oklahoma Press.

Olsen, Tillie, "I Stand Here Ironing." Copyright © 1956 by Tillie Olsen. Originally published in the *Pacific Spectator*. Reprinted by permission of the author.

Pedrick, Jean, "Hats." From *Pride and Splendor*, Alice James Books, © 1976 by Jean Pedrick.

Piercy, Marge, "To Be of Use." From *To Be of Use,* copyright © 1969, 1971, 1973 by Marge Piercy. Reprinted by permission of Doubleday & Company, Inc.

Replansky, Naomi, "A Good Day's Work." From *Ring Song,* Charles Scribners Sons. Copyright 1952 by Naomi Replansky. Reprinted by permission of the author.

Reznikoff, Charles, "Amelia." From *By the Waters of Manhattan,* copyright 1941 by Charles Reznikoff. Reprinted by permission of New Directions Publishing Corporation.

Rich, Adrienne, "Phantasia for Elvira Shatayev." Reprinted from *The Dream of a Common Language* by Adrienne Rich by permission of W. W. Norton & Company, Inc. Copyright © 1978 by W. W. Norton & Company, Inc.

Shore, Wilma, "The Butcher." Copyright 1941 by Houghton Mifflin Company. Reprinted with permission of the author.

Smith, Barbara, "The Bowl." Copyright © 1975. Reprinted by permission of the author.

Tafolla, Carmen, "Allí por la calle San Luis." Copyright © 1976 by Carmen Tafolla. Reprinted by permission of the author.

Voigt, Ellen Bryant, "Farm Wife." Copyright © 1972 by Ellen Bryant Voigt. Reprinted from *Claiming Kin* by permission of Wesleyan University Press.

Walker, Alice, "Women." © 1972 by Alice Walker. Reprinted from her volume *Revolutionary Petunias and Other Poems* by permission of Harcourt Brace Jovanovich, Inc.

Walker, Margaret, "Girl Held Without Bail." From *Prophets for a New Day,* copyright © 1970 by Margaret Walker. Reprinted by permission of Broadside Press, Detroit, Michigan.

Walker, Margaret, "Lineage." From *For My People,* copyright 1942 by Yale University Press. Reprinted by permission of the author.

Photograph Acknowledgments

Pages 24–25. **Willa Cather:** Nickolas Muray; from the New York Public Library Picture Collection. **Ranice Henderson Crosby:** courtesy of Mary Mulrooney. **Mary Wilkins Freeman:** Culver Pictures, Inc. **Nikki Giovanni:** © 1978 by Jill Krementz. **Naomi Replansky:** courtesy of Charles Lewis. **Charles Reznikoff:** © by Gerard Malanga. **Anzia Yezierska:** The Quigley Photographic Archives, Georgetown University Library; courtesy of Alice Kessler-Harris.

Pages 92–93. **Toni Cade Bambara:** © 1978 by Jill Krementz. **Judith Higgins:** courtesy of Ned Higgins. **Zora Neale Hurston:** Carl Van Vechten; James Welden Johnson Memorial Collection of Negro Arts and Letters, Collection of American Literature, Beinecke Rare Book and Manuscript Library, Yale University. **Sarah Orne Jewett:** courtesy of the Maine Women Writers Collection, Westbrook College, Portland, Maine. **Rikki Lights:** courtesy of Norm Gilliam, Philadelphia, Pennsylvania. **Alice Marriott:** courtesy of the Marriott-Rachlin Photo Collection. **Jean Pedrick:** courtesy of Laurence Kefferstan. **Barbara Smith:** courtesy of Koby Studio. **Margaret Walker:** New York Public Library Picture Collection.

Pages 166–167. **Sheila Ballantyne:** courtesy of Jennie Arndt. **Rosellen Brown:** courtesy of Ann Alexander. **Patricia Cumming:** courtesy of Marcia J. Kasabian. **Alice Marriott:** courtesy of the Marriott-Rachlin Photo Collection. **Tillie Olsen:** © 1978 by Jill Krementz. **Wilma Shore:** courtesy of Edward Stevenson. **August Strindberg:** Culver Pictures, Inc. **Carmen Tafolla:** courtesy of Joe E. Herrera. **Ellen Bryant Voigt:** courtesy of Betty Sheedy.

Pages 232–233. **Sholem Asch:** courtesy of the Asch family. **Sue Davidson:** courtesy of Don Normark. **Edward Field:** courtesy of Gary Heinz. **Dorothy Canfield Fisher:** courtesy of The Wilbur Collection, Bailey Library, University of Vermont. **Meridel Le Sueur:** courtesy of Meridel Le Sueur. **Marge Piercy:** courtesy of Robert Shapiro. **Adrienne Rich:** © 1978 by Thomas Victor. **Alice Walker:** © 1978 by Jill Krementz. **Margaret Walker:** © 1978 by Jill Krementz.